'UNDER GOD'S VISITATION'

*A Study of the City of Wells
from the Civil War to the Restoration*

'UNDER GOD'S VISITATION'

*A Study of the City of Wells
from the Civil War to the Restoration*

ANTHONY NOTT

To my father, Leonard Nott 1904–84,
who loved Wells and its history

First published in Great Britain in 2010
Published by Anthony Nott

Copyright © Anthony Nott 2010

The right of Anthony Nott to be identified as the Author of the Work has been asserted by him in accordance with the Copyright, Designs and Patents Act 1988.

All rights reserved. No part of this publication may be reproduced, stored in a retrieval system, or transmitted, in any form or by any means without the prior written permission of the publisher, nor be otherwise circulated in any form of binding or cover other than that in which it is published and without a similar condition being imposed on the subsequent purchaser.

A CIP catalogue record for this title is available
from the British Library.

ISBN 978-0-9565835-0-5

Typeset & printed by
Taylor Thorne Print Ltd, Somerset
www.taylorthorneprint.co.uk

FOREWORD

This book arose from the work done by Joan Hasler and Anthony Nott in transcribing and editing the Wells Corporation's Convocation Acts Books 1589-1644 and 1662-65. This work was published by the Somerset Record Society as Volumes 90 and 91 in 2004. It was felt at the time that although there were general studies of the history of Wells and various monographs on particular aspects, a study of how the entire city was affected during the period of national political instability from 1640-1665, would be interesting and informative. The present work seeks to provide that.

The title of this book is a quotation from an entry in the parish register of the church of St Cuthbert, Wells. It was written in 1648 by the curate, Francis Standish, who saw the suffering and social disruption of the Civil War as a sign of God's punishment of a sinful society.

The following conventions have been followed in the text: round brackets have been used for explanatory comments; and where a word or letter has been missed from a quotation or an elucidation is necessary, square brackets have been used. As the New Year in the seventeenth century began on 25 March, any dates given between 1 January and 24 March show the old and new style dating. In the notes and bibliography, all titles are given in italics. Finally any errors are solely the responsibility of the author.

ACKNOWLEDGEMENTS

The author would like to thank in particular Joan Hasler for her encouragement of the project and for arranging for the compilation of the index; Tony Scrase for sharing his research on Wells properties and for allowing one of his maps to be customised; and Brian Luker for his detailed and helpful comments on the text. The author would also like to thank William Smith, the Wells City Archivist, and Anne Crawford, the Wells Cathedral Archivist, for their help; Jean Imray, a former Wells City Archivist, who generously allowed the author to read her unpublished research on the Wells Almshouse in the seventeenth century and Patrick Kirkby who gave valuable technical assistance to the author with the illustrations and maps. Thanks should also be given to the staff of the Somerset Record Office who allowed the author always to read the original documents. Finally my thanks go to my wife Jenny who has supported my endeavours and my son, Andrew who made sure that all my many textual revisions were saved electronically.

The author would also like to thank the National Portrait Gallery for licensing the use of the portraits of the William Seymour, 2nd Duke of Somerset, Sir Ralph Hopton and Prince Maurice; the National Army Museum for the photograph of the mounted figure of Major Richard Atkyns, Prince Maurice's Regiment of Horse 1643; the British Library for the title pages of *The Declaration of John Robins* 1651, Thomas Collier's pamphlet *A Looking-Glasse for the Quakers* 1657 and the Plan of the City of Wells 1735 by William Simes; the Bishop's Palace, Wells for the portrait of William Piers, Bishop of Bath and Wells 1632-70; the Wells Cathedral Library for title page of Ludolphus's *De Vita Christi* and St Cuthbert's Church for the Royal Arms of Charles I.

CONTENTS

PROLOGUE: **'And Hey and Down Go They'**   1

CHAPTER 1: **'A Pleasant City'**   9
   The Social and Political Scene
   Economic matters
   Gentry
   The Clergy and Ecclesiastical Office Holders
   The Corporation
   Catholic Recusants

CHAPTER 2: **National Government and Local Affairs 1625-40**   29
   Religious Affairs in the City
   'In a Mist of Ceremonies'
   Ship Money
   The Militia and Billeting

CHAPTER 3: **'To the Service of the Country'**   49
   'An Impious and Turbulent Pilate'
   'Liable to Bear Office'
   Moral Turpitude
   Subsidies
   The Protestation

CHAPTER 4: **'the Combustion at Wells'**   67
   The Protaganists: the Royalists
   The protagonists: The Parliamentarians
   Monday 1 August – Saturday 6 August

CHAPTER 5: **The Dangerousness of the Times: Parliamentary Wells August 1642 – June 1643**   87
   Sir Edward Rodney
   'For the Defence of King, Parliament and Kingdom'
   'Havock'
   The Royalist Victory: June 1643

CHAPTER 6: **Royalist Wells: July 1643 – July 1645**   105
   Paying for the War
   The case of the Postmaster
   The Threat to the Cathedral Establishment
   Demands, Threats and Murder
   The 1644 Campaign
   The End of the War
   The Effects of War

CHAPTER 7: **The Aftermath: 1645-49**   127
   'The Sickness'
   The Economic Crisis
   National Politics 1645-9
   County Politics
   City Politics
   Punishing the Royalists
   A Parliamentary By-Election
   Church Affairs: 'A Parish of Above Ten Thousand Souls'
   Social problems
   'Villanously Murdered'
   Church Affairs: The Cathedral
   The Purchase of the Bishop's Rights and Lands
   The End of the Decade

CHAPTER 8: **'Broyles and Sharp Contentions'**   159
   'Though the Crown Should Hang on a Bush, I Charge You Forsake It Not'
   National and Local Government 1649-59
   'Every Rayling Shimei'
   'A Vexatious, Frivolous and Contentious Jar'
   Dissension in the Cathedral

CHAPTER 9: Society and Religion: 1649-59   179
- Society and the Church
- Indentured Servants
- 'Reading, Writing and casting Accounts'
- 'Very Aged and Impotent and Like to Perish'
- 'Proud Wifelings'
- Toleration
- 'A Master Sectarie'
- 'The Old Ranters, Garment and Robins'
- The Quakers

CHAPTER 10: Restoration and Reaction 1659-1665   203
- The Elections to the Convention Parliament
- The Restoration; The Bishop and the Cathedral
- St Cuthbert's Church
- Baptists and Quakers
- Making Adjustments
- 'An Act For the Well Governing and Regulating of Corporations'
- The Construction of the New Market House/Town Hall
- Exits and Entrances
- Epilogue

APPENDIX Mayors of Wells   225

BIBLIOGRAPHY   229

INDEX   235

LIST OF ILLUSTRATIONS

Between pages 50 & 51
William Seymour, Marquis of Hertford
Sir Ralph Hopton
Sir Edward Rodney
Parliamentary Pamphlet August 12 1642

Between pages 82 & 83
William Piers, Bishop of Bath and Wells
Part of the title page of Ludolphus's *De Vita Christi* (Antwerp 1618) showing the handwritten account of the damage done to Wells Cathedral by parliamentary soldiers in 1643.
Major Richard Atkyns, Prince Maurice's Regiment of Horse 1643
Prince Maurice

Between pages 114 & 115
A page from the Wells Corporation Receiver's book showing the signatures of the leading parliamentarians on the Wells Corporation in 1652-3
The Crown Inn; Wells Market Place in 1665
Lechlade's House now 17 The Liberty where William Walrond lived
The Canonical House called The Rib; The Deanery

Between pages 146 & 147
'The declaration of John Robins: the false prophet otherwise the Shakers' God'
Thomas Collier's pamphlet 'A Looking-Glasse for the Quakers' 1657
Wells Market place, the Cathedral, Bishop's Palace and Liberty (from the plan by William Simes 1735)
St Cuthbert's church, Wells from the plan by William Simes, 1735.
The Royal Arms of Charles I in St Cuthbert's Church, Wells

MAPS

A street map of Wells in 1642, page 7 (by kind permission of A. J. Scrase from his 'Wells: a Study of Origins and Early Development' p10)

Map illustrating 'the Combustion at Wells' in the summer of 1642, page 66 (Patrick Kirkby with permission from Ordnance Survey)

ABBREVIATIONS

BL	British Library
BRS	Bristol Record Society
CAM	Calendar of the Committee for the Advancement of Money
CCC	Calendar of the Committee for Compounding
CSPD	Calendar of State Papers Domestic
DNB	Dictionary of National Biography
EHR	English Historical Review
HMSO	Her Majesty's Stationery Office
JHC	Journal of the House of Commons
JHL	Journal of the House of Lords
NA	National Archives
PCC	Prerogative Court of Canterbury
SANHS	Somerset Arcaeological and Natural History Society
SDNQ	Somerset & Dorset Notes and Queries
SRO	Somerset Record Office
SRS	Somerset Record Society
WCL	Wells Cathedral Library
WTH	Wells Town Hall

PROLOGUE

'AND HEY AND DOWN GO THEY'

On the afternoon of Thursday 28 July 1642, William Seymour, Marquis of Hertford, bearing the king's Commission of Array, rode down the long hill from the Mendip plateau through College Lane and then via the Liberty to the city of Wells. (Map 1) He was accompanied by a group of loyal Somerset gentry with their servants and retinues. His military strength was weak consisting only of three troops of horse (180 men), a small troop of dragoons (30-40 men) and 100-foot soldiers commanded by a professional soldier, Lieutenant Colonel Henry Lunsford. Hertford received no official welcome from the Wells Corporation but it is inconceivable that the mayor and senior members of the corporation, worried by the show of military force, did not try to ascertain what his plans were and for how long he intended to remain in Wells. Hertford's first requirement was suitable accommodation for himself and his entourage and he commandeered the deserted Bishop's Palace for his headquarters. There is no information in the corporation records concerning the accommodation of the royalist troops but it seems likely that they would have been billeted on the citizens although some soldiers may have camped out in the open, possibly in the Bishop's Park on the southeast side of the city. The inns probably did very good trade on that Thursday evening![1]

Hertford's arrival in Wells was the result of the rift between king and parliament that had become so serious by the summer of 1642 that both sides were considering armed conflict. Those who supported the king although they may have had reservations about the wisdom of his political and religious policies, saw parliament's attempt to wrest control of the armed forces from him as a step too far. Charles I was head of the militia and his supporters were suspicious of the motives of the radical group in parliament who wished to take away his control of it. For the king's opponents in parliament, all trust in the king had disappeared and they felt it essential that he should not be allowed to control the armed forces of the kingdom without parliamentary check.

Six months earlier, the king had left London for Windsor and in February had retired to York preparing to meet his parliamentary enemies with force. The additional fact of an Irish Catholic rebellion that had broken out in the previous November, turned the control of the armed forces into a burning issue. As there was no large standing army, the bulk of any forces raised would have had to come from the local militias. Consequently parliament attempted to control these militias by passing the Militia Ordinance giving it the sole power of raising the militia. The king countered this by issuing Commissions of Array, an old feudal device for raising troops. The scene was set for a military confrontation and it was in Wells that one of the first confrontations between king and parliament was to take place in July.

Hertford, the commissioner appointed by the king for the south-west to raise troops for the royalist cause through the Commission of Array, had been in confident mood as he left Beverley in Yorkshire on 10 July 1642. In a letter to Queen Henrietta Maria then in Holland, he wrote, 'His Majesties affaires, are now I hope in a prosperous way. And the affections of His People, breaks out every day more and more; who begin to have their eyes open, and will I believe no longer be deluded with the imaginary fears and jealousies ... I am with all speed to repair unto the West, to put His Commissions of Array in execution, which I make no doubt to perform without any great difficulty; If God prospers Us, as I trust he will in so good a cause, We shall then shortly (I hope) be blessed and cheered up with Your Majesties long wished – for presence, *And hey then down go they.*' [2]

Hertford's confidence was misplaced. Opposition to his arrival was mounting; on 19 July, during his journey south, parliament authorised Alexander Popham to proceed to Somerset to raise troops under the parliamentary Militia Ordinance. Hertford's first attempt to raise support for the king in the south-west was at Marlborough in Wiltshire. It was a town in an area where he was a substantial landowner, and on the outskirts of which his brother, Sir Francis Seymour, had his principal residence. To his discomfiture, Hertford was met by a riot. Many of the townspeople according to a royalist source 'prepared to enterteyne him with a tumult, rising, just as the Marquesse was within view of the Towne, and in a Rebellious manner breaking open the Churchdoores and possessing themselves of the County-Magazeene that was there kept: But assoone as the Marquesse was come to Town and alighted at the Lord Seymour's house, the Corporation attended their Lordshipps with a dissembling submission, but made noe restitution of the magazeene, and the Lords having noe considerable strength, about them, did wisely passe it over, hopeing by gentle meanes to reduce them to their dutyes.' The report to parliament from the opposing side gave a different view: 'The Marquesse of Hertford and the Lord Seymor ... in attempting to seise upon their Magazine ... were opposed and most courageously resisted by the greatest part of the County [who] will by no meanes give way nor suffer the Commission of Array [to be] put in execution.' The signs for the royalists were becoming ominous!

Further problems awaited the Marquis in Bath. He arrived to find 'the Summer Assizes beginning, and a great assembly of Gentlemen the most part of the better sort verie well affected.' This royalist account did not present a true picture. Hertford was received by the mayor and corporation quite cordially but sheriff Sandford of Somerset on 25 July, empanelled a grand jury of Somerset packed with gentlemen who supported parliament, which drafted a petition to the king claiming that the Commission of Array issued by him was illegal and should be recalled. The petition argued that the Commission of Array had 'issued forth in an unusuall manner unto diverse lordes and others, contrary ... to Magna Carta, The Peticion of Right [1628] and liberty of the subject, which breedes many distempers, distraccions, and jelousies throught this country [county] ... to the great disturbance and tranquillity of the people.' The grand jury also petitioned the assize judge, Sir Robert Foster, in like vein. Foster later assured the king that he had given no opinion on the legality of the Commission of Array, 'although I find the contrarie in print.' At the same time there arrived in Bath an order from parliament appointing some of the leading gentry, mostly from northeast Somerset, to raise 'horse, horsemen and arms, for the defence of King and both Houses of Parliament.' The association of the king's name with parliament was included for constitutional and political reasons but did not reflect the reality of the situation. A military confrontation could not long be delayed.[3]

It had now become clear to Hertford that Bath, in the north of the county, was an unsuitable place to further the king's cause. The question was where the centre of royalist operations should be. Bristol was an obvious possibility 'being a great, rich and populous city; of which being once possessed, they should be easily able to give the law to Somerset and Gloucestershire.' Lord Clarendon who wrote a contemporary history of the civil war, felt in hindsight that this would have proved the best option. However Bristol was rejected because ' there being visibly many disaffected people in it, and some of eminent quality; and if he [Hertford] should attempt to go thither, and be disappointed, it would break the whole design.' Of equal importance was the fact that Denzill Hollis, one of the five members of the House of Commons whom the king had tried to arrest for treason in January 1642, was lieutenant of the city and in command of the militia. Sensibly, Hertford did not want to precipitate a military clash so early in his mission. He was not to know however, that Hollis was about to return to London for a short while to assume command of an infantry regiment in the parliamentary army being formed under the Earl of Essex. Consequently after some further discussion, Wells was chosen as a base for the Marquis's operations in the county it' being a pleasant city, in the heart and near the centre of that county.'

Hertford's confidence had been severely dented by the events in Marlborough and Bath but his morale was raised when on the Mendip plateau above Wells he ' was mett by a considerable number of people of all quallityes.' His morale boosted by this support, he entered Wells with a false optimism.[4] Sir Ralph Hopton, his senior military commander did not share the same feelings and later bitterly regretted the decision to make Wells the base for the Marquis's campaign. In his view 'Wells (lying in the middest of that County) was unhappily chosen.'[5]

How far was Hertford's confidence justified in his decision to make Wells the centre of operations? How much support for the royalist cause was he likely to find there? He would have been certainly known by reputation amongst the citizens but it is unlikely that he had ever visited the city in any official capacity – there is no record of it in the city archives. His grandfather, the Earl of Hertford had visited the city officially in 1601 as Lord Lieutenant of the county and had in 1609 through a personal appeal to Lord Chancellor Ellesmere, helped to ameliorate the punishments meted out to some residents by Star Chamber. In his letter to the Lord Chancellor he had referred to the mayor and masters of the city as his good friends and revealed that the recorder of the city was 'one neere unto me' and that the late mayor's son was his household servant. The memory of this successful intervention may have lingered on but to the majority of the citizens of Wells, Hertford, although a landowner in the county, must have appeared a remote figure. He had been appointed lord lieutenant of Somerset in March 1639 and in the summer of 1642 held the post jointly with Lord Philip Herbert. He was also an absentee landlord and was not popular amongst some local residents because of his enclosure of common pasture land on Godney Moor some three miles west south west of Wells. Sir Edward Rodney, in an attempt to diffuse the situation, had acted as intermediary between Hertford and the affected tenants of the manor of Wells and on 20 March 1640/1 an agreement was reached stating that by 10 April, some of the enclosed ground was to be 'thrown open' to the commoners to enable them to pasture their cattle. This compromise was evidently unsatisfactory to some commoners because in May 1641 it was reported that 'some have in disorderly, and in a riotous Manner, broken down several Parcels of the said Inclosures, and put their Cattle into the said 160 acres [those retained by Hertford] and give out threatening Speeches, that they will use Violence to any man that shall offer to oppose such their Doings.' These rioters were small freeholders and prosperous farmers with communal grazing rights who would have almost certainly brought their produce to Wells market for sale.[6]

Wells was not a good choice strategically because of its proximity to the clothing districts of north-east Somerset where support for parliament was strong and where parliamentary supporters would soon be mobilised by the local gentry. It was also not a good defensive site; it had no fortifications and was overlooked by the Mendip Hills. It was however a city where there was much royalist sentiment but this was conditioned by a pragmatism, which in practice meant that the city corporation was always careful not to offend whichever side was in the ascendancy.

NOTES
[1] The road alignment on the northern outskirts of Wells was different in 1642 from the modern one. The modern A 39 road to Bristol was then the main road to

Chewton (Mendip) and Bath. It deviated north west from the present road just to the north of the hamlet of Walcombe and proceeded straight up the Mendip scarp joining the modern road near the site of the present Pen Hill televison mast. The road to Bristol followed the modern Old Bristol Road via the hamlet of Milton and was accessed from New Street. As these two main roads were only connected by a minor side road it is almost certain that the Marquis of Hertford would have entered Wells on the then Bath road going via College Lane (modern College Road). He could then have turned right into the Back Liberty and then left into New Street and so to the city or continued via the East Liberty turning right into the Front Liberty (now Cathedral Green) and entering Sadler Street and the city via Brown's Gate. The only other seventeenth century account of a person of importance entering Wells from Bath is that of July 1613 when the consort of James I, Queen Ann, visited the city. Then the city corporation met the queen 'near about Brownes gate' which suggests that the queen's route may have been via the East Liberty and Front Liberty. See Nott A & Hasler J (eds), *Wells Convocation Acts Books 1589-1665, Part 1 1589-1629,* SRS Vol 90, Taunton 2004, p 251. For these road alignments and other major roads entering and leaving Wells in 1642 see Map 1.

2 *The Lord Marquesse of Hertford, His Letter, Sent to the Queen in Holland.* London, 1642, p A2, BL, HMNTS e. 109 (24); 'And hey and down go they': Hertford may have been adapting a popular royalist song of the time 'Hey boys and up go we.'

3 Underdown, D, *Somerset in the Civil War and Interregnum,* Newton Abbot, 1973, p 32; Wroughton, J, *The Civil War in Bath and North Somerset,* Bath, 1973, pp 38-40; Cockburn, J S (ed), *Somerset Assize Orders 1640-59,* SRS Vol 71, Taunton, 1971, pp 53-55.

4 Clarendon, Edward, Earl of, Macray, W D (ed), *The History of the Rebellion and Civil Wars in England,* Oxford, 1888, Vol. II (Books V & VI), pp 294-6; Lynch, J, *For King and Parliament,* Stroud, 1999, pp 18-19.

5 Chadwyck Healey, C E (ed.), *Bellum Civile,* SRS Vol. 18, Taunton, 1902, pp 1-2.

6 Stokes, J, (ed), *Records of Early English Drama: Somerset, Vol.1, The Records,* Toronto, 1996, p 359; *JHL. Volume 4, 31 May 1641,* History of Parliament Trust, 1802, pp 261-262; Williams, M, *The Draining of the Somerset Levels,* Cambridge 1970, p 89; Unnamed Miscellany Book, WTH, pp 281-3.

'AND HEY AND DOWN GO THEY'

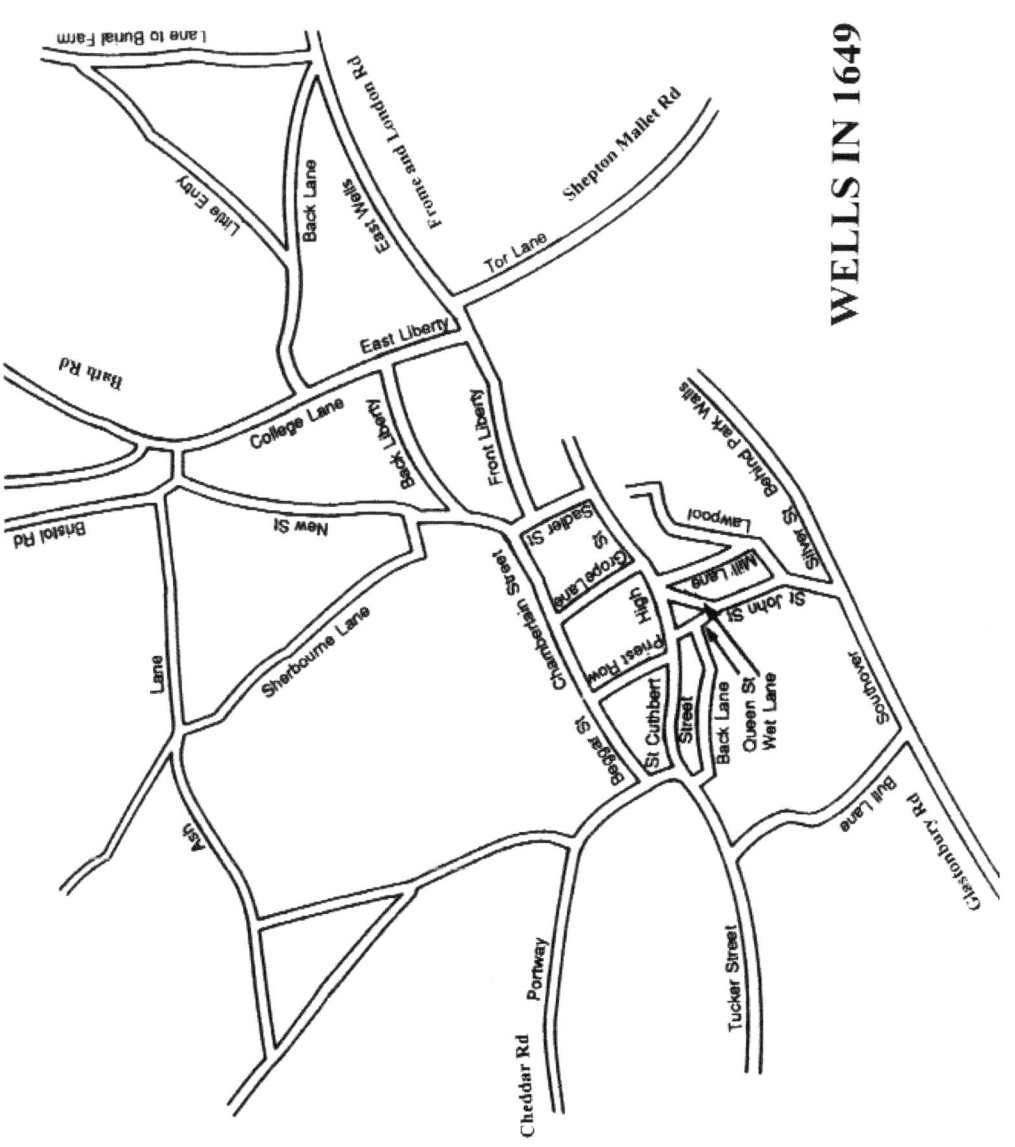

CHAPTER 1

'A PLEASANT CITY'

To Hertford and his followers Wells must have seemed, despite certain strategic reservations, an eminently suitable place as the centre of royalist operations in the county. It had the largest population of any town in Somerset at just over 2,600, a magazine containing stores of gunpowder, bullets and match and was a natural meeting place for the gentry and for trade. As he rode into the Market Place Hertford could not have failed to appreciate the fine stone architecture built by fifteenth and sixteenth century bishops that enhanced it. He would have passed the conduit built by Bishop Bekynton in 1450 that supplied the city with fresh water from the springs in the grounds of the Bishop's Palace. Dwarfing the conduit and with its tower visible above the roofs of the town was the splendid Late Gothic market cross built by Bishop Knight in 1542 and partially paid for by money left him by the late dean, Richard Woolman. On the north side of the Market Place was a row of stone buildings called the New Works again erected by Bishop Bekynton in the mid fifteenth century. Going through the great gatehouse at the east of the Market Place, he would have seen the Bishop's Palace which was to be his base for the next ten tumultuous days. He may have reflected on the sad decline in the temporal wealth of the bishopric since the mid sixteenth century and the position of the present incumbent Bishop Piers, recently imprisoned and now living in retirement on his estates.

He would have been cheered no doubt by the reception he received from the royalist gentry who lived in the Liberty around the cathedral and reassured by the royalist inclined corporation and the general political passivity of the city's inhabitants – a contrast to what he had experienced in Marlborough.

THE SOCIAL AND POLITICAL SCENE

Hertford probably saw little of city life during his brief stay in Wells. Immured in the Bishop's Palace away from the city, associating mainly with the gentry, he would not have met the ordinary citizens or seen their living conditions. In the High Street a typical tenement was only 27 feet 2 inches wide but stretched back 90 feet from the roadway. It contained one hall, one chamber, one small shop and one kitchen. There were also several other small rooms plus specialist rooms such as a salthouse and milk house as well as a stable and saddlehouse. In such houses people were acutely aware of their neighbours. This awareness often resulted in quarrels but it could also engender social solidarity when trouble loomed. For the inhabitants of the High Street the degree of the noise and smell of the market was a measure of the city's prosperity. In the Middle Row, constructed in the centre of the High Street in 1571, were the two fish shambles, the pig market and six meat shambles. Cattle were driven into the city to be sold at the Wednesday and Saturday markets; local farmers brought in butter and cheese and the Wells tradesmen displayed their wares in a market that spread from the the lower part of the High Street as far as the bishop's great gate in the east. The cobbled High Street could be cleansed by water emanating from the Bishop's Palace and channelled in a 'kennel' or deep gutter running down the north side of the street but it rarely was. The street was invariably dirty: coal ash, wood ash, rubbish, dirt dung and filth were regularly dumped there and trampled and ground into the surface by the horse drawn wheeled carts – the High Street being the main traffic artery of the city. Travellers through the city going towards Glastonbury having navigated the High Street, had to pass through the odorous suburb of Southover with its tanners, cobblers and smiths before reaching the clearer air. Most of the leading tradesmen of the city lived in these conditions and consequently the cultural and social gap between them and the aristocratic Hertford was a wide one. They would be deferent towards him as the social code demanded, generally supportive of the royalist war effort but they would not go out of their way to help him.

In the years before the civil war, social relations between the citizens and the resident gentry and clergy were relatively tranquil.

Although separated geographically and to a considerable extent socially – the gentry and clergy living for the most part in the north east of the city in the Liberty – the three groups shared the same devotion to traditional customs and this formed a unifying bond between them. This had been demonstrated unequivocally when they had supported the holding of a church ale with traditional pageants and feasting at midsummer 1607 in defiance of the local Puritan county JPs. An attempt between 1607-1609 by the Puritan stocking maker and burgess, John Hole, to attack traditional customs and to destabilise the corporation by issuing a bill of complaint against some of its members in the court of Star Chamber, although technically successful, had failed in its broader aim of establishing a Puritan political and cultural regime in the city and the government of the city remained in the hands of moderate men. Although the holding of a church ale was not repeated between 1607 and 1642, the constructing and decoration of maypoles, a popular custom which Hole and his supporters detested, continued. There is also evidence suggesting that the city's trade companies may still have held traditional parades in the streets in the years before the civil war. In 1640 the only surviving accounts of a trade company that of the Cordwainers, mention a 'new greene silke streamer with a staff our old silke streamer the Arms of the Company' and in 1642 it still possessed 'one silke Streamer and the Crowne.' This desire to perpetuate long established customs inclined the majority of the inhabitants of Wells to support passively the existing traditional political establishment embodied in the person of Charles I. [1]

ECONOMIC MATTERS

Another reason why Wells in 1642 was a stable city was that it had survived the economic recession of the 1620s better than some other larger towns. It had been able to diversify its economic activities and not remain dependent on one main trade – the manufacture of cloth. While it experienced the same general rise in population as the rest of the country in the eighty years before the civil war, it did not have such serious economic problems as larger cathedral cities like Exeter, Gloucester and Salisbury. Gloucester, for instance, suffered a prolonged economic depression throughout the 1620s and 1630s linked to problems with coastal trade, disruption of its exports due to foreign war, interruption of its inland trade because of plague and the clash between its puritan ruling elite and the resident and visiting county gentry who were important consumers.

Wells on the other hand did not suffer to the same extent. It drew its economic strength from being the centre of a more compact hinterland than Gloucester and was recognised to be the economic, social, cultural and religious centre for the northern part of the county. It is true though that like Gloucester there had been a decline in cloth manufacturing in Wells during the early seventeenth century. In 1622 during a time of a national depression in the cloth industry, the Wells Corporation had petitioned the Privy Council that 'the trade of clothing and generally all other trades which heretofore have been the means to relieve and set at work the poor, are now decayed ... that riots are constantly threatening,' but it is clear that by 1642 the Wells clothing industry had to some extent recovered, its main products being the lighter worsted cloth and stockings. Two clothiers were members of the corporation and at least three others can be identified. The total of outworkers employed in the cloth industry many of whom were women, is not known but even if the stocking maker John Hole's claim in 1607 that he employed between 400 and 500 outworkers weekly was exaggerated, the numbers could still have been significant. Indicative of this is the formation of a new clothiers' company between 1613 and 1636 to replace the shearmen and tuckers and weavers who were subsumed into it. Stocking making was still flourishing in 1642 with two major manufacturers in the city and this helped to keep unemployment in check. Wells was also lucky in that its economic activity was little disrupted by plague during the early seventeenth century. Only on 1 October 1625 did the corporation take the extreme step of postponing the St Calixtus Fair due to be held on 11 October because of 'the grievous sickness of the pestilence.' Also in Wells there was no serious conflict between the corporation and the cathedral clergy and resident gentry who were employers and cash buyers and thus an important part of the city's economy. [2]

While the clothiers provided large-scale employment, more employment opportunities were provided by the artisans and retailers in the city the most important of which were the tanners, shoemakers, tailors, chandlers, pewterers and smiths, while the retail trades were represented by the mercers (woollen and linen drapers), haberdashers, grocers, butchers, and bakers who sold their wares at the twice-weekly markets and the six annual fairs. Some of these men were quite wealthy: Richard Casbeard a shoemaker must have employed other shoemakers to be able to supply 200 pairs of shoes for the royalist army in July 1644 and possibly another 500 pairs demanded in the autumn of 1644 while the linen draper William Bull was able in 1622 to buy the rectorial manor of Shapwick for his eldest son and send him to be educated at one of the inns of court in London. The other trade that increasingly expanded during the first half of the seventeenth century and provided employment was that of innkeeper. Ten new inns appeared between 1600 and the 1640s. Their prosperity is registered by the growth in the rents charged to the innkeepers: the annual rent for the Swan Inn in Sadler Street rose from £4 in 1605 to £10 in 1642. These inns were an integral part of the economy of the city providing as well as refreshment in a hard drinking age, a place where business could be transacted and bargains struck. The large number of separate meeting rooms in the Christopher Inn in the High Street owned by the Vicars Choral and leased to the mayor Robert Morgan in 1642 is one illustration the facilities available for business. [3]

Although poverty in the city grew in the 1630s owing to a substantial rise in inflation and a drop in the real value of wages, it would have been to a certain extent ameliorated by the poor rate administered by the churchwardens of St Cuthbert's church but the lack of surviving records makes it difficult to assess its extent with any degree of accuracy. The poor rate was supplemented by charitable bequests. Many of these bequests were small amounts that were distributed immediately after the death of the testator: in 1604 John Colles, the town clerk, left the 24 residents of the Bubwith Almshouse 6d each and James Godwin in 1616 gave the poor of the town and the Almshouse £5 to be distributed after his death Other bequests were in the form of long term investments: Elizabeth Bowerman gave the corporation £30 in 1602 with the interest to be used to buy coal for the poor. There were many more of these small bequests that provided the corporation with an income to alleviate poverty. In January 1632/3 the corporation revealed that it was holding £620 13s 4d that it had received from charitable benefactions. From this sum lent out at 8%, the corporation derived an income of nearly £50 per annum to spend on poor relief and other projects. However it is doubtful if this sum were ever received in entirety owing to the inability of some burgesses to repay their loans with the accrued interest on time if at all! [4]

Provision for the 'respectable' poor was also improved in the early seventeenth century. The bequests by Bishop Still (1608), Henry Llewellyn (1614) and Walter Brick (1636) increased the almshouse provision from 24 places to 40. A workhouse was established by the corporation in the stable next to the prison in 1623 but it was only small and was supplemented by a burling chamber to provide employment for boys on 5 January 1631/2. (Burling was the taking out of knots and other objects that might have become embedded in the cloth.) An attempt however to build a more commodious workhouse in Priest Row in 1632 was stymied by the refusal of the parish to give up the house and the intransigence of Hugh Mead, the appointed overseer of the work, who refused to cooperate in the realisation of the project. Nothing further was done. [5]

The corporation also attacked the problem of poverty and the resultant social instability by attempting to control the 'dangerous poor' of the city through the establishment of a small house of correction in the prison loft in 1624 and by closely monitoring the economic and social status of younger people in the city as well as the constant flow of visitors. Further, more drastic steps, were taken to avoid people falling into poverty in 1635 when the corporation ordered 17 unmarried women to find masters and three young men were sent to the newly colonised West Indian island of St Kitts as indentured servants for four years.[6]

The recovery of the city's economy in the 1630s, the absence of extreme poverty and the lack of a providential cataclysm so eagerly seized upon by Puritans as a sign of God's anger such as a disaster like the great fire at Dorchester, mediated against the development of Puritanism in Wells. Although the Puritan view of life was present in the city in 1642, it remained very much a minority one. Between 1642 and 1645 Wells was to remain predominantly royalist in sentiment.

GENTRY

Although united by their adherence to traditional culture, both groups – gentry/clergy and citizens were separated socially. As a rule the gentry and clergy took little part in civic affairs and then only as outsiders acting as county JPs or tax commissioners. They tended to worship and be buried in the cathedral and chose their friends from amongst their own group. They were however dependent on the city for provisions, labour for their building projects and for their servants: consequently the citizens usually treated them with respect. The corporation for its part although its main centre of worship was the parish church of St Cuthbert, did have reserved seats in the 'quire' of the cathedral for special occasions and would have had some social interaction there with the gentry and cathedral clergy.

Although third amongst the county's towns for overall wealth in the Lay Subsidy returns of 1641, Wells boasted the largest number of men paying the tax on land. Most of these men supported the royalist cause in the coming conflict and those more deeply involved were heavily fined by the victorious parliamentarians. Some were professional lawyers; others were lay servants of the bishop or the dean and chapter; while others simply enjoyed living in Wells which, because of its plentiful accommodation, was the social and business centre for the central and northern parts of the county as well as being one of the four venues for the quarter sessions. Residents and visitors could find congenial company there, discuss local and national politics and business, educate their children at the Cathedral Grammar School and if they wished, follow their chosen profession. Residents were often bound together by family connections and by friendship. Most of the genteel sort lived in close proximity in the more fashionable north-eastern part of the city in the Cathedral Liberty, the Market Place, New Street, and the eastern end of Chamberlain Street. The Liberty (comprising what is now the North and East Liberties, Cathedral Green and St Andrew's Street,) was outside the jurisdiction of the city and had been developed in the mediaeval period to provide accommodation for the cathedral clergy. In 1642 most of the large stone built houses belonged either to the dean and chapter or to the see of Bath and Wells in the gift of the bishop and one belonged to the vicars choral. Some were leased to resident cathedral clergy, others to the gentry. The dean and chapter also owned other property in the city, especially the New Works in the Market Place, that they leased out to their lay officials and others. The houses in the Liberty were stone built with stables and outhouses and extensive walled gardens between half an acre and an acre in area. These houses compared favourably with the long and narrow tenement houses lining the High Street in the city that were mostly constructed of wood.

Some of the lessees of the properties in the Liberty were gentlemen involved in the government of the county and supporters of the king. Eminent amongst them was the county JP William Walrond from Isle Brewers (10 miles southeast of Taunton) who leased Lechlade's House (now 17 The Liberty.) Walrond with his son George were to be staunch supporters of the royalist cause in the civil war. Walrond was also linked by family ties with the cathedral hierarchy being the father-in-law of the cathedral treasurer and later dean and bishop, Robert Creyghton. His kinsman Humphrey Walrond (either his nephew or great-nephew) another royalist, lived in a canonical house (now the Wells Cathedral Music School) on Cathedral Green. The wealthy royalist barrister, Edward Wykes who came from an established Wells family and was for a brief time in 1644 recorder of the city, lived on the site of what is now 23 The Liberty. He was active on the royalist side between 1642 and his death in 1644 and in that year issued a warrant to the Wells Corporation to levy £100 for the royal army. He again had cathedral links being the brother-in-law of Dr Paul Godwin a resident canon at the cathedral. His wife Jane was the daughter of Dr Gilbert Bourne who had been the vicar general of the diocese of Bath and Wells in the early 1590s and she was also a great-niece of the Marian bishop, another Gilbert Bourne. Another lawyer, the royalist barrister John Baber, recorder of the city from 1625-1644 lived at what is now 25 Market Place in a property belonging to the dean and chapter. Like Wykes, he was active in the royalist administration of the county between 1642 and 1644 co-signing a warrant with William Walrond in 1644 for the provision of gunpowder and ammunition for the city's magazine in St Cuthbert's church (in the thirteenth century church treasury accessed from the north aisle. It is now the choir vestry). Other country gentry had moved to Wells taking up the available accommodation in the Liberty: men such as William Prowse of Compton Bishop, and the royalist Valentine Trym the eldest son of David Trym who was leasing the Wookey manor house and demesne from the Rolle family. Trym was a great friend of the royalist barrister Edward Wykes having been the servant of his father Nicholas Wykes. Also living in the Liberty in what is now the Dean's Lodging was Samuel Powell, the son of a former cathedral prebendary and archdeacon of Bath, Dr William Powell. Powell although no doubt having royalist sympathies, was not fined for his royalism and remained the tenant of the house until 1660. [7]

Outside the Liberty there were well-established minor gentry families with connections to the cathedral who had settled permanently in the city such as the Bower family. Its representative in 1642 was Edmund Bower (2) son of Adrian Bower and nephew of Edmund Bower (1) whose father Walter Bower had been a canon of the cathedral. Bower was to be fined by the victorious parliamentarians for his support for the royalist cause after the civil war. Andrew Bowerman who lived in modern 78 High Street whose great uncle had been the sub dean of the cathedral and whose father had been clerk of the courts of the dean and chapter, was also a royalist sympathiser. His son, a clergyman, was to be fined after the civil war for his royalism. Another royalist family well established in the city was the Coward family. Thomas Coward (died 1621) had moved to the city on inheriting a mansion house in Chamberlain St from his uncle John Whiting of Axbridge. He subsequently became mayor of the city in 1611/12 and 1619/20. His sons Thomas and William were not so politically active. In 1642 both were resident in Chamberlain Street; Thomas, the captain of the Wells militia, was to be fined for his support of the royalist cause after the civil war while his brother, William, who before 1662 had taken no official part in city government was, after the purge of parliamentary supporters, to be mayor of Wells in 1663-4. While the Coward brothers' views remained in harmony, the civil war caused the Morgan brothers, Robert and William, to take different sides Both were grandsons of John Still (Bishop of Bath and Wells 1593-1608) and sons of William Williams alias Morgan of minor gentry stock who had been a woollen draper and pursued a long and successful career as a capital burgess on the corporation. Robert (see below) was to become an active parliamentarian whereas William remained a rather reluctant royalist. William Morgan however, throughout the conflict and afterwards stayed on good terms with men who supported parliament citing in his 1654 will two staunch parliamentarians, William Smith and the town clerk John Standish as his particular friends.

None of these men described above with the exceptions of Edward Wykes, William Coward and Robert Morgan ever became burgesses of the city and Wykes became one only in 1644 when he was appointed recorder. From the evidence of the surviving wills it is clear that the wealthier families resident in the Liberty such as the Walrond, Wykes and Evans (see below) did not mix socially with the tradesmen of the city. Edward Wykes in his will cited as his friends Dr. Paul Godwin, his brothers-in-law the Bournes and William Bull of Shapwick; while Walrond had his own clique of family and friends in the Liberty. Those minor gentry who lived in the city such as Andrew Bowerman, Edmund Bower and William Coward on the other hand did integrate socially with the more influential men in the city. Bowerman's will was witnessed by the town clerk Bartholomew Cox and the republican John Casbeard; the Bower brothers, Adrian and Edmund, were especially friendly with George Bull, Walter Brick, William Smith and Robert Rowley all of whom served on the corporation; and William Coward's will was witnessed by the innkeeper Ralph Coniers and Richard Thomas again both members of the corporation. [8]

THE CLERGY AND ECCLESIASTICAL OFFICE HOLDERS

In that July of 1642 the position of the church establishment in Wells was under threat. The Bishop of Bath and Wells, William Piers had been imprisoned in London in December 1640 for his Laudian policies and after his release was now living in semi-retirement on his Oxfordshire estate. The administration of the diocese was mainly delegated to his registrar, Alexander Jett, whose surviving correspondence reflects the uncertainty and stress of the times especially as the abolition of episcopacy was being actively discussed in parliament.

    The Wells Cathedral clergy were also under threat. They were led by the dean, Walter Raleigh, a nephew of the famous Sir Walter. He had been in office for just over a year and was a royal chaplain who was to suffer disastrously for his royalist sympathies. The other key cathedral clergy resident in Wells were Dr Gerard Wood, archdeacon of Wells, Dr Robert Creyghton the treasurer, Dr Sebastian Smith, the precentor and the resident canon, Dr Paul Godwin, son of Thomas Godwin. (Bishop of Bath and Wells 1584-90) Also under threat of possible loss of livelihood in the event of a parliamentary victory and resident in the Liberty were the lay officials of the diocese of Bath and Wells and of the dean and chapter. Dr Arthur Duck, the bishop's vicar general although mainly resident in London on business for the Archbishop of Canterbury, William Laud, leased a house in the Liberty. Other church functionaries were residents such as Robert Chute, steward of the dean's manors in Somerset. In the Market Place at modern 16 lived Alexander Jett who later 'trailed a pike in the royal army' and was registrar general to the bishop; Mark Tabor the registrar of the archdeaconry of Wells lived at modern no 19 and at modern 21 was Tristram Towse, deputy chapter clerk, registrar of the peculiars of the dean and chapter and registrar of the archdeaconry of Bath, who was later fined for his royalism. Arthur Mattock, the bishop's receiver general also lived in the Liberty while William Crosse, the bailiff of the bishop's manor of Wells leased modern 6 and 8 High Street from the Wells Corporation. These men provided a solid base of royalist support in the city. [9]

THE CORPORATION

While there was much support for the royalist cause in Wells during the civil war, there was a minority on the corporation that supported parliament and a small number of burgesses were in arms for parliament. In the spring of 1642 of the 829 adult males registered in the city at the time of the signing of the Protestation (see below), approximately 150, the more substantial tradesmen in the city, were burgesses. The city was ruled by a corporation of 24 capital burgesses: a self-perpetuating oligarchy which to replenish its ranks, chose men from the limited pool of the 150 who had paid the burgess fee (ranging from 7s to 20s) plus gifts of wine, wax and gloves.

The Wells Corporation although it had existed de facto since the fourteenth century, had been formed by a royal charter of 1589. Its members were made up of a mayor (also a master), seven other masters and 16 capital burgesses making 24 in all. Added to this total was a recorder, the legal officer of the corporation, who could also be a capital burgess and master. The corporation members were all, with the exception of the elderly town clerk Bartholomew Cox, involved in trade in the town.

A majority on the corporation in the summer of 1642 was

favourable to the royalist cause but the members were also pragmatic men who although often swayed by personal rivalries, realised that the good government of the city and its economic survival was to the advantage of their own business interests. The arrival of the Marquis of Hertford and his armed party in the city and the mobilisation of the parliamentary response to the north and east were worrying developments and it was the corporation's responsibility to find a way to save the city from the consequences of war.

The eight masters were the most influential men on the corporation and of these, the most venerable was the tanner Henry Foster. He had been a capital burgess for 41 years and in 1642 was over 70 years of age. He had been an instigator of the 1607 midsummer shows and had been cited in John Hole's bill of complaint in Star Chamber but not punished. Foster would undoubtedly have been favourable to the royalist cause but he was not a popular member of the corporation: initially he had been passed over for a mastership no doubt because of his violent temper and his frequent tendency to use insulting language against his colleagues. When younger he had beaten the sergeant at mace with a pair of shackles and had had to be reprimanded by the corporation. Despite these faults, Foster had played an active part in corporation business and continued to do so during the civil war. He died in 1646.

Another influential figure but of a more idiosyncratic kind was Bartholomew Cox who had been a burgess and town clerk since 1604, becoming a capital burgess and master in 1623 and mayor for the first time in 1625/6. Cox was the type of person who could accommodate himself to any political situation providing his own interests were secured. Over all these years he had dedicated himself to maintaining and exploiting his own position on the corporation and his ambition had even led him to aspire to become MP for Wells in 1625. He had overtly supported neither side in the 1607 church ale controversy although he had confiscated a possibly libellous ballad then circulating but this was probably to safeguard his own position as town clerk. From 1628 he also acted as clerk to the dean and chapter and was deputy sheriff for the county in 1629/30. He had some experience of the world outside Wells having travelled to London on corporation business on three separate occasions during the 1630s as well as many local journeys. However his assiduous dedication to his own financial advancement had led him into a damaging conflict with the recorder, John Baber who in 1629 alleged that Cox had neglected the city's government, extorted money for alehouse licences and broken the terms of the 1589 charter. Baber's intention to prosecute Cox in the Star Chamber court galvanised the corporation into reversing its original suspension of Cox and asking Baber to drop the case because any punishment of the town clerk would reflect badly on the corporation. It is significant that only 15 members out of the 24 were present on the 5 November 1631 to exonerate Cox. By 1642 Cox was 67 years old and less physically active than he had been. In 1641 he had been asked by the corporation to accompany Robert Lane to London to procure a legal opinion regarding the interpretation of the 1589 charter but had declined 'both for his weakness in body and business he has here in the country.' However he remained active on the corporation until increased decrepitude forced his retirement from active affairs in 1650. He died in 1653. His career suggests that he was unlikely to express any firm political opinions being mostly concerned with keeping his social and professional position and cultivating his business interests outside the city.

Walter Brick, another master in the conservative mould, is of little consequence in the civil war narrative because his last appearance at a corporation meeting was on 10 October 1642. Increasing age and ill-health meant retirement from active local politics until his death in 1649. Two other masters were the baker/clothier Thomas Jones and the mercer William Baron both moderate conservative figures who were to remain in office throughout the vicissitudes of the civil war and its aftermath. Jones died in February 1652/3 but Baron remained in office throughout the Interregnum. He was not purged in 1662 and remained on the corporation until his death in 1668. The seventh master, Robert Rowley, a victualler, had definite royalist sympathies. He was another newcomer only becoming a capital burgess in June 1641, a master two months later and mayor on 30 September 1642. He was however still a member of the corporation in November 1647, but whether or not he continued as a member until his death in 1651 is unclear because of lack of evidence. Thus of the eight masters on the corporation six, although pragmatic and moderate, were likely to be royalist supporters between 1642 and 1646.

The same pattern of moderation and pragmatism can be found in the majority of the capital burgesses who in 1642 comprised two mercers, three clothiers, four tanners, two victuallers/innkeepers, one vintner, one chandler, one miller, one saddler and one shoemaker. Of these, four: John Cox, Robert Creese, John Hill and William Taverner died of natural causes during the period of the civil war and one, Thomas Foster, the son of Henry Foster was murdered. Of the remaining 11, one, Ralph Ciniox, left the town in 1644 not to return and of the remaining 10 only one, the innkeeper William West, fought for the royalists. Of the remaining nine, three: Robert Hill, William Atwell and Richard Casbeard continued to hold office after the defeat of the royalists whilst the three others: William Hiett, William Lewce and Robert Lane were members of the corporation in September 1644 but died shortly afterwards. The remaining two masters and three capital burgesses can be clearly identified as supporters of parliament, the chief of whom was Robert Morgan.

Morgan was a relatively new member of the corporation in 1642. As has already been noted, he was the grandson of a bishop and son of a capital burgess. His father had been a supporter of the Wells church ale of 1607 and a prominent opponent of the Puritan group that had attacked it. Robert Morgan became an attorney at law with business interests in malting and brewing but his career prior to 1639, seems to have been centred outside Wells. He was however an ambitious and astute man. By 1639 he was a widower with two children and in that year he evidently determined to establish himself in Wells where he could expect, because of his antecedents, to enjoy a career in local politics. To facilitate this, in August 1639 he married as his second wife Frances Cordwent the widow of the prosperous Wells innkeeper Humphrey Cordwent who had died the previous year. Morgan's rise to a position of authority on the corporation was swift. On 30 October 1640 he became a burgess, on 1 July 1641 he became a capital burgess and master and on 29 September 1641, mayor of the city. Morgan was obviously the kind of person the corporation was anxious to recruit especially as he now had an economic stake in the town controlling through his marriage three inns all in the High Street, the George (on the site of the present Nat West Bank), the Christopher (the property east of modern Guardhouse Lane) and the Hare and Hounds. (now 33 High Street) Despite his traditional background, Morgan was to become in the autumn of 1642 a committed parliamentarian and was imprisoned by the royalists in 1643, losing his place on the corporation. The reasons for his political stance are not fully clear but judging from his later career it seems that as well as being ambitious, he had the knack of backing the winning side. It is likely that his experiences as mayor in the tense standoff between the royalist and parliamentary forces at Wells in late July and early August 1642 and the success of the parliamentary cause in Somerset in the autumn of the same year, convinced him of the ultimate success of parliament. He also probably had Puritan religious sympathies but they do not seem to have been the prime cause for his political allegiance – he never became a Presbyterian elder in the parish church after the expulsion of the vicar of St Cuthbert's. A prestigious political career in county politics was his main aim and in that he succeeded. After the civil war, he became a member of the Somerset County Committee and a county JP; he died in 1653.

Robert Morgan and his four other allies on the corporation were to become increasingly important figures in the administration of the city during and after the civil war. Next in importance to Morgan was Stephen Haskett, the eighth master. He had been a servant to the wealthy linen-draper William Bull (d. 1623) and then had set up in business as a mercer. Haskett was a reluctant member of the corporation. In May 1641 he initially refused to become a burgess and showed the same reluctance a little later when approached to become a capital burgess. On being threatened with a heavy fine he gave in and soon became a master in September 1641. Haskett's reluctance to serve stemmed from his Puritanical religious views (he became a Presbyterian elder after the civil war) and his radical political opinions were out of step with those of the majority of his colleagues. He also may have wished not to take up the burdens of local office. Although he signed the petition in support of episcopacy soon after his appointment as master, he was soon recognised by his colleagues to be a firm supporter of parliament. On the royalist reconquest of Somerset from the parliamentarians in 1643, because of his assiduity in collecting parliamentary taxes, he was ejected from the corporation along with Robert Morgan on the information of the royalist commanders the Marquis of Hertford and Sir Ralph Hopton. He returned to local politics after the parliamentarians retook Somerset in 1645 rejoining the corporation after 1647 and became mayor in 1655/6. He was again finally excluded from the corporation in the royalist purge of 1662.

Two of the other parliamentary supporters on the corporation were also drawn from the clothing trades. The two clothiers on the corporation, Thomas Salmon (from 1646 a Presbyterian elder) and Richard Fryer, were to become active supporters of parliament during the coming years although remaining in the town. They were linked to the Puritans who had supported John Hole in 1607. Although initially unpopular amongst the majority of the city's leading citizens, these Puritans had remained a recognisable group mutually supporting one another while integrating with the traditionalist majority. The two main supporters of Hole, the pewterer Hugh Mead (d 1639) and the grocer Humphrey Palmer (d 1641), pursued long careers on the corporation. Mead in later life was concerned to be considered a gentleman and consequently became a worshipper at the cathedral where he claimed his soul had received much comfort while Palmer, after his unsuccessful attempt to become mayor in 1616, made an attempt at enforcing strict Sunday observance during his mayoralty in January 1623/4 that was not repeated. However he soon became embroiled in a controversy over missing supplies of gunpowder and became discredited. The Puritan influence continued through Thomas Mead, Hugh's son, who became a leading member of the corporation in the 1650s and was described by Cornelius Burges, his rival in the purchase of the deposed bishop's lands, as 'an arch incendiary.'

Fryer and Salmon were men of more moderate views than Thomas Mead. Fryer was the apprentice of Christopher Croker (d 1624) who had been Hole's apprentice and who gave evidence for Hole in the Star Chamber investigation. Croker was also a surety for Salmon when he became a burgess in 1622 and Salmon married the daughter of Joseph Hill a clothier and supporter of Hole in 1607. Joseph Gallington who during the Interregnum became a leading member of the corporation, was an apprentice of Salmon and both Fryer and Salmon sponsored the Puritan Croscombe clothier William Whiting when he became a burgess in 1636. Whiting became a capital burgess after 1648 and mayor in 1658/9. Salmon died in 1658 but Fryer survived the restoration purge of 1662 and remained a member of the Corporation until his death in 1664.

The retail cloth trade was represented by two mercers. William

Smith the more important one was a supporter of parliament. He was the son of the grocer, Edward Smith (d 1623) who had opposed the corporation's attempt to attack John Hole in Star Chamber and who left a will in which he emphasised his Puritan views at length. However his son, William, was another man of moderate views and although active in Commonwealth and Protectorate politics, retained his seat on the corporation until his death in 1663.

Whatever their political allegiances, it was in the interest of all 24 men on the corporation in a time of civil disturbance to sustain the local community, to defend its rights, to maintain law and order and to preserve the economic viability of the city increasingly dependent on attracting visitors to its markets, fairs and inns. Friendships between them cut across religious and political allegiances: it is interesting to note that Hugh Mead in his will in 1639 mentioned his "beloved friends" as being Thomas Salmon and William Smith the later parliamentarians, Robert Lane, a moderate and William West who later was in arms on the king's side. Local solidarity was also engendered because the corporation also needed to keep its large portfolio of properties and its charitable funds secure, as it was from these sources that it derived much of its income. Thus the corporation as far as possible presented a united front to whichever of the warring parties was in the ascendant despite any difference of opinion amongst its members. [10]

CATHOLIC RECUSANTS

The small group of resident catholic recusants in the town played little overt part in town affairs but were accepted members of the community living in the Liberty and the northern area of the town. Occasionally they were fined for non-attendance at church by the ecclesiastical or civil authorities but only when their absence from church services had become blatant; this was the only punitive action taken against them. During the Civil War they kept a low profile and only one was fined after it.

Chief among the recusants was the long established Godwin family: its representatives in Wells 1642 being James Godwin and his cousin Joseph Godwin son of Robert Godwin who was leasing Wookey rectory and its lands. Joseph was the son-in-law of the JP

William Walrond. James Godwin owned extensive estates including that of St John's Hospital in Wells. Unlike his father James Godwin d 1616, he did not become a burgess. Another recusant family resident in the town at modern 17 New Street, was the Beaumont family in the persons of Anthony and John Beaumont. They were friendly with the Wookey Godwins; their father William (d 1633) had made Joseph Godwin's father Robert one of the executors of his will along with Edward Wykes, Robert Toope, another Liberty resident, and William Bellamy, secretary to Ezekiel Barkham, the bishop's receiver general. The Beaumont brothers concentrated on running their stocking making business and managing their land portfolio and took no part in town government. The Evans family was the third, living at what had been the college for chantry priests on the site of what is now 15 the Liberty. William Evans was the son of another William Evans who had been the master at the Cathedral Grammar School. He showed no overt allegiance to the royalist cause, his recusancy was drawback enough. In June 1651 the Committee of Compounding (the committee established by parliament to fine royalist supporters) laconically remarked of him "long since sequestered for recusancy, never having been in arms." As with the Evans family, recusancy was no bar to holding an office connected with the church. Maurice Lund another recusant and a resident of the Liberty, had with his father been granted the offices of keeper of the Bishop's Palace, bailiff of the bishop's stock and warden of all his woods. Other recusants briefly resident in the city at this time were the Cottingtons, father and son, possibly relatives of Dr James Cottington a precentor of Wells who had died in 1605.[10]

As for the commonality of the city, little record remains of their views on the momentous events going on around them. Civil war could only bring hardship and disruption to lives. Victories that promised a peace which could be lasting would be celebrated, armies passing through the city would be endured, new opportunities for business cultivated and social cohesion maintained whatever the difficulty.

NOTES
[1] For Hole's biography see Nott, A, & Hasler, J, (eds), *Wells Convocation Acts Books 1589-1665, Parts 1 & 2 1589-1629 & 1629-44; 1662-5*, SRS Vols 90 & 91, Taunton 2004, p 977; for an account of the Wells festivities of 1607 see Stokes, J, (ed), *Somerset, Records of Early English Drama, Vols. 1&2*, Toronto

1996, pp 719-728, Nott, T, *Poxe, Puncke and Puritane,* History Round Wells, Issue 4, Wells 2001, passim &; Scrase, A, *Wells: A Small City,* Stroud 2006, pp 83-89; for the Cordwainers' Accounts see Stokes, J, *The Wells Cordwainers' Show: New Evidence concerning Guild Entertainments in Somerset,* Comparative Drama 27. 2, 1993, pp 176-196.

[2] Clark, P, *The Ramoth-Gilead of the Good: Urban Change and Political Radicalism at Gloucester 1540-1640* in Barry, J, (ed) *The Tudor and Stuart Town: A Reader in English Urban History 1530-1688,* London 1990, pp. 244-273; for Exeter see Stoyle *From Deliverance to Destruction,,* Exeter 1996; for Salisbury see Slack, P, *Poverty and Politics in Salisbury, 1597-1666,* in Clark, P and Slack, P, (eds) *Crisis and Order in English Towns 1500-1700,* London 1972; for Dorchester see Underdown D, *Fire From Heaven,* London, 1992; Underdown, D, *Riot, Revel and Rebellion,* Oxford 1985, p 56; Nott & Hasler, SRS.Vol 90, op cit, pp 31, 420-1; Stokes, J, (ed), *Somerset Records of Early English Drama,* Vol.1 op cit p. 263.

[3] Scrase, A, *Wells: A Small City,* op cit pp. 91-92; Hill, R, *The Christopher Inn,* History Round Wells Issue 5, 2002; Nott & Hasler, SRS Vol 91, op cit, pp 871 & 884.

[4] NA Prob. 11/105 & 11/128; Nott & Hasler, SRS Vol 91, op. cit., pp. 587-602.

[5] Nott & Hasler, SRS Vol 91, op. cit, pp 580-1. 584, 666, 949-950, 986-987, 1019-1011; SRS Vol 91, op cit, pp 335-6.

[6] Nott & Hasler, SRS Vol 90, op cit, p 381; Nott & Hasler, SRS Vol 91, op cit, pp 565, 667-669; Slack, P, *Poverty and Policy in Tudor and Stuart England,* London, 1988, pp 61 & 91.

[7] For information on the gentry living in the Wells Liberty see Bailey, D S, *The Canonical Houses of Wells,* Gloucester 1982, p 21 passim; Bailey, D S, *Wells Manor of Canon Grange,* Gloucester 1985, p. 3 passim; I am grateful to A. J. Scrase for personal information and analysis of the 1642 protestation returns.

[8] The gentry wills cited are as follows: Edward Wykes NA Prob 11/200; William Walrond NA Prob 11/309; Adrian Bower NA Prob 11/157; Edmund Bower NA Prob 11/143; Andrew Bowerman NA Prob 11/200; William Coward NA Prob 11/324.

[9] For the careers of the capital burgesses on the Wells Corporation see Nott & Hasler SRS Vol 91, op cit, pp 938-1024.

[10] I am grateful to A J Scrase for the list of recusants in the 1642 protestation returns; individual wills are William Evans NA Prob 11/162; William Beaumont (father of Anthony & John) NA Prob 11/163; John Lund (brother of Maurice Lund) NA Prob 11/170.

CHAPTER 2

NATIONAL GOVERNMENT AND LOCAL AFFAIRS 1625-40

During the period 1625-40, Wells like other places was adversely affected by the religious, financial and military policies of the government of Charles I. The high church policy of the new Archbishop of Canterbury, William Laud, enforced locally by William Piers, Bishop of Bath and Wells from 1632, irritated the cathedral clergy and was unpopular in the diocese generally. Piers on his arrival in the diocese not only proceeded to attempt to enforce this policy of 'the beauty of holiness' on the churches under his control but also pursued a more aggressive and intrusive policy into what he considered were his rights and in the process alienated the Wells Corporation. The unrest engendered by these actions was exacerbated by the government's policy of non-parliamentary taxation in the form of benevolences, loans and ship money. The imposition of billeting on the city in 1628 and the inefficiencies of militia organisation between 1638 and 1640 also caused resentment and irritation. These factors had the effect of making the citizens of Wells become more conscious of the national political scene by 1640 and led some of them to become more active politically than they had been in the past.

RELIGIOUS VIEWS IN THE CITY

While local people were irritated by what they perceived as royal misgovernment in taxation and the preparations for war, 'it was the force of religion that drove minorities to fight and forced majorities to make reluctant choices.'[1] From the hundred or so surviving Prerogative Court of Canterbury wills of the more affluent Wells citizens, it can be seen from the preambles that the majority of the testators were probably conservative in matters of religion in that their references to God were expressed in traditional form. These people, mostly men, had grown up used to the tolerant and moderate approach of their diocesan bishops in the first quarter of the seventeenth century. In particular, Arthur Lake (Bishop of Bath and Wells 1616-1626) had opposed extreme religious views. He had argued that prolonged speculation on the doctrine of predestination was not pastorally profitable and had urged his ordinands to adopt the view that God's grace was universal. He had however patronised a preaching ministry and so kept the evangelical preachers in Somerset inside the church organisation. This tolerant attitude was to change in the 1630s.

Religion however was not just a private matter in Wells. The corporation was linked institutionally with the parish church of St Cuthbert. It appointed one of the churchwardens, had its own special seats in the nave, processed there on important feast days and appointed a priest to assist the vicar. People were bound by the penal laws to attend Sunday worship there and often prosecuted in the petty sessions court if they did not. It was therefore of importance to local people who the vicar of St Cuthbert's was and what his religious affiliations were.

ST CUTHBERT'S CHURCH

The vicar of St Cuthbert's church from 1634 was Thomas Westley. Appointed by the dean and chapter on the nomination of Dr Timothy Revett, archdeacon of Bath, Westley was from a London gentry family. It is likely that his appointment was the result of intervention by Bishop Piers who was a personal friend. In 1659 Westley's wife was to be buried in Walthamstow in the Thorne chapel in the church of St Mary at Walthamstow, the same church where the bishop and his second wife were to be buried in 1670 and 1679. Westley had in fact known the future bishop since his time at Oxford. Both Westley and Piers had been educated at Christ Church, Oxford. Westley was there from 1617 until 1625 and met Piers at that time; Piers had a canon's stall in Christ Church Cathedral from 1616 and was vice-chancellor of the university from 1621-4. During his time at Oxford, Piers had promoted the high-church doctrines that Westley supported. Westley was to remain as vicar of St Cuthbert's until April 1646 when he was forced to resign due to his support for the royalist cause and his high church views by the then mayor Richard Casbeard. At the Restoration he was rewarded for his loyalty by the King with a prebendary's stall in the cathedral. During Westley's incumbency at St Cuthbert's there were to be no Sunday afternoon preachers – a custom that was growing in popularity in some more evangelical churches; the congregation of St Peter and Paul at nearby Shepton Mallet for instance had appointed a Sunday afternoon preacher despite the opposition of the rector John Couth. Evidence from the pre-war years showed that Westley's relationship with the corporation was somewhat prickly. Having been engaged to preach one of the four annual sermons for which money had been provided in earlier years by testators, he showed his reluctance when he claimed that he had not been spoken 'unto by any to make it [and] demanded 3s 5d more to make up his salary for his pains, 10s in the whole.' If he had to preach then he would be adequately paid for it. On 16 March 1637/8 he attended a corporation meeting and restated his demands: 'he will have 10s for every sermon that hereafter is to be preached for any money given to the corporation wherefore sermons are to be preached, except Mistress Small for which he will have but 6s 8d.'

Westley was assisted in his ministry at St Cuthbert's by a curate appointed by the corporation. The curate usually held the post of governor of the adjacent Bubwith Almshouse and his appointment as governor needed also to be approved by the dean and chapter. The curate was paid £7 per annum by the corporation to conduct morning prayer in the church. The combined posts of governor and curate had been held by Richard Deane until his death in 1641. Deane was succeeded by Daniel Buckley in May 1642 with the approval of Thomas Westley and the dean and chapter. Buckley however died on March 23 1642/3 and was replaced by Francis Standish one of the vicars choral. Standish was appointed solely by the corporation to both the curacy and governorship of the almshouse. The dean and chapter could not be consulted because according to the corporation record they were absent from the city.[2]

Westley's high church principles were not shared by all his

parishioners. The preambles to surviving wills reflect a diversity of religious experience amongst people in the city. There were the more radical Puritans, one of the leaders of whom was the pewterer Hugh Mead. In his 1639 will, he clearly expressed his more extreme Protestant views bequeathing his soul 'into the hands of Jesus Christ Saviour and Redemmer stedfastlie believing to be saved by his alone merits, passion and bloodshedding and by noe other meanes or wayes whatsoever ... one day to behold him my blessed Saviour sitting at the right hand of God the father in glory in the daie of the resurrection of the dead.' He also revealed in his will that he had attended divine worship in the cathedral where no doubt he enjoyed the preaching of the Puritan archdeacon of Bath, Gerard Wood. A small group of men expressed Calvinistic views. Andrew Bowerman, in 1647 left a will showing his belief in predestination referring to the 'elect children of God' of whom he considered himself one. Thomas Baron a wealthy mercer in 1634 had the same belief trusting in 'eternal life with other the elect children of God.' These wills however were exceptions and amongst the surviving wills of the artisans, shopkeepers and minor gentlemen, such as those of the astute shoemaker Richard Casbeard, the cooper Thomas Fatt and the gentleman John Bradford, the preambles are generally fairly brief, the testator placing his or her soul into 'the hands of Almighty God ... assuring myself of salvation through the merits of Jesus Christ my redeemer,' before proceeding with the bequests.[3] This suggests that as far as the evidence allows, the more prosperous Wells testators were a fairly levelheaded group and not prone to religious extremism. A literate minority were interested in theology nonetheless. The Puritan John Hole had a collection of books most of which he left to his great-nephew 'except my best Bible and book of martyrs,' The town clerk, Bartholomew Cox gave theological works to the library of the vicars choral and the Wells MP Sir Edward Rodney wrote his own theological works: which survive in the British Library: "On Divine Providence" and "Meditation on the Lord's Prayer" amongst others.[4]

BISHOP PIERS

The policies of Bishop William Piers soon caused opposition and dangerous resentment. He had been appointed Bishop of Bath and

Wells on the 26 November 1632 and his enthronement took place on the 4 January 1632/3. The relationship of the corporation with the new bishop was problematic from the start. It was unfortunate that the corporation was embroiled in a lawsuit with the recorder over its alleged mismanagement of charitable funds when the bishop arrived in Wells and neglected to present him with the customary silver bowl. On 21 July 1634 the mayor informed the corporation 'my lord bishop takes it unkind that he has not been presented with a gift as four ... others of his predecessors have had and desires an answer.' Nothing was done to redress the situation until 24 October when the corporation disassociated itself from the recorder's attack on the bishop for shutting his water gates, thus cutting off the supply of water from the palace to the town, and hastened to present him with the customary bowl and a pair of gloves for his wife.

Bishop Piers was much more intrusive in the affairs of the city than his predecessors had been and soon the corporation was treating him with a certain amount of suspicion. When Piers wished to see Bishop Bekynton's 1450 grant of the water for the conduit, the corporation refused to part with it but was prepared to make a copy which the bishop's solicitor could come to the council house to view if he so wished. When the bishop on 17 January 1638/9 required a record of the town sessions since he had become bishop, the corporation replied that if he wished to see any particular article, he would have to pay a fee to the town clerk for copying it. Again on 11 March 1638/9 the corporation saw its liberties threatened when the bishop arrested Thomas Jones, the profligate son of one of the masters, and sent him to the quarter sessions and then to the assizes for contempt. Further trouble erupted at about the same time when the bishop interfered in the appointment of the parish clerk for St Cuthbert's and insisted that his servant James Sandford should be chosen. His wishes were opposed by the parishioners and he was forced to go to the assize judge who on 11 March 1638/9 ordered that Sandford should be established in the office of parish clerk and that 'yf any shall oppose him therin, then the next justice of the peace is desired by this court upon sight of this order to bynde over to the assizes all persons whoe shall oppose the said Sandford in executing of the same office and to be of good behaviour.' This threat did not stop some of the local Puritans from expressing critical opinions about the church establishment. In the following year, on 23 March 1639/40, two

Wells shoemakers, Henry Hutchins and Henry Attwood were bound over at Chard assizes 'for speaking of scandalous and opprobrious words against my Lordes Grace of Canterbury and being now called in open court have not appeared but have made default.' They were in fact attacking the bishop's superior, William Laud who had been bishop of Bath and Wells from 1626-28. The local JPs near Wells were ordered to apprehend them and commit them to the county gaol where they were to remain until the next assizes. Their names do not appear again in the record. [5]

The opprobrious words the two shoemakers used are evidence that a minority of people in Wells were adopting more extreme Puritan views. The bishops were criticised for their high church policies and for supporting the re-issue by the king of the Book of Sports which promoted traditional Sunday pastimes as long as the obligatory attendance at church had been observed. On 24 March 1633/4 Ralph Haines a Wells shoemaker, was reported as saying 'that my lord Curle [Bishop of Bath & Wells 1629-32] was blind & did not understand the scripture in respect he suffered maypoles to be sett upp in the Towne of Wells.' Some traditionalists however persisted in honouring the May customs even profaning the Sabbath with them. The ecclesiastical authorities in the form of the archbishop's visitation had to act when the actual Sunday service was profaned and in 1634-5. Richard Lovell, a cutler, and John Mayne, an itinerant musician, were presented in the ecclesiastical court for 'hewinge and trimmeing of a maypole upon a Sabbath daie in the morninge when the bell tolled to prayer, and that a Maypole was sett upp before eveninge prayer contrarie to his Maiesties Declaration And that there was a drumbe beate upp att the setting upp of the maypole.' Despite the royal support for Sunday sports outside the times of divine service, the disapproval shown by the vociferous Puritan minority supported by local Puritan JPs helped to accelerate the decline in traditional entertainments that had begun in 1608. The dissatisfaction with the established church as manifested by the Puritan element at St Cuthbert's and the cathedral, led a few men and women from Wells to travel to Bristol to worship with the newly formed Broadmead congregation, later to be a Baptist church. There was also every opportunity for the Wells Puritans to slake their thirst for sermons by travelling outside the city to hear them. A visiting preacher such as the suspended Welsh minister William Erbury preached for four hours at Chew Stoke in 1640 with only a break for a psalm. He attracted "divers strangers from Bristol" and even some from Wells may have attended. When Erbury preached at Burrington one of the churchwardens reported seeing 40 strangers in the church from Chew Stoke, Blagdon, Ubley and other places. It is clear that Erbury aroused much excitement in the neighbourhood and beyond. There was indeed no shortage of Puritan preachers to the north and east of Wells to satisfy the spiritual needs of Wells Puritans. [6]

'IN A MIST OF CEREMONIES'

In 1642, the established church as represented by the cathedral hardly presented a picture of harmony. For most of the 1630s there was an ongoing dispute between the Puritan inclined cathedral clergy and the Laudian dean and bishop. The dean, George Warburton, a royal chaplain and also a protégé of William Laud had been appointed on 25 August 1631. He had been at Oxford at the time when Laud was there and had been a royal chaplain to James I and Charles I. Warburton who had held no major clerical appointment before coming to Wells, was also appointed as dean of Gloucester at the same time. It is clear from his correspondence with Laud that Warburton had a mandate to ' reduce things [in the cathedral] to the ancient and comelie form [in] discharge of my dutie, and of that trust, which it hath pleased God and his Majestie to recommend to me.' Laud and his followers, supported by the king believed that a church should be a place where worshippers should be able 'to behold His [God's] glory and majesty in the stateliness and beauty of the building, in the richness of the sacred vessels and ornaments, ... the various fruits of the blessed sacraments and the dignity, holiness and sacred pomp of his ministers.' External ceremony and worship were at the centre of their vision. Preaching and sermon based evangelism were frowned upon and the emphasis placed on prayer and the sacraments.

Warburton's first act was to produce a letter from the Secretary of State, Sir John Coke, dated 11 June 1632 telling him that 'His majestie is informed that the communion table in your church [which had been placed at the east end of the quire and railed off since 1592] is not furnished with such decent ornaments as are requisite and as in other cathedral churches are supplied.' Warburton was informed that the king wished for a 'spedy redresse'. The royal information as to the state of the cathedral ornaments undoubtedly came from Warburton himself and his presentation of the letter to the chapter was a *coup de main*.

The dean was soon in open conflict with the archdeacon of Wells, Dr Gerard Wood. Wood was a Cambridge man, a moderate Puritan and so he inevitably disliked the high church policies of Warburton. Warburton described him as 'of a stirring spirit, and one that never yet, that I have seen or heard, either kneeled at prayer, or did anie reverence either toward the Altar, or at the name of Jesus.' Wood was also a personal friend of Bishop Curle, soon to be promoted from Bath and Wells to the see of Winchester. Warburton found he had little support from Curle in his efforts of 'reform' and so corresponded with Laud over the head of his bishop. On 30 September 1632 Warburton wrote to William Laud, then Bishop of London, stating that on his appointment as dean the previous year he had found the state and order of the cathedral 'much out of frame.' He had endeavoured to reform matters but had been frustrated by Archdeacon Wood's determination to preach the endowed sermons from a wooden pulpit in the 'quire' instead of from Bishop Knight's stone pulpit in the nave which the dean wanted used. The dean considered this preaching in the 'quire' to be 'a late upstart practize' and his main reason for wanting the sermon moved to the nave was to restore cathedral worship to what he considered was 'the ancient order.' The 'quire' was now 'pestered with seates and forms quite through, and manie of them (indeed allmost all) sett across the Quire from North to South.' Some of these seats and forms were used by the corporation and had been in place since September 1604. In October 1619, extra seats had been placed in the 'quire' for the masters' wives and removing them would be an affront to the corporation. Bishop Curle, a friend of Wood's, declined to intervene conclusively and the confrontation dragged on. Behind the dispute lay a difference of view between the dean and the archdeacon about the nature of divine worship. On one occasion Dr Wood preached on the text 'Jesus said againe, I am the light of the world,' Warburton further informed Laud, 'whereupon he taxed those that went about to obscure the light of the gospel with a mist of Ceremonies and an hypocriticall and vain-glorious shew of religion and devotion; and prest it farther that it was not the glorious light of Candles but the light of the gospel that was there meant and must enlighten us.' Warburton also reported that Wood had intimated to him some dislike of the organ. Warburton said he intended to come to court and petition the king for a commission of certain bishops for 'the settling of peace.' [7]

Petty quarrels between the dean and the chapter continued during the winter of 1632/3 but it seems clear that after the initial battles the chapter recognised that the dean had a powerful patron in Laud, elevated to Canterbury in 1633 and open opposition to royal church policy amongst the cathedral hierarchy declined. Reformation of the worship in the cathedral continued when Laud, on 1 April 1635 ordered that all seats were to be removed from the nave to which the chapter unanimously agreed. In the same month there is evidence of the continued animosity between Warburton and Wood. On 18 April 1635 Bishop Piers reported to Laud about a quarrel between Warburton and Wood over what was a very trivial matter. Wood had pulled down an ancient stable in the Camery (the area to the south of the 'quire') of the cathedral and replaced it with a new one also adding a wash-house. Warburton maintained that the Camery was consecrated ground and so unsuitable for such mundane buildings. Piers stated that the site of the stable was not consecrated ground but that the washhouse was an addition. The resolution of the case is unknown. On 1 October Laud ordered that the dean and chapter should consult together for providing ornaments for the cathedral to which the chapter readily agreed. The canons knew very well that the dean was in constant contact with Laud and the king and on the same day agreed unanimously 'that such daies as Mr dean shall spend waiting on his majesty or in travelling towards him or home from such service, shall be allowed as parte of the daies of his residence.'

During the 1630s, Bishop Piers came to be reviled by his Puritan opponents in the diocese. His impact on the city of Wells while irritating seems not to have been overly contentious except for the St Cuthbert's incident already referred to. Where friction did occur was when the Bishop enforced his rights over the diocese by court action. Piers was engaged in a reformation of administration and a general tightening up of ecclesiastical discipline such as the Beckington case of 1638 when the churchwardens there, who had refused to move the altar in the parish church from the middle of the chancel to the east end of the church, were punished. The citizens of Wells would have seen the humiliation of the churchwardens of Beckington as they were forced to make their submission to the bishop at the High Cross in Wells. In the spring of 1640, Piers interfered again in the cathedral. He had already secured the appointment of his son as archdeacon of Bath in 1638, a piece of nepotism readily agreed to by the chapter; but by 1640 the relationship between the bishop and the chapter had again soured. Archdeacon Wood and Paul Godwin (a canon and son of Bishop Thomas Godwin 1584-90) who were both Puritans, led the opposition to Bishop Piers in the cathedral alleging that he was attempting to infringe their liberties and jurisdictions, to dispose of seats and to cite canons residentiary before his consistory court. In March Piers demonstrated his power over the chapter by making orders and decrees concerning two chapter members in dispute in the chapter house and forbade any canon resident from preaching in the cathedral – an obvious attack on Wood and Godwin who learnt a week later that the bishop had disliked some sermons they had preached in the cathedral. Piers continued his attack on Wood on 4 August by citing Mark Tabor, Archdeacon Wood's notary public, in the consistory court for some minor extortion and Wood himself was presented in the following year (27 July 1641) for similar offences. The decision by the chapter to forget its differences with the bishop made on 24 October 1640 was thus of short duration. Soon however Bishop Piers was engulfed in his own troubles when the Long Parliament met in November 1640 and his ability to influence cathedral affairs waned. [8]

SHIP MONEY

People have always paid taxes reluctantly and seventeenth century taxpayers were no exception. To understand the town's reaction to the imposition of the un-parliamentary imposition of ship money it is necessary to describe the previous experience of Wells taxpayers. National taxation was irregular in the early seventeenth century and for the Wells citizens in the 1630s the main type of national taxation that they had experienced was the parliamentary subsidy. This was a traditional and familiar tax that had always been collected in time-honoured fashion. In Wells just over 100 people paid this tax which was assessed on the gross value of a person's land owned and any goods or money owed for goods above the minimum threshold of £1 for each category. It is likely that in common with the rest of the country, the tax yield in Wells was scandalously under-assessed as the eight assessors for the city were all local men, four of them being members of the corporation. Collection of the tax was a leisurely business: Wells taxpayers had paid parliamentary subsidies in 1606, 1610, 1621, 1624, 1625 and 1628 and they were used to the payments being staggered – usually in four or six separate instalments over about 6 months. The writ for the subsidy was given to the corporation by two local JPs and the corporation usually appointed eight collectors, two for each of the four districts or 'verderies' in the city who were supervised by the two city constables.

Un-parliamentary taxation was not popular. After the failure of the 1614 parliament to vote subsidies, James I had appealed for a voluntary loan or 'benevolence'. The Wells Corporation received the order for the loan on the 4 August 1614 and ordered 'a note to be made of all the inhabitants who are subsidy men and other men of good ability.' Collectors were despatched but met with some resistance and were unable to give a full return. By the 14 October the corporation had had enough of the procrastination of the taxpayers and ordered the collectors to certify to the corporation 'the names of these which do refuse so to give their benevolence.' Presumably the recalcitrant citizens paid up because there is no further reference to the loan in the record. [9]

In 1622 the Privy Council had requested a "voluntary" loan for the defence of the Palatinate. This money was never collected in Wells and when in 1631 the Privy Council demanded the money, the Wells Corporation replied 'we cannot find any record of any such letters directed to any officer ... neither can we say what sums of money [were] given and collected for that purpose.' These were blatant lies but effective ones because Privy Council gave up the search for the missing money.[10]

In 1626 Somerset along with other coastal counties had been ordered to supply money to provide ships for the fleet. Sir Edward Rodney the MP for Wells when addressing a meeting at Axbridge in 1626 had to deal with the main local objections to this un-parliamentary taxation posed to him in two questions by his audience. The first was: 'Why should we give since the parliament did not think fitt, shall wee bee wiser than the parliament?' The second was of a more practical nature and concerned the money given in previous benevolences that had remained in the sticky hands of the collectors and had not reached the government. Rodney attempted to mollify his audience but his refutation of the first argument was authoritarian and hardly tactful relying as it did on the operation of the royal prerogative. In a sitting of parliament the king allowed his subjects to argue – outside of parliament no such liberty was to be allowed. With regard to the second argument Rodney conceded that in the return of the benevolence the JPs would add in all the money remaining in the collectors' hands. These arguments were of little avail for, when pressed in March 1627 for the money, the Somerset justices were unwilling to collect it because they considered that it would "beget upon us and our posteriors the presidente of a chardge which [neither] wee, nor our predecessors did ever beare." This was a warning for the future! In 1629 un-parliamentary taxation was roundly condemned by parliament just before its dissolution. Parliament was not to be called for another eleven years. [11]

The corporation's reaction to the levying of un-parliamentary ship money between 1635 and 1640 showed how this new government policy could raise tensions and some resentment in the local community. The corporation used the familiar strategies of delayed collection and a challenge to the rating assessment to show its dislike of the new tax. However the first four ship money taxes were eventually paid showing that there was not so much resentment to the tax in Wells as in other parts of the county.

Taxation to provide Charles I with ships to protect the fishing fleets in the English Channel from privateers was first demanded in 1634. £2166 13s 4d was imposed on Somerset and it was paid without any problems because taxpayers could see the reason for the imposition. It is unclear if the taxpayers of Wells contributed because there is no reference to the collection of the tax in the city's records. When the government saw that this first measure of un-parliamentary taxation had been successful, it determined to make ship money an annual tax and this it what caused trouble. In 1635 the government raised the amount of tax required to £8000 for the county of Somerset, the equivalent of five parliamentary subsidies. The first ship money warrant for Wells was dealt with quite efficiently and quickly. It was received by the corporation on 31 August 1635 and as with the subsidies, the corporation collected the required £60 from the more substantial householders in the city and the Liberty (nearly 60 in all) by the 22 December and the receipt for the cash from the Treasurer of the Navy was received on 23 February 1635/6. It must be borne in mind that the £60 collected from Wells was under half of that collected later in the 1641 subsidies. It was the annual incidence of the tax and its un-parliamentary nature rather than its amount that generated some tension in the city.

The collection of money from the second warrant received on 12 December 1636 was a more difficult operation. This time there was some resistance in the city. A former mayor, George Bull, refused to come to the convocation meeting to discuss the ship money warrant and the constables had to confiscate the goods of two burgesses while other citizens initially refused to pay. The corporation members wisely took precautions against any trouble that might ensue regarding non payment: 'Whereas the two constables have bestowed and taken great labour in collecting the rate for the ship money unpaid upon this town and have taken some distresses viz of Thomas Middleham, John Wokey and John Mayne and have demanded of others the rates who answered that they have not any money; it is therefore ordered and consented unto by all persons named here present that if any trouble or charge should happen against the mayor constables or any other officers about the rating or collecting or taking of distress or for imprisonment of any persons that is refractory the defence thereto shall be at the charge of the commonalty.' Too much must not be made of the non-payers. George Bull had had a difficult relationship with the corporation. In 1627 he had refused to be admitted a burgess and to take 'such offices upon him as may be imposed on a burgess.' He had only relented and become a burgess in 1635 also being master and mayor in the same year. Thomas Middlham's refusal was possibly due to a recent altercation he had had with the corporation. On the 9 September 1636 Middleham had been fined 20s because, although not a capital burgess, he felt that he was as worthy as any member of the corporation to sit on the forms specifically provided for the corporation in the 'quire' of the cathedral. After all he was the son of the chaplain to the former Bishop of Bath and Wells, Bishop Godwin! On the 14 of August 1637, the constables took a silver box from him that they appraised at 52s 4d in lieu of his ship money. Wokey, the licensee of the Swan Inn in Sadler Street had also been in trouble with the corporation and had on 25 October 1630 been fined £20 and bound over to the next petty sessions for foul speeches. Nothing is known about John Mayne except that he was a minstrel often absent from the city. £52 was paid in on the 26 July 1637 and the remaining £8 in the following January.

The collection of money for the third imposition of ship money in 1637 took 19 months to collect and was bedevilled by a dispute between the corporation and the hundred of Wells Forum (bigger than the out parish of St Cuthbert and including Evercreech, Wookey and Litton) because the hundred wanted to incorporate the Liberty payment (formerly included in the city's payment) in its own assessment. The reason for this was that the officers of the hundred considered their assessment to be too high because in assessing the rate charge for the hundred, the county sheriff simply used his discretion and did not take the advice of local assessors as he did in the city. Consequently the officials of the hundred sought to lower its payment by incorporating the £12 paid by the Liberty into the total for the hundred. The dispute was settled in the corporation's favour on the 13 July 1638 by the bishop and four county JPs acting at the behest of the Privy Council but the ship money for 1637 was not paid in to the Treasurer of the Navy until the 22 May 1639. By this time the fourth ship money writ had already been received on 28 November 1638.

The 1638 ship money county payment was this time only £2,800 and on the 18 December 1638 the mayor, one of the constables and a sergeant at law were summoned to Taunton to receive the ship money rate for the city which was fixed at £21. In March 1638/9 the corporation was ordered by the sheriff to collect the tax by 24 June 1639. By 27 July the money had still not been paid to the sheriff and it took a letter from the Privy Council on 6 December 1639 to galvanise the corporation into action. £18 was paid in on 21 December but the final £3 not until February 1639/40.

The fifth and final warrant was received on 2 January 1639/40 and on 21 February at the prompting of the sheriff the mayor agreed to start a collection. However a week later the news came that a parliament was to be summoned, the first for 11 years and the collection of the tax stopped while the corporation waited on events. It was never to be resumed and just over a year later on 2 April 1641 the recorder advised the corporation that any ship money collected should be returned. Ship money was finally abolished by act of parliament on 7 August 1641. [12]

THE MILITIA AND BILLETING

The government of Charles I also became unpopular because of its imposition of billeting on local communities in the later 1620s occasioned by the war with France and its mishandling of the militia in the Bishops' Wars against the Scots between 1638 and 1640.

Between February 1626/7 and September 1627 around 1000 men from Somerset were pressed for service in the army. The ensuing expedition to help the French Protestants against the Catholic king of France proved to be a dismal failure but Charles I and his favourite the Duke of Buckingham made matters worse by keeping the remnant of the defeated army in being and by quartering it on the local population in the south western counties. Wells was forced to receive a company of soldiers under the command of a Lieutenant Gates by an order from the deputy lieutenants of Somerset received on 10 January 1627/8. A local gentleman, Adrian Bower, was appointed by the deputy lieutenants as receiver and was ordered to pay 3s 6d weekly for each man. No money was forthcoming from the government for this rate and the burden of paying the allowances to the troops fell upon the local community. There is no evidence in the corporation records of any local tax imposed on the city to pay for the billeting and the expenses fell on individual householders. The corporation was directed to billet the chief officers of the company 'in the best men's houses' and it was this that caused the most serious problem. The corporation naturally suggested that the seven men concerned should be billeted outside the city in the Liberty. All seven gentlemen who were approached, refused. By April 1628, the billeting of troops in Wells became a national issue. The county MP Sir Robert Phelips, no doubt because he had been excluded from the deputy lieutenant-ship of the county, launched an attack on ' the oppression of deputie lieutenants' in the House of Commons on 2 April. He attacked the deputies' practice of sending out warrants to raise money locally for billeting as an attack on the "proprietie of goods and libertie of person." In particular he attacked the Wells MP

John Baber who as recorder of Wells had authorised the billeting of the company of troops in the city on the orders of his fellow MP and county deputy lieutenant, Sir Edward Rodney. Rodney now spoke in support of Baber in parliament and argued that the soldiers who had come to the county were in a poor physical state with 'weapons by their sides, and merit in their hands from the King's service in France, and with necessity and hunger in their bellies. All we did was to make them subsist. No man will starve.' Technically Baber as recorder (the chief legal officer of the city) should have had a legal warrant for billeting soldiers in Wells but he unwisely based his arguments on necessity and not the law. He said he had thought it best to arrange the billeting 'for the ease and relief of the town…they were all English and necessity commanded me to yield to nature rather than the law.' Baber was immediately subjected to vociferous criticism: members complained that he had not satisfied them and that faced with an illegal demand, he should have refused to billet the troops; he was also condemned for forsaking the law, acting with 'superofficiousness', being a coward and forsaking his profession. The Commons decided however to act 'with great moderation' simply sequestering him and not expelling him. Baber was not allowed to resume his seat until a petition against him from Samuel Powell (living at what is now the Dean's Lodging, 25 The Liberty) and an accusatory letter from William Bushell another resident of the Liberty (soon to be appointed keeper of the Bishop's Palace in Wells) were submitted to the House of Commons for consideration. The complaints were finally rejected as 'not having tendered any proof' against Baber and he was reinstated to his seat in the House on 17 July 1628. However by this time the Wells residents had long since taken matters into their own hands and in mid April had ejected the company of soldiers and its officers from the city.[13]

When Charles I embarked on a war against the Scottish Presbyterians in 1638, the memories of billeting were still relatively fresh in people's minds and the use of the militia by Charles I in connection with the second Bishops' War against the Scots soon became a further bone of contention. The first Bishops' War in 1638/9 had little impact on Somerset. In November 1638 when the king and council believed that hostilities were imminent, all the lord lieutenants were ordered to hold immediate musters. Soldiering in the Wells militia contingent, which up to now had been an annual summer activity, was unpopular in the late autumn weather. Only a small number of men were kept under arms during the winter and they returned to their homes in July 1639 when hostilities ended.

When the Second Bishops' War commenced in March 1640, militia training began in earnest. The Wells city contingent of around 40 men under their captain Thomas Coward was to be drilled by professional soldiers. In April the Privy Council urged the deputy lieutenants to hurry with the levying of men because the general rendezvous was to be at Bruton on 10 May. The absence of their colonel Sir Edward Rodney must not have been conducive to the morale of the Wells men. He had refused to serve when the Privy Council summons came on the technical legal ground that, since the new commission of the lord lieutenant had been issued the previous year, he needed a new commission too and until he received it he would be unable to act in his role as deputy lieutenant. [14]

The plan of the three deputy lieutenants who unwillingly took on the job, was for the drilling of the 2000 troops (all pressed men) to last until the 16 May and it was planned to march the troops off towards the north of England on 20 May – pay was at 8d a day. However on the 16 May the deputy lieutenants received a letter from the Privy Council delaying the date of the rendezvous. They replied on 26 May as follows: 'but on the 16th present we received your letters dated 6th transmitting a copy of the Council's letters dated the 3rd signifying the King's express command that the soldiers should not be brought to the rendezvous till 1st June, when they had been there already by the former directions full seven days and a great part of the money provided for the pay already spent, so by reason that these last letters were detained from us so long, we your deputy lieutenants, the whole country and the 2000 soldiers have been put to more trouble and expense than was needed.' They also pointed out that 'this whole service,' was 'the greatest that ever happened in our times.' The late arrival of the royal letter, the waste of at least £600 of taxpayers' money and the impossibility of raising more in the short term, led the deputy lieutenants to send the militia home with instructions to rendezvous again on June 1.

When 1 June came only about 1600/1700 arrived. They were quite tractable as long as the money held out and the two deputies always in attendance had to find £100 of their own money to pay them. More men deserted and when the soldiers finally marched north on

11 June about a third of the original 2000 had deserted.

From nearly every county in the south of England came reports of mass desertions, vandalism and murder. In Somerset at Wellington, the Devon troops turned on a hapless Roman Catholic lieutenant named Eure, devastated his quarters, flayed him to death and dragged his remains through the streets of the town while the constables and townsfolk stood and watched. Some of the Devon rioters walked home and boldly informed their deputy lieutenants what they had done and told them if they were to hang one they were to hang all. The remnant of this troubled Devon contingent, 36 men in all, arrived in Wells on 17 July 1640 and were billeted in the town until the following Monday. The town clerk's laconic comment in the convocation book gives no hint about the public reaction to the arrival of the soldiers but it must have been one of some concern. One of the pressed soldiers left a problem in Wells when he was marched off to the war. On 16 April 1641 Joan Foster confessed to the petty sessions court in Wells that she had a 'bastard born of her body wherof she accused Thomas [she didn't know his surname] of being the father who was pressed as a soldier in the Northerly.' [15]

NOTES

[1] Morrill, J, *The Religious Context of the English Civil War*, in Cust, R, & Hughes, A, (eds), *The English Civil War*, London, 1997, p 161.

[2] White, P, *The Via Media in the early Stuart Church*, in Fincham, K, (ed), *The Early Stuart Church, 1603-1642*, Stamford, California, 1993, pp 211-230; The moving and railing off of the cathedral altar can be found at *Calendar of the Manuscripts of the Dean and Chapter of Wells Vol.II*, H.M.S.O. 1914, p 325; Wesley's career can be found in Matthews, A G, (ed), *A Revision of John Walker's Sufferings of the Clergy during the Grand Rebellion, 1642-60*, Oxford 1948, p 321 and in Foster, J, (ed): *The Members of the University of Oxford, 1500-1714*, 1891-2; Nott & Hasler, SRS Vol 91 pp 653,668. Nott & Hasler, SRS Vol 90 op cit p 144.

[3] NA Probates 11/200, 11/181, 11/312, 11/237.

[4] BL Add 34239, 5a, b.

[5] Nott & Hasler, SRS Vol 9, op cit, pp 638, 640-643, 751-753; Barnes, T G (ed), *Somerset Assize Orders*, SRS Vol 65, Taunton 1959, no 160, p 47.

[6] Stokes, J, (ed), *Somerset Records of Early English Drama*, Vols. 1&2, Toronto 1996, pp 381, 384-5; Hayden, R, (ed), *The Records of a Church of Christ in Bristol, 1640-1687*, BRS Vol 27, Bristol 1974, p 97; Stcig, M, *Laud's Laboratory: The Diocese of Bath and Wells in the Early Seventeenth Century*, London and Toronto, 1982, pp 288-289.

[7] Robinson, A, (ed), *Laudian Documents*, in Palmer, T F, (ed), *Collectanea II* SRS Vol 43, Taunton 1928, pp 178, 184-7, 191-217; Lake, P, *The Laudian Style:*

Order, Uniformity and the Pursuit of the Beauty of Holiness in the 1630s, in Fincham, K, *The Early Stuart Church, 1603-1642 op cit,* pp 161-185..

[8] *Calendar of the Manuscripts of the Dean and Chapter of Wells Vol II, op cit,* pp 412-413, 422-424; Bruce, J, (ed), *CSPD. Charles I 1635,* London 1872, pp 32-51.

[9] Nott & Hasler, SRS Vol 90, op cit, p 262.

[10] Nott & Hasler, SRS Vol 90, op cit, pp 351-2; Nott & Hasler, SRS Vol 91, op cit, pp 567-8.

[11] Barnes, T G, *Somerset 1625-1640: A County's Government During the "Personal Rule,",1625-40,* London, 1961, pp 161-7 & p 204; *BL. Add 34239 5c.*

[12] Nott & Hasler, SRS Vol 91, op cit, p 655 passim.

[13] Nott & Hasler, SRS Vol 90, op cit, p 467; *JHC. Vol. I 1547-1629,* London 1802, pp 880-881, 898-899, 906, 914; Russell, C, *Parliaments and English Politics 1621-1629,* Oxford 1979, p 75; Barnes, T G, *Somerset 1625-1640: A County's Government During the "Personal Rule",*op cit, pp 254-8.

[14] Nott & Hasler, SRS Vol 90, op cit, pp 467-8; Barnes, T G, *Somerset,1625-40: A County's Government During the "Personal Rule,"* .op cit p 256.

[15] Bruce, J, (ed), *CSPD. 1635 op cit, pp* 203, 220-221, 313, 318, 436-437; Nott & Hasler, SRS Vol 91, op cit, p 784; WTH, *Wells Corporation Sessions Book 1625-50,* folio 129v.

CHAPTER 3

'TO THE SERVICE OF THE COUNTRY'

There is no doubt that the decision by Charles I in late 1639 to call a parliament in 1640 was greeted with joy and pleasure by the ordinary people of Somerset. Edward Phelips of Montacute declared that there was 'much joy amongst all country people.' It was generally felt that there were problems that only the king working through parliament could solve. Wells usually sent two burgesses to parliament and so the interested parties started their preliminary manoeuvres at once. The news of a calling of a new parliament reached Wells in December 1639 and Bishop Piers immediately requested 'that the corporation would have him in mind when the election of burgesses of parliament should be.' Sir Edward Rodney who had been MP for the city in the parliaments of the 1620s and recorder John Baber wrote in similar vein. [1]

In Wells, the mayor William Baron, a linen draper, received the news of the date of the forthcoming election in late February 1639/40 and on 29 February at a general convocation of all burgesses, requested them to accompany him to Ilchester for the contested election of a knight of the shire for Somerset. This was an unprecedented move. There is no mention of this happening in any previous election and the mayor's request reflects the great interest amongst the more prominent citizens in the election and the desire to participate directly in national politics. It had been the practice for all burgesses to vote for the Wells MPs at a general convocation when there were more than two candidates but it was quite unusual for burgesses to attend the county election. At the meeting in Ilchester, those burgesses who accompanied the mayor would have met and discussed politics with burgesses from other towns in Somerset and with the substantial property holders in the villages. On 17 March the mayor received from the sheriff a warrant for the election of two burgesses to represent Wells in parliament. Two days later the corporation chose Sir Edward Rodney (one of the city's MPs between 1621 and 1629) and the recorder John Baber who had represented the city in the last parliament called by Charles I, that of 1628/9. Rodney, a deputy lieutenant and vice admiral of the county since 1625, was also a county JP and colonel of the northwest division of the Somerset militia comprised of about 200 men. Sir Edward was a popular man in the city. He owned a large house in Chamberlain St (at modern 38-44) and leased from the corporation land adjacent to it on the north side of Chamberlain Street (modern Portway Avenue and land to the east) on which were situated the butts for archery practice which Rodney was to repair when necessary. He also owned the manor of Rodney Stoke, leased lands in Westbury including the bishop's park and was currently resident at Pilton Park, which he had also leased. [2]

The choice of John Baber as MP in early 1640 would have been more controversial. It was usual for the Wells Corporation to choose its recorder as one of its MPs but Baber's case was slightly different. He had been recorder since 1625 but since then had caused trouble for the corporation by suing the town clerk Bartholomew Cox in Star Chamber in September 1629 and trying for the next seven years to get him sacked. Baber had accused Cox of neglecting the city's charter, extorting money for alehouse licences and breaking the city's charter. On 26 August 1630 he had then appeared in the bishop's consistory court to inform the bishop about the alleged misuse by the corporation of money left for charitable purposes, a dispute that dragged on for several years reaching Star Chamber in 1632. In 1634 he had had one of the capital burgesses, Richard Bourne arrested. His choice as MP in March 1640 could have been because no other suitable candidate had presented himself or it could be construed as a definite snub to Bishop Piers who had asked to be consulted over the choice of candidates. It was Baber after all who had offended Bishop Piers in October 1634 by protesting at the petty sessions for the city against the 'nuisance to be offered to the inhabitants of this town by your lordship that the water gates of your lordship's palace have of late been shut and barred, by reason whereof the inhabitants and other concourse of people coming to this town could not take the commodities of the way and water there as in former times.' The Wells Corporation had hastened to disassociate itself from the

William Seymour, 1st Marquis of Hertford and later 2nd Duke of Somerset, 1588-1660. Supreme royalist commander of the western counties 1642-43. (National Portrait Gallery)

Sir Ralph Hopton 1596-1652. Senior royalist general in the south-west 1642-46; MP for Wells 1640-42. (National Portrait Gallery)

Sir Edward Rodney 1590-1657. MP for Wells 1625-9 and 1640-42; colonel in the Somerset militia. (Author's photograph from an effigy in the church of St Leonard, Rodney Stoke, Somerset.)

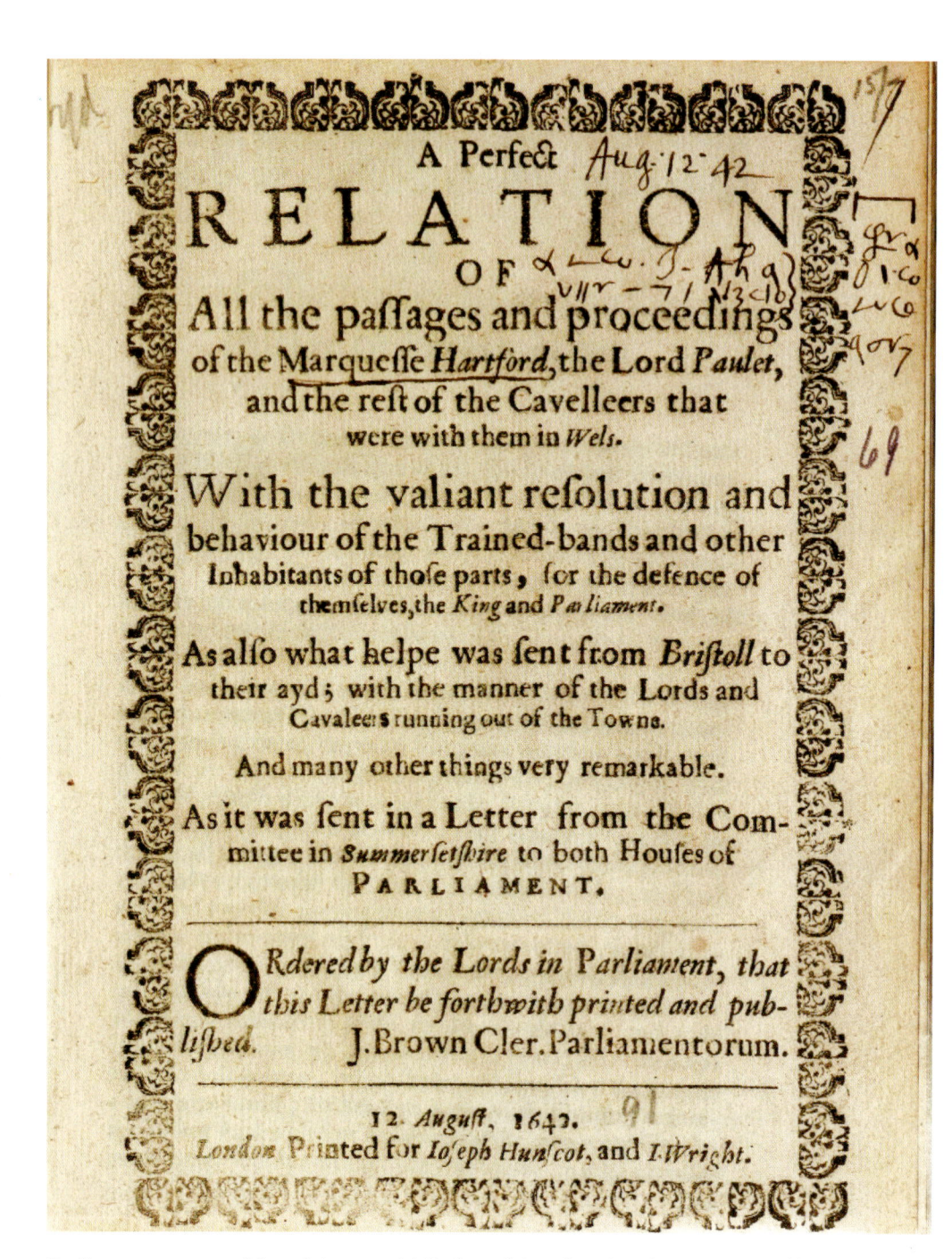

A Perfect
RELATION
OF
All the passages and proceedings
of the Marquesse *Hartford*, the Lord *Paulet*,
and the rest of the Cavelleers that
were with them in *Wels*.

With the valiant resolution and
behaviour of the Trained-bands and other
Inhabitants of those parts, for the defence of
themselves, the *King* and *Parliament*.

As also what helpe was sent from *Bristoll* to
their ayd; with the manner of the Lords and
Cavaleers running out of the Towne.

And many other things very remarkable.

As it was sent in a Letter from the Committee in *Summersetshire* to both Houses of
PARLIAMENT.

ORdered by the Lords in Parliament, that this Letter be forthwith printed and published. J. Brown Cler. Parliamentorum.

12. *August*, 1642.
London Printed for *Ioseph Hunscot*, and *I. Wright*.

Parliamentary pamphlet of August 1642 describing the 'Combustion at Wells.'
(Author's copy)

recorder's charge but by 1639 relations between the bishop and the city had so deteriorated that the choice of the recorder as MP could be seen as the city's reposte to an unpopular bishop. [3]

This first parliament (soon to be known as the 'Short') of 1640 met on 13 April 1640, lasted three weeks and was dissolved by the king on 5 May. It did not grant him any money and insisted on redress of grievances before dealing with royal financial demands. The Wells Corporation was however officially concerned only about local matters. On 14 April, the mayor proposed to the members of the corporation that he had been 'moved' by Sir Edward Rodney to ask them if they wished to take advantage of the present sitting of parliament to have something (unspecified) done about the city's trading companies. As the parliament was soon dissolved nothing was done about this matter. The summer saw the fiasco of the militia but was noteworthy in retrospect for the election as burgess of the Puritan shoemaker David Barrett, who was to play a leading and controversial part in Wells affairs during the Interregnum. After the dissolution of the Short Parliament, London was subjected to much political unrest mainly from apprentices and the Archbishop of Canterbury came under sustained attack for the changes in church worship he had implemented. In the autumn of 1640 Dr Arthur Duck, who was now also the chancellor to the Bishop of London, came under attack because the diocesan visitation that he had been charged with overseeing in London, had proved to be very unpopular. Duck was well known in Wells. He had been vicar-general to the Bishop of Bath and Wells from 1616 to 1623 and from 1635 onwards; he had also from 1629 taken out a lease on a house in the Liberty from the dean and chapter that was renewed on 1 April 1642. During his time as vicar-general, Duck had been active in the ecclesiastical courts of the bishop as presiding officer. Duck was publicly insulted in London and on two occasions and forced to flee for his life. His woes were pilloried in a series of publications one of which was called 'Duck's Coranto,' and his surname led to endless plays on words. It is highly likely that Duck's humiliation became known in Wells as there was a regular carrier service from London to Wells which acted as a conduit for news; also the registrar of the Bishop of Bath and Wells, Alexander Jett was receiving regular correspondence from the bishop's officials in London which he no doubt disseminated to his circle of friends.

There was indeed a growing news culture in 1640 that sharpened the political awareness of Wells citizens. Travelling chapmen and tinkers attending the Wells markets and fairs were a source of news and with the breakdown of government censorship in the 1640s, printed broadsheets providing news were regularly available in the provinces. The members of Wells society who were still illiterate were also able to hear the latest news from their more literate neighbours who often read the latest news to them at the inns, and alehouses of the town. Wells was also a popular resort for the gentry who visited the city for the January quarter sessions and at many other times of the year for business and pleasure. They often received information by letter from relatives and friends either resident or visiting London and even paid individuals known as "intelligencers" to inform them about the latest political events in London. [4]

THE LONG PARLIAMENT

The summer of 1640 saw the ill-fated military campaign against the Scots ending in the defeat of the poorly prepared English army by the Scots at the battle of Newburn on 28 August with the result that the Scots were able to occupy the north east of England. The government of the king was humiliated and the king, chronically short of funds, had no option but to summon another parliament. On 1 October 1640, the mayor Thomas Jones, informed the Wells corporation that a new parliament was to be called. This caused an explosion of interest amongst the burgesses as the prospect of county and borough elections loomed. On 6 October, the corporation received a letter from Sir John Stowell of Cothelstone (near Bishop's Lydyard) asking for support for his candidature as knight of the shire for Somerset in the forthcoming election. Stowell wrote: 'having a purpose to offer myself to the service of the country for the approaching parliament, I shall receive more than ordinary encouragement therein if those resolutions may be seconded by your friendly assistance: And hereof I am the more confident, having formerly received favours from your town of the like nature of which I am you're your debtor and which I shall willingly acknowledge in this public employment by the best office of friendship that shall be required of your loving friend and servant.' On Friday 16 October the mayor reported to the corporation that as well as Rodney and Baber (the city's two MPs in the recent Short Parliament), Sir Ralph Hopton of Witham had offered himself as a candidate to represent the city in the new parliament to be convened in November (later known as the Long Parliament). Hopton was held in high esteem in the city. His late father Robert had been a burgess whose entry fine had been waived on 1 October 1625 'on account of the favour and affection' he had shown to the corporation. Robert Hopton was also to overlook in 1626/7 some of the corporation's negligence in failing to provide adequate gunpowder supplies for the city's magazine and usually signed his letters to the corporation 'your loving friend, your assured friend.' It is also possible that Sir Ralph , a deputy lieutenant of the county since 1629, had been able to show favour to the corporation over Recorder Baber's charges of negligence against it as he had been a member of the commission of enquiry chaired by the bishop. On the same day, a general convocation of all burgesses was held and Hopton and Rodney were chosen to represent the city in parliament. The corporation ratified this choice the following day. The following December, the unpopular Baber resigned as a capital burgess in high dudgeon. At another general convocation held on Sunday 18 October 32 burgesses indicated to the corporation their intention to ride to Ilchester the following day to support Sir John Stowell in his bid to become a county MP. No capital burgess went and the burgess group represented a variety of opinions from the haberdasher John Niblett who was to resign from the corporation in 1649 for 'being in arms against the parliament' to David Barrett who was to lose his burgess-ship in 1643 for being in 'actual rebellion against his majesty.' Political expectations were intense. [5]

When Hopton and Rodney arrived in London for the opening of what became known as the Long Parliament on 3 November 1640, they found London in a state of political turmoil. Their political patron was William Seymour, Earl of Hertford and Lord Lieutenant of Somerset. Hertford had been one of group of 12 peers led by the Earls of Warwick and Bedford who had encouraged the Scottish invasion of England in August 1640 as a means of putting pressure on the king to call a parliament and signed a petition to that effect. Seymour was a second cousin of Rodney's and the two men had been great friends from their youth. Rodney had aided Seymour in his failed attempt to effect a clandestine marriage to Arbella Stuart, a cousin of James I in 1610, and had shared a brief exile with him in France until the king's anger had cooled. He had also shared lodgings in London with Hertford's younger brother Sir Francis Seymour, also now an M.P.[6] Both Hopton and Rodney were in sympathy with Hertford's views and wished for reform. Rodney who had enthusiastically supported the royal policy of un-parliamentary taxation in the 1620s thereby suffering 'envy, reproaches and the raking of ill tongues' had distanced himself from his royal master's policies by 1640 and as has been already noted, had conspicuously absented himself from the recent assembly of the militia of which he was one of the colonels. Hopton who had in 1639 commanded a troop of horse in the campaigns against the Scots, had disliked the idea of fighting fellow Protestants and had been appalled at the poor organisation and performance of the royal army. [7]

The state opening of parliament by the king took place on 3 November 1640 and both Rodney and Hopton were soon involved in the attack on the king's principal advisor the Lord Lieutenant of Ireland, Thomas Wentworth Earl of Strafford, who was accused of conspiring to bring an army from Ireland to overcome the king's political enemies. On 30 November, they became members of the committee of the House of Commons constituted to draw up articles of impeachment against Strafford. Other members of the committee with whom they conferred were interestingly John Pym the leader of the radical element in the House of Commons who led the attack on royal policy, John Hampden, Sir Francis Seymour and the Earl of Hertford's steward, Edward Kirton. On 30 December 1640 they also became members of a committee considering a most important piece of legislation attacking the royal prerogative – 'The Act for the Yearly Holding of Parliaments.' But it was in December that an issue arose that was to have important local repercussions: that of the future of episcopacy. [8]

'AN IMPIOUS AND TURBULENT PILATE'

In December 1640 a petition was presented from Somerset to the House of Commons charging the Bishop of Bath and Wells, William Piers, with 'innovations and acts tending to the corruption of religion.' This petition was not signed by anyone from the cathedral or the city and emanated from Puritan gentry in the county who had been offended by the bishop's policies. Among the most important charges against Piers were the placing of communion tables at the east end of churches, railing them and incarcerating those churchwardens who refused; upholding wakes and church ales; enforcing the reading of the 1633 Book of Sports in the churches and suspending and censuring the clergy who refused; opposing Puritan lecturers and finally urging diocesan clergy to contribute financially to the Scottish wars.

On 18 December 1640, Piers was impeached in the House of Lords and bound by heavy bail to appear at the bar and answer the charges preferred against him. The articles of impeachment described him as 'a desperately prophane, impious and turbulent Pilate, unparralled for prodigiously prophane speeches and actions in any age, and only fit to be cast out and trampled under foot.' A committee was set up to investigate the charges and Piers was one of the 12 bishops who signed the protest against the legality of all proceedings of parliament in their enforced absence. The bishop's officials feared for his safety and at Christmas 1640, William Bellamy the secretary to Ezekiel Barkham the bishop's receiver general, wrote to Alexander Jett in Wells that he was afraid that the bishop would be sent to the Tower because on 24 December the House of Commons journal had noted that 'several informations [from Piers's opponents in Somerset] and complaints [have been] made against Bishop Piers … heinous crimes, tending to the corruption and subversion of the religion in his diocese.' The bishop's woes increased when his son William, archdeacon of Bath was summoned to appear before the House of Commons on 4 January 1640/1 for 'very malicious and wicked words by him spoken against the last Parliament,' before three witnesses. Evidently the archdeacon was alleged to have said of some of the members of the Short Parliament: 'a pox of God take them all for a company of puritanical factious fellows … and that the king should never be quiet till he had taken off twenty or more of their heads.' Although Archdeacon Piers, on his knees before the bar of the House of Commons, denied that he had said these words, he was imprisoned and was not granted bail until April 1641. [9]

During the next six months the attacks on the bishops intensified. William Bellamy wrote to Jett from Doctors Commons in London on 29 May 1641: 'I can write you no good news: tis very doubtful whether the bishops shall continue or not, or what government we shall have; the parliament are now very hot upon it. There is a bill passed in the House of Commons this day against pluralityes of benefices.' This was worrying news for the cathedral clergy because most held more than one ecclesiastical office. Soon the situation became even more critical when a Presbyterian divine, Cornelius Burges (later to become the *bete noir* of the Wells corporation), urged the conversion of episcopal land to private use; an ominous proposal to the bishop's servants who had been granted leases of episcopal land. By July 1641 the situation of the bishops was grim and the House of Commons voted for a bill abolishing the bishops' voting rights in parliament and their temporal jurisdiction. Bellamy, clearly worried about their futures told Jett: 'Yesterday was a fatal day for the bishops. They are voted down and their lands to be seized into the King's hands. What will become of ecclesiastical jurisdiction is yet uncertain; some report we shall have some doings, though not as we have had; others that the causes of our courts and probates of wills shall be turned to the common laws. What to think of it I know not, but in the Act suppressing the High Commission Court, which is now in print, there is a clause which most concerns to reach to the suppressing of all ecclesiastical judges after the first of August next.' His first fear about the seizing of bishops' lands was not to be realised at that time but the act abolishing the Court of High Commission was passed by the House of Lords and the effect of this had quite an impact on Wells, the seat of the bishop's jurisdiction. The court set up in 1559 with officers appointed by the crown, exercised jurisdiction over ecclesiastical affairs. Its brief was 'to visit, reform, redress, order, correct and amend all ... heresies, errors, schisms, abuses, offences and contempts' and its sanctions and punishments backed up the local ecclesiastical courts such as the bishop's consistory court and the archdeacon's court which dealt with clergy discipline, moral offences amongst the laity and religious deviation.

The attack on the bishops was also very worrying for all those who had a financial interest in Bishop Piers's administration in that it presaged an end to a way of life that had obtained for centuries. The physical presence of the bishop in Wells was obvious for all to see as the bishop was the lord of the manor of Wells and owned the twice-weekly market and most of the fairs; he was also the source of much business. An historian of the Bishops of Bath and Wells in the sixteenth and seventeenth centuries has vividly described the scene before the bishop's great gate at the eastern end of the Market Place: 'Here every quarter day, or even for the general audit at Michaelmas came bailiffs and reeves of the bishop's various manors, bringing the money rents in bags and the rents paid in kind ... So too ... came the country gentry and yeomen farmers seeking leases, or the renewal of leases, jostling with notaries burdened with parchment rolls, clerics seeking ordination and justices of the peace coming to consult the bishop.' It was this traditional way of life that was now under threat. Alexander Jett like others of the bishop's officials was worried about his position; he had invested a lot of money in his office as bishop's registrar. On 19 July 1641 he wrote to the bishop's secretary James Sandford in London expressing his fears for his office which: 'for ought I can perceive is likelie to come to an end. God give me patience and that all things may work to the best: I shall heartily rejoice to hear good news from London, especially from you.' Five days later Jett wrote again: 'we daily hear of our downfall, and it is reported here for credit [that] ecclesiastical jurisdiction will utterly be taken away, which if it be, my loss you know will be very great. God almighty give me patiently to endure it, which I trust of his mercy he will.'[10]

The late summer and autumn of 1641 brought no better news for the bishop's officials but a fight back by the moderate supporters of episcopacy was launched and a petition to keep episcopacy was signed in Wells on Friday 8 October 1641 as part of a county petition. The signatories were the following members of the cathedral chapter: the archdeacon of Wells Gerard Wood, Paul Godwin, Thomas Walker, William Piers archdeacon of Bath, Sebastian Smith the precentor and Robert Creyghton the treasurer. The petition was also signed by seven of the eight masters on the Wells Corporation including later parliamentary supporters Robert Morgan and Stephen Hasket. Walter Brick the other master was absent. He had attended the 1 October meeting and did not reappear until 11 November. Only eight of the 16 capital burgesses signed but this is probably not significant because amongst the signatories there were men who within 18 months would hold differing political views. The Somerset petition was presented in the House of Lords by the Marquis of Hertford with 14,000 signatures. It was moderate in tone – it accepted punishment of evil doers, bishops included: 'We wish the wittingly and maliciously guilty of what condition soever they be (whether bishops or inferior clergy) may receive condighn punishment.' It did not accept that episcopacy was divinely instituted and wanted it reformed but not abolished. The petitioners complained that the use of the Prayer Book had been interrupted and despised by some misled people and demanded the 'silencing of all who under a veil of religion, publish pamphlets conducing to confusion and rebellion.' [11]

The petition could not save Bishop Piers. He with 11 other bishops had protested against all the proceedings of parliament during his enforced absence from the House of Lords and in consequence he and his colleagues were committed to the Tower of London in December 1641 and not released on bail until the 6 May 1642. Piers compared his treatment to that of the apostle St Paul. In a sermon preached in the Tower in February 1642 he said: 'All the afflictions of the people of God are but pricks and thorns. Oh welcome, thrice welcome, these bitter sweets, these loving chastisements, these indulgent visitations, these pleasant crosses, these comfortable calamities, these wholesome miseries, these glorious trials.' The bishop had a nice taste in oxymorons if nothing else! Meanwhile episcopal business had to continue; on 4 March 1641/2, the bishop wrote to Jett from the Tower giving instructions concerning 'my Lord of Cork' and others. Once released from captivity the bishop retired to his manor at Denton, Oxfordshire and remained there. [12]

Meanwhile the business of the diocese continued but there was a worrying sign of dissent – a harbinger of things to come. On 8 April 1642 there seems to have been a premeditated attack on one of the symbols of the late Dean Warburton's Laudian policy when Richard Allen arrived at the cathedral for his institution into the living at Batcombe, a notoriously Puritan parish. Allen was accompanied by his brother, another clergyman and an unnamed Londoner, another Puritan. 'There being a very faire crucifix at the upper end of the south end of the cathedral …behind the quier, this Londoner most maliciously threw a stone at it and broke it, the two said Allens standing at the lower end of the ile and beholding it, and watching that none came the whiles.' [13]

Bishop Piers was not able to visit his diocese in July 1642 for the visitation and his Vicar General, Dr Duck warned Jett on 2 July that he would have to manage the visitation using surrogates. Two days later William Bellamy wrote to Jett from London enclosing directions about the visitation and telling him to ride to Denton to confer with the bishop and to make sure that he 'came not back without a fat buck for those that do my lord's visitation.' More worryingly he also enclosed the articles of impeachment against the bishop. However political events were moving too quickly; the civil war was about to start, the visitation did not happen and the bishop remained unscathed. Wells was soon to be under the control of parliament. [14]

'LIABLE TO BEAR OFFICE'

The years 1641 and 1642 were also difficult years for the Wells Corporation. The political news from London, whether from the bishop's servants or by carrier, was unsettling. The trial of the Earl of Strafford, the much reviled Lord Deputy of Ireland, had started on 22 March 1641 and both Wells MPs, Rodney and Hopton, had attended the sessions in Westminster Hall. It is highly likely that both men sent back reports of the trial's progress to their friends at home; William Bellamy was also in correspondence with the recorder, John Baber but unfortunately no letters survive. The corporation, worried by the national political emergency, decided on 9 March 1640/41 to attempt to procure another charter from the king confirming the liberties already granted in the 1589 charter and adding some more. The first new liberty sought was seen as a way to solve the problem the corporation was experiencing in recruiting new members. Men were becoming increasingly reluctant to serve because of the general political uncertainty and the cost in time and money especially in the increasingly difficult economic climate. The corporation was therefore keen to enlarge its area of recruitment by making the wealthy inhabitants of the Liberty liable to bear office. Secondly the corporation was keen to stop outside JPs from interfering in the city's affairs. At a meeting on 2 April 1641 the corporation nominated the chandler, Robert Lane, to ride to London 'to procure the liberties that we have to be renewed and others which may be procured to put into a new charter.'

When Lane arrived in London, the Strafford trial was reaching its climax and he may still have been there when Strafford was publicly executed on 12 May 1641. He was certainly there until 10 May (the date of the advice he received from the city's legal counsel in London), but he had returned to Wells by the 24 May. No doubt the members of the corporation were avid to hear at first hand of the dramatic developments in London as well as to receive the lengthy legal opinions on the possible renewal of charters. The legal advice that Lane brought back was somewhat ambiguous. One legal counsel, Thomas Malett, who was to suffer during the civil war for his royalism, took a robust view and was of the opinion that any inhabitant of the city or Liberty could be made to serve on the corporation whereas the other counsel Henry Rolle, a later parliamentarian, was more circumspect. He advised that the corporation could compel any free burgess to take office but not 'every inhabitant that uses no trade nor takes benefit of privileges granted to the town as gent.' Malett however from his vantage point of London advised caution and warned against attempting to procure another charter because the corporation was unlikely to be granted any increase in its judicial powers by parliament. The expense of obtaining a new charter would also not be commensurate with the advantages that might be gained. The corporation soon tested out the new advice by electing Stephen Haskett, a mercer in the city as a capital burgess. As has already been described Haskett's initial refusal to serve was soon overcome. The corporation was not so successful when it attempted to follow Malett's advice by forcing Richard Phillips to become a capital burgess. Phillips had been household steward to Arthur Lake, (Bishop of Bath and Wells 1616-1626) and had been one of the collectors of ship money in 1635 but was not a trader in the city. The corporation's threat of a fine or a prosecution failed to move Phillips to accept and on 1 July 1641 he was excused election 'for diverse reasons by him alleged such as infirmity of body and other things.' As Phillips was fit enough to act as an assessor of the lay subsidy on 30 September 1641, the corporation must have reluctantly seen the sense of Rolle's advice. The subsequent choice of Robert Morgan in Phillips's place had important consequences for the city in the future. [15]

MORAL TURPITUDE

It is also noticeable at this time that the petty sessions court of the corporation was taking a greater interest than before in breaches of conventional morality and imposing more draconian punishments. This was partly because of the decline in authority of the local church courts caused by the ongoing attack in parliament on the authority of the bishops and the Court of High Commission previously described, but also to the presence of a latent Puritanism amongst some corporation members which was now emerging in the currently charged political atmosphere. On 16 April 1641 one particular case of bastardy is noteworthy for the severity of the punishment inflicted. In previous cases the punishments meted out to the man and the woman were unequal: the father was usually only forced to pay for the upkeep of the child and if he refused was imprisoned until he was able to pay the necessary 6d a week whereas the mother was publicly punished and humiliated.. In the case of Elizabeth Phelps and Edward Browne the justice William Baron decreed a more even-handed though severe punishment by sentencing both parents to be 'whipped naked from the girdle upwards from the prison to the crosse, roundabout the crosse and from there to the prison.' This even-handed punishment was unusual because Katherine Lee who confessed to conceiving a child in the Bishop's Park was also whipped and imprisoned but the same punishment was not meted out to her lover Richard Duffett who was only committed to prison. Baron was also severe on the prostitute Ann Morgan who was to be 'imprisoned until Saturday morning market and then to be set in the stocks ... at the upper end of the market ... and after that time to be washed in the moat [of the Bishop's Palace] and then to be brought down to the prison and there to remain during the pleasure of the mayor and justice.' Her clients were left unpunished. Amusingly the justice declined to become involved in an argument between the tanner Richard Atwell and Elizabeth Whiting. Evidently Elizabeth had beaten Richard and called him an 'old toade.' Baron was quite happy to refer the case to the recorder John Baber who, as has been seen, was out of sympathy with the corporation. [16]

SUBSIDIES

On 2 April 1641, John Baber, the city recorder, sent a message to the corporation that in his view the ship money which had been paid and was still in the local receiver's hands, should be repaid. However gratifying this was to the taxpayers involved, there was soon to be a great increase in taxation. The Scottish army still in northern England had not been paid since January and just over £1,000,000 was needed to pay the Scots and the English army. Parliament resorted to the usual device for raising money by subsidy and four subsidies were voted with an estimated yield of £300,000. With only £300,000 raised from the customs revenues there was a shortfall of £400,000. The House of Commons made up the discrepancy by the expedient of a poll tax to be imposed on all subjects and 'graduated according to social rank, from £100 for a duke down to a minimum of sixpence for every person above the age of 16 not in receipt of parish poor relief.' Parliament was thus trying to raise in 1641 four times the cost to the taxpayer of the ship money of the 1630s and more than double the tax take of any parliament in English history.

The commissioners for the new taxes arrived in Wells on 30 September 1641 and summoned the eight local assessors appointed by the corporation to appear before them in the guildhall (the hall in the Bubwith Almshouse) in Wells on Saturday 2 October at 'eight of the clock in the forenoon.' The assessors were to 'accomplish all such things as unto them in that behalf of his majesty for the better executing of the said commission shall be injoined. And that you show the warrant to every of the inhabitants whom you shall warn for this service.'[17]

THE PROTESTATION

Rodney and Hopton were active in parliament in the cause of reform throughout 1641. With the other MPs they signed the Protestation of 3 May 1641. This was parliament's riposte to the discovery on the previous day of the king's abortive plot to release the Earl of Strafford by force from the Tower of London. The oath taken by each MP committed him to 'maintain and defend, as far as lawfully I may with my life, power and estate, the true reformed protestant religion expressed in the doctrine of the Church of England, against all Popery and popish innovation within this realm, contrary to the said doctrine and according to the duty of my allegiance, I will maintain and defend His Majesty's royal person and estate and also the power and privilege of Parliaments [and] the lawful rights and liberties of subjects.'

Rodney continued to sit on parliamentary committees until mid-December 1641 but after that took little part in parliamentary activities and his name does not appear in the Commons Journals.

More is known about Hopton's stance. He was still in favour of reform in December 1641 and was appointed by the House of Commons to present the Grand Remonstrance to the king on 1 December 1641 at Hampton Court. This document described as 'inflammatory' and 'wildly tendentious' by some modern historians, consisted of 204 clauses attacking the 'abuses' of the royal government in the 1630s, praising the record of the Commons' achievements since November 1640 and lastly setting out what the Commons intended in the matter of religion: reducing the power of bishops by debarring them from sitting in the House of Lords and placing the king's power as supreme governor of the church under the control of parliament. The king received the delegation and Hopton kneeling before him, presented the Remonstrance. The king promised to give his answer 'with as much speed as the Weightiness of the Business will permit.' On 13 December Sir Ralph was given leave by the Commons 'to go into the country' where he possibly was able to give up-to-date news to his Wells constituents. He was soon back in London after Christmas and on 5 January 1641/2 was present when the king with an armed retinue, attempted unsuccessfully to arrest the five MPs who were his main opponents in the House of Commons. The king's actions were defended by Sir Ralph who 'excused the Kings coming hither with soe great a number and soe unusually armed, because wee our selves had divers of our servants attending in the Lobbie without the doore of this howse armed in an unusuall manner also with Carabins and Pistolls, and that the speech his Majesty made was full of grace and goodness.' Hopton's innate loyalty to the king now came into play and he could not agree that sole power over the militia should rest with parliament and not the king.

His final breach with his erstwhile allies in parliament came on 4 March 1641/2 'when he gave great offence, laying an Imputation upon the Committees of both Houses that the tenth clause [of a new declaration] prepared and brought in from the Committees of both Houses, did accuse the King, for being an Apostate from his Religion, not only in his own Person, but endeavouring to bring his people to the same Apostasy and Idolatry or words to that Purpose, and did desire, that such things might not pass without very good Proof, whereas no such thing could be collected out of that clause.' The House of Commons resolved that Sir Ralph should be brought to the bar of the House to receive his sentence of imprisonment in the Tower of London. Sir Ralph appeared, was duly sentenced and sent to the Tower where he stayed for two weeks. After his release he took no further part in parliament and by July was reported to have returned to the country.

The king's attempt to arrest the five MPs in January 1642 had another result – the imposition of the Protestation of 3 May 1641 throughout the country. Throughout January 1641/2 copies of the Protestation were paraded in front of the Parliament House by London apprentices. On 20 January, the Speaker of the House of Commons ordered the county sheriffs to see that the protestation oath was taken by all adult males over the age of 18. During late January and early February printed copies were received in the localities. The mass signing done in Wells in late February and early March 1641/2, was organised by a group of thirteen men, ten of whom were from the city. The group was led by the vicar of St Cuthbert's, Thomas Westley. He was assisted by his curate Daniel Buckley and by his churchwarden Josias Cooke. The city representatives were the mayor Robert Morgan, the justice Thomas Jones and the two constables William Hiett and Robert Hill. Three other prosperous citizens helped to make up the number: the mercer Joseph Plummer, Henry Jones a member of the hammermen's company and Thomas Meade one of the overseers of the poor. The other three men came from the out-parish. There is no evidence as to how this was organised but as the team was led by the vicar, the signings may have taken place in church after divine service. The Wells returns were divided into three parts: the first was headed St Cuthbert's Parish (in) and comprised the city including Tor Street; the second was for the Liberty and the third the villages/hamlets in the out parish of St Cuthbert in which modern St Thomas Street was included. 869 adult males are recorded as signing in the city and Liberty. Only a group of 22 men did not sign, 18 of whom were Catholic recusants, the other four being musicians who were absent from the city. Four recusants lived in the Liberty: they were the Francis Cottingtons, (elder and younger,) William Evans and Morris Lund while the other 14 lived in the city. The most important of the city dwellers were the Beaumont brothers, John and Anthony, and three members of the wealthy Godwin family. Their names were duly noted. [18]

During the troubled summer of 1642 the city got on with its normal activities until July when the citizens were suddenly thrust into the events that were to lead to four years of disruption and civil war.

NOTES

1. Underdown, D, *Somerset in the Civil War and Interregnum,* Newton Abbot 1973, p 24; Nott A & Hasler J, (eds), *Wells Convocation Acts Books 1589-1665, Part 1 1589-1629, Part 2 1629-44; 1662-65,* SRS Vols 90 & 91, Taunton 2004, p 774.
2. I am grateful to A. J. Scrase for information on Sir Edward Rodney's property in Chamberlain St.; Scrase A J & Hasler, J (eds), *Wells Corporation Properties,* SRS Vol 87, Taunton 2002, p 215.
3. Nott & Hasler, SRS Vol 91, op cit, pp 941-942.
4. Nott & Hasler, SRS Vol 91, op cit, pp 782 & 785; Cressey D, *England on Edge: Crisis and Revolution,* Oxford, 2006, pp 258-262; *Calendar of the Manuscripts of the Dean and Chapter of Wells Vol. II,* HMSO London 1914, pp 370, 391; Bailey, S, *The Canonical Houses of Wells,* Gloucester 1982, pp 56-57; Stokes, J (ed), *Somerset Records of Early English Drama, Vols. 1 & 2,* Toronto, 1996, pp 392, 878; for a detailed account of the news culture see Fox A, *Oral and Literate Culture in England 1500-1800,* Oxford ,2001 passim.
5. Gristwood, S, *Arbella: England's Lost Queen,* London 2003, pp 331-380.
6. Nott & Hasler, SRS Vol 91 op cit, pp 793-796, 802, 945, 995.
7. Bruce, J, (ed), *CSPD 1625-1626,* London 1858, p 444; Edgar, F T R, *Sir Ralph Hopton,* Oxford 1968, p 17.
8. *JHC Vol. 2* London 1802, 30 November 1640, p 39; *JHC Vol. 2 op cit,* 30 December 1640, p 59.
9. *DNB Piers, William;* S.R.O. DD/O/ C/1878 Box 2; Cressey, D, *England on Edge op cit* p 268.
10. SRO DD/O C/1878 Box 2; Hembry, P, *The Bishops of Bath and Wells 1540-1640: Social and Economic Problems,* London, 1967, pp 9, 244-248.
11. Cressey, D, *England on Edge, op cit,* p 268; Underdown D, *Somerset in the Civil War and Interregnum, op cit,* pp 26-27;
12. *SRO DD/OC/1878 Box 2.*
13. *Calendar of the Manuscripts of the Dean and Chapter of Wells, Vol. II, op cit,* p 426.
14. *DNB Piers, William; JHL, Vol. 2,* 6 May 1642; Cressey *England on the Edge,* op cit, p 257.
15. Nott, & Hasler, SRS Vol 91 op cit, pp 803-814.
16. WTH. *Wells Corporation Sessions Book 1625-50,* fos 84,129 &130.
17. Adamson, J, *The Noble Revolt,* London 2007, p 323; Nott & Hasler, SRS Vol 91 op cit, p 815.
18. Gardiner, S R, (ed), *The Constitutional Documents of the Puritan Revolution 1625-1660,* 3rd edition 1906, p 155; Edgar, T F R, *Sir Ralph Hopton op cit,* pp 20-24; Woolrych, A, *Britain in Revolution 1625-1660,* Oxford 2002, p 200; Fletcher, A, *The Outbreak of the English Civil War,* London 1981, p 209; Howard A J, & Stoate, T L, (eds), *Somerset Protestation Returns and Subsidy Rolls,* Almondsbury, 1974, pp 126-133.

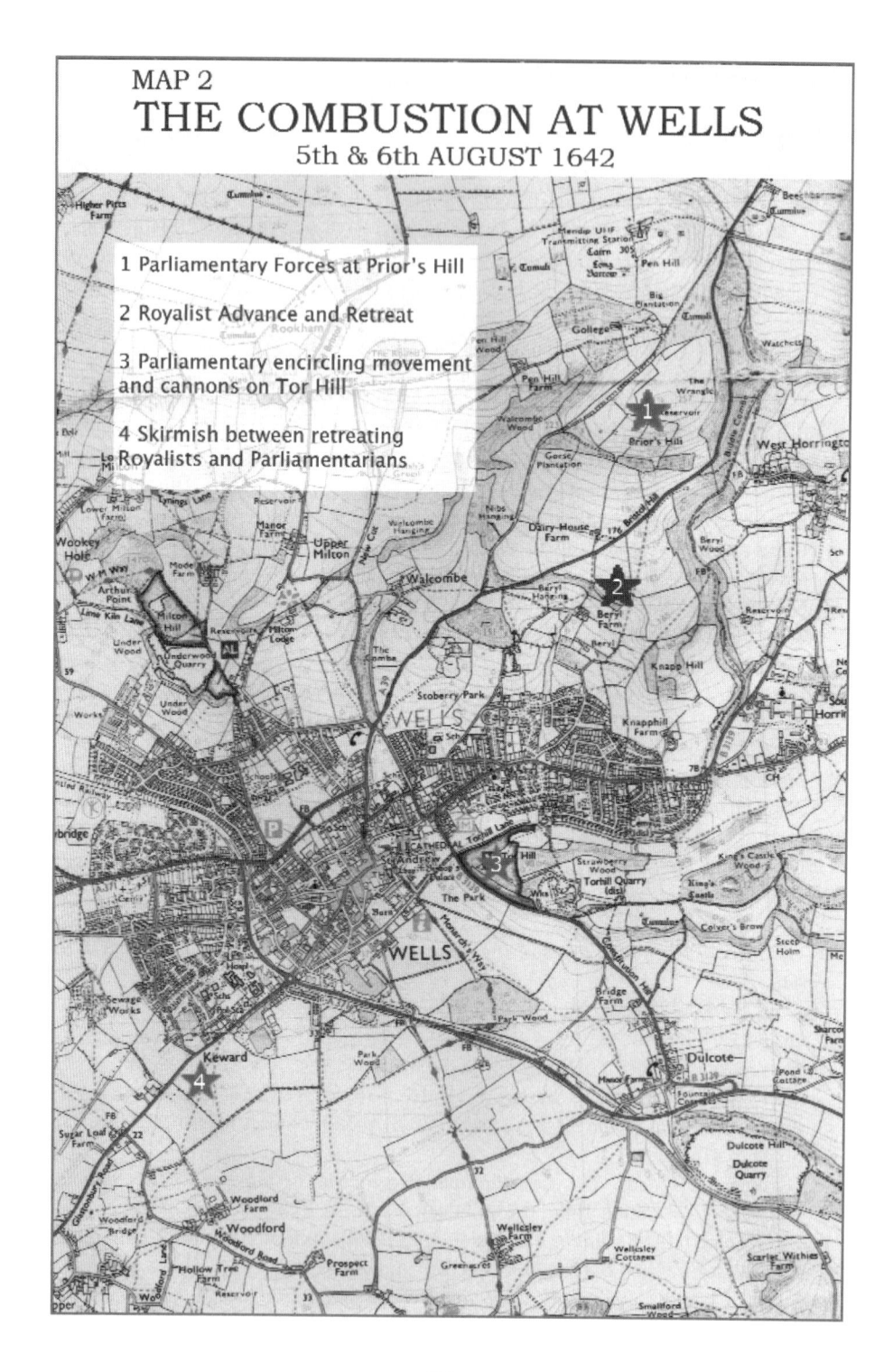

MAP 2
THE COMBUSTION AT WELLS
5th & 6th AUGUST 1642

1 Parliamentary Forces at Prior's Hill

2 Royalist Advance and Retreat

3 Parliamentary encircling movement and cannons on Tor Hill

4 Skirmish between retreating Royalists and Parliamentarians

CHAPTER 4

'THE COMBUSTION AT WELLS'

It was an uneasy city that watched the royalist troops enter on 28 July 1642. The main reason for its apprehension was the knowledge that the Somerset gentry loyal to parliament were also collecting troops in the north-east of the county and that a confrontation at or near Wells was likely to ensue. For some of the gentry involved it meant a severing of old friendships: for the yeomen, artisans, labourers and their families, a time of fear, rumour and dislocation.

THE PROTAGONISTS: THE ROYALISTS

Hertford was an unlikely war commander. Although a great lord, he had no real military experience and was a conciliator, the epitome of moderation. In the summer of 1640 he had allied himself with the reformist peers led by the Earls of Bedford and Warwick and with his brother-in-law the Earl of Essex (later to be commander of the parliamentary army), had been one of the twelve peers who on 28 August 1640 had signed a petition to persuade the king to summon a parliament. On 7 September 1640 Hertford had argued before the Privy Council that 'the very summoning of a parliament would win the hearts of the people.' During 1641 the king gradually detached him from the reformist group of peers by appointing him a member of the Privy Council in February and advancing him to the marquisate on 24 April. Hertford was described at that time as being ' very gracious to the people' and was still respected by the main reformist groups within parliament. In July 1641 the king appointed him governor of the person of the eleven-year-old Prince of Wales. John Pym, the king's chief parliamentary opponent, considered that the prince was safe with Hertford who would 'secure him from all plots.' In December 1641, moderate parliamentarians still considered him 'a good lord.' In February 1642, Hertford refused parliament's offer of appointment as lord lieutenant of Somerset on its behalf and went north to join the king in York. But as late as June 1642 when conflict between king and parliament seemed inevitable, he joined with Sir John Bankes, Chief Justice of the Common Pleas, in expressing his disapproval to the king of the royal order of 20 May for all Yorkshire men possessed of a horse to rendezvous with the king. However, a month later he was on his way from Yorkshire to Somerset to raise troops for the king in the south-west – the battle lines had been drawn.

Hertford was not to be a particularly inspiring or decisive commander. In the opinion of his friend the politician and historian Lord Clarendon, he was 'a man of great honour and fortune.' His deep sense of honour is exemplified in his offer in January 1649 to suffer execution in the king's place because the king had followed his advice. Clarendon went on to write: 'though he was a man of very good parts, and conversant in books both of Latin and Greek languages, and of a clear courage [exemplified in a duel in 1635] of which he had given frequent evidence, yet he was so wholly given up to a country life where he lived in splendour, that he had an aversion, and even an unaptness for business … He was of an age [54] not fit for much activity and fatigue, and loved, and was even wedded so much to his ease that he loved his book above all exercises.' Clarendon also commented on his 'laziness of mind' and his dislike of argument, qualities that were to cause problems with his somewhat volatile subordinate commanders during the civil war. [1]

Among the group of gentry accompanying Hertford were some of the most important men in Somerset including the two Wells MPs, both men of steady judgement in an emergency. They were his cousin and close friend Sir Edward Rodney of Rodney Stoke and Pilton. and Sir Ralph Hopton, the latter being the only member of the gentry present who had had real experience of war. Hopton had fought the the Thirty Years war in Bohemia and the Low Countries and was to take a leading role in the campaigns in the west of England during the next four years.

Hertford was not well served by some of the other leading gentry who accompanied him. Of dubious value was John, Baron Poulett of Hinton St George, the only peer resident in Somerset. Poulett, a man of undoubted personal courage, has had a bad press from the leading historian of this period of Somerset history who has described him as 'lazy and not exceptionally intelligent', disliking hard work and rash in speech and action. Aged 59 in 1642, Poulett suffered severely from gout and this tended to make him somewhat irascible; its ravages had also curtailed his employment in command of a ship in the royal fleet in 1635. In a letter from York in the spring of 1639 when he was with the king in the campaign against the Scots, he wrote to his son-in-law Thomas Smyth of Ashton Court, near Bristol: ' I am come to my crutches after having been carried between men's hands and in a chair almost three weeks.' Although he tended to treat his 'inferiors with a considerable disdain,' he was capable of extreme kindness and tenderness in his own family. He was very fond of his son-in-law Thomas Smyth and before his journey to join the king at York in April 1639, he had written to Smyth: 'Sonne I was so harte swollen at parting that I made my expressions to you more by signes than wordes for which you will excuse me.' However his intemperate words at Wells proved a godsend to his parliamentary opponents who publicised his remarks throughout the country. In a pamphlet published on 22 August 1642 by parliament, Poulett's opponents reported: 'My Lord Paulet [at Wells] ... with many imprecations oaths and execrations in the height of fury declared that it was not fit for any yeoman [a royalist source reported that the term peasant had been used] to have allowed him from his own labours, any more than the poor moiety of ten pounds a year ... that when the power should be totally on their [the royalist] side, they [the yeomen] shall be compelled to live on their allowance.' These remarks initially circulated orally, were considerably embroidered in the telling. The men in the parliamentary forces soon came to believe that Poulett's remarks referred to all men 'under the degree of gentlemen.' It was reported by the parliamentarians that 'my Lord Poulett is hated of all men ... [and that] the people hearing such inhuman propositions ... attempted to lay violent hands on him ...they have resolved rather to lose their lives than be slaves.' Many ordinary people in north-east Somerset, it was claimed, decided 'that there was no way to ... preserve themselves from this insupportable tyranny than by adhering to Parliament and submitting to the ordinance of the militia, which was purposely prepared to enable them to resist these horrid invasions of their liberty.' Although Poulett's remarks were no doubt exaggerated by his opponents, his undoubted intemperance had done the royalist cause a great disservice. [2]

The other leading gentry with Hertford in Wells although courageous, were more characterised by bellicosity than good sense. Sir John Stawell of Cothelstone, who had solicited help from the Wells burgesses in his bid to become a county MP in 1640, was a case in point. He has been described as having 'a choleric unevenness of ... temper and ... impatient rashness and wrath.' His 'only personal distinction was a dilettante's passion for medicine, the rules of which he followed to the extent of never eating breakfast.' This was a judgement made of his behaviour in a time of peace. Sir John, although eccentric, was however to show his bravery and utter commitment to the royalist cause very soon, even though it finally led to his incarceration and utter financial ruin. John Coventry, the second son of the late Lord Keeper, Thomas Coventry, has been characterised as vacillating and often petty and who during the course of the civil war, managed to disrupt the whole royalist camp. Sir Francis Dodington, brother of a later recorder of Wells was a violent and vindictive man: after a successful assault at Woodhouse near Longleat in July 1644, he hanged 14 of the defenders after having violently assaulted them, much to Sir Ralph Hopton's disgust. Added to this group of volatile characters was Sir John Digby of Sherborne, second son of the Earl of Bristol, another outspoken and quarrelsome man more of a liability than a help. However one cannot but feel some sympathy for Thomas Smyth of Ashton Court, possibly a more reluctant recruit to the royalist cause. A personal friend of Alexander Popham who was emerging as the commander of the parliamentary forces, he was overshadowed by his father-in-law John Poulett and his aged but energetic stepfather Sir Ferdinando Gorges, the colonial entrepreneur who despite his advanced age of 76, was to prove that he had lost none of his aggression in the events of the first week of August 1642. Among those also supporting Hertford were Sir Charles Berkeley of Bruton, Sir Henry Berkeley of Yarlington, Colonel Edmund Wyndham, Sir Francis Hawley and Edward Kirton, Hertford's steward. More professional military expertise was present in the person of Colonel Henry Lunsford. According to Sir Ralph Hopton, Lunsford 'was come to him [Hertford] with Officers for a Foot Regiment and Commission from the King to raise for his Brother Sir Thomas Lunsford a Regiment of Foote in that County, in hope that hee should there recover the most part of his old Regiment which hee had there raysed for his Majesties service in the north, two yeares before.' Considering the local unpopularity of the war against the Scots, the problems encountered by the militia and the mass desertions of 1640, Lunsford was perhaps being a trifle optimistic in hoping to be able to raise a substantial force for the king in north Somerset. Also any mention of his brother was not advantageous to the royalist cause because Colonel Thomas Lunsford, controversially appointed by the king as Lieutenant of the Tower of London in December 1641, was an abrasive and arrogant man with a reputation for violence who was hated and feared by parliament. Hertford's tasks of coordinating his somewhat volatile supporters and of developing a successful strategy for dealing with his parliamentary opponents, were not going to be easily carried through. [3]

THE PROTAGONISTS: THE PARLIAMENTARIANS

On hearing that the royalists had arrived in Wells, the local parliamentary gentry on Friday 29 July countered this move by ordering a general muster of the north east Somerset militia at Shepton Mallet for Monday 1 August. They had received their authority from parliament on 20 July giving them power 'to assemble and call together all such persons as they shall think fit, within the county of Somerset at such convenient times and places as they shall appoint ... concerning the raising of horse, horsemen and arms for the defence of the King and both Houses of Parliament.' At first glance, the parliamentary gentry would have appeared to have been inferior in numbers, prestige and experience when compared with the royalist gentry. They were led by Alexander Popham, the MP for Bath, who lived at Hunstrete House near Compton Dando. He was the eldest surviving son of Sir Francis Popham the extremely wealthy MP for Minehead and grandson of the Elizabethan Lord Chief Justice, Sir John Popham. Educated at Balliol College, Oxford and the Middle Temple, Popham would have seemed to be a natural supporter of the king. However his support for parliament seems to have been based on political and religious convictions. He did not trust the king and feared an extension of arbitrary royal power. He was also a Puritan by conviction, his father having taken a leading part in the establishment of Puritan colonies in Virginia and New England. His family although prominent in Somerset gentry society was unpopular. His father Sir Francis a county JP and deputy lieutenant, was particularly mean and anti-social in a society where the leading gentry were expected to provide an outward show of hospitality and conviviality. He was also 'acquisitive, always ready to go to law [and] moved suits in a most vexatious manner.' [4]

Alexander Popham was supported by William Strode of Barrington Court. Strode was the son of a Shepton Mallet clothier and had been wealthy enough to buy Barrington Court from Sir Thomas Phelips of Montacute, then deeply in debt. Despite his acquisition of this estate, he was considered an upstart by the main gentry families in Somerset. Popham's three other main supporters were his uncle Sir John Horner of Mells, John Ashe, the wealthy clothier from Freshford also an MP and John Pyne. Horner had been a JP since 1614, sheriff of the county in 1614 but by 1639 both he and William Strode were considered by the Privy Council as unfit to serve as sheriffs, being 'refractory.' John Ashe had made a fortune as a clothier employing thousands of outworkers in the manufacture of lightweight 'Spanish Cloth' along the Avon valley in the north of the county. Although he was richer than many of the gentry, he was also regarded by them as a social upstart and was never chosen to act as JP, deputy lieutenant or sheriff of the county. John Pyne of Curry Mallett was a wealthy Presbyterian gentleman. His father Hugh had been opposed to the king and his favourite the Duke of Buckingham in 1626 and his scathing verbal attack on the king had nearly brought him to the gallows. Thus the main parliamentary leaders were men who felt that they had been excluded from the county government either for their Puritan religious views, opposition to the crown or because they had made their fortunes by trade. The royalist historian Clarendon was perceptive enough to realise this. He wrote: 'yet ther were a people of an inferior degree, who, by good husbandry, clothing, and other thriving arts, had gotten very large fortunes, and by degrees getting themselves into gentlemen's estates, were angry that they found not themselves in the same esteem and reputation with those whose estates they had; and therefore, with more industry than the other, studied all ways to make themselves considerable. These from the beginning were fast friends to the Parliament.' [5]

From the beginning of the confrontation at Wells, the royalists were outmanoeuvred by their parliamentary opponents. The royalist document of authority, the Commission of Array, was written in Latin and so the parliamentary leaders were able to use this fact to distort its meaning to their supporters. Clarendon describes the difference in tactics between the two opposing groups. He writes that the parliamentarians 'always had this advantage of the King's party and his counsels, that their resolutions were no sooner published than they were ready to be executed, there being an implicit obedience in the inferior sort to those who were to command them.' In contrast to this 'all the King's counsels were with great formality deliberated before being concluded: and then with equal formality and precise caution of the law, executed.' Consequently Hertford and his supporters were always reacting to events whereas his parliamentarian opponents took an aggressive and energetic stance from the beginning of the confrontation.

As soon as news reached Popham of the royalists' arrival in Wells, he, Ashe, Horner and Strode swung into action. On Saturday 30 July they visited Shepton Mallet and organised the sending out of 'tickets' inviting their supporters to meet them on Monday 1 August at Shepton Mallet and as an incentive promised them a feast of venison for their trouble. On Sunday 31 July Hopton intercepted some of these 'tickets' and took them to Hertford and the other gentlemen. Hopton reports that he (Hopton) had 'a more serious consideracion of the consequences of it, then for the present, hee could prevayle with them to entertaine.' In Shepton Mallet the royalist parson, John Couth was worried and according to his parliamentary opponents insinuated in a sermon to his parishioners in the parish church on that Sunday that the parliamentarians intended 'to fire their houses, and make their Streets run with bloud.' On the very same day Couth, supported by five other leading residents, sent a petition to Hertford appealing for protection. This spurred the Marquis into action. First, in order to arm the foot soldiers whom Lunsford hoped to recruit, he sent a small group of troops to Wincanton with carriages to fetch the arms stored there and secondly decided that Sir Ralph Hopton with 100 gentlemen volunteers and a cavalry troop should confront the parliamentary leaders in Shepton Mallet on the next day, Monday 1 August. Despite this show of energy on the Marquis's part, Hopton later criticised Hertford's lack of decision writing that 'the error of uneffective and unfinished consultations began betimes and hath constantly attended the business throughout' This was to be borne out on the following day. [6]

MONDAY 1 AUGUST

The royalist plan was for Hopton with Gorges and some more gentlemen volunteers to arrive in Shepton Mallet with a troop of horse early in the morning. Unfortunately because the gentlemen volunteers did not get up very early, Hopton did not arrive in Shepton Mallet until nearly 11 am. Immediately after Hopton had left Wells, the Marquis of Hertford began to worry about a possibly violent confrontation with the parliamentarians and sent an urgent message to Hopton by Thomas Smyth ordering Hopton not to take any troops into the town but just to enter it with the gentlemen volunteers, which he did. Hopton dismounted in the Market Place by the Market Cross and called the townspeople together to discuss the petition sent to the Marquis by John Couth. At that moment, William Strode rode into the Market Place with (according to him) his son and four servants two of whom were armed. According to Hopton, Strode was accompanied by eight to ten horsemen well mounted and armed. Hopton ordered Strode to dismount and hear the petition read to which Strode (according to a parliamentary source) replied that 'he came not to hear petitions but to suppress insurrections and tumults and required as one of the committee of both houses the said three gentlemen and the rest in the name of the King and Parliament to depart the town, as they would answer at their perils.' Hopton was incensed by Strode's remarks and, according to him, he rose from where he sat, pulled Strode from his horse, confiscated his pistols and arrested him for high treason. A royalist source claimed at this point that as soon as Hopton laid hands on Strode, 'a man of Mr Strode's presented a pistol to him ready cocked, and had killed that noble gentleman, had it not been prevented by one Mr White then waiting on him, who snatched the pistol out of this fellows hands'. Strode, to cover his discomfiture at being unceremoniously bundled from his horse, later claimed that both Hopton and Smyth had pulled him from his horse while Gorges struck at him with a halberd and some of the 'Cavaliers' held their sword points to his body forcing him to alight. He also claimed that the armed gentlemen threatened his servants with loaded pistols to stop them coming to their master's assistance. Hopton then completed Strode's humiliation by committing him into the custody of the constable George Milward who, unfortunately for Hopton, was a friend of Strode and who released Strode as soon as Hopton had left, although a royalist source maintained that Milward was forced to release Strode 'by the multitude ... or lose his life.' Hopton then proceeded to read the petition again but only one of the eight signatories appeared, some indication of the amount of hostility there was in Shepton Mallet towards the king's cause.

Hopton was then informed that the parliamentary levies were advancing on Shepton Mallet from the north-east. He hastily remounted his horse and rode with his followers down Town St, then turned right until he came to the Swan Inn where he intended to meet some more royalist gentry with whom he hoped to oppose the parliamentary advance. None however arrived and he was forced to return to the main body of his troops south west of the town, leaving a guard in the town. By this time the town constable had released Strode who went to meet Popham and Horner. They then rode into town, the royalist guard presumably retreating before them. The royalists now, according to their opponents, succeeded in recruiting some more men from the local militia under Thomas Strode, one of Sir Edward Rodney's captains. By noon about 2000 Parliamentary horse arrived in Shepton Mallet with about 100 foot soldiers some of whom had been attacked by the royalists and relieved of their powder and bullets. Sir Ralph Hopton now drew his troops together and reinforced by the troop of horse under Sir John Digby that had come from Sherborne, set them in battle order against the parliamentary troops whom he called 'an unruly rabble'. This caused the parliamentary troops to withdraw to a field on the east side of town to avoid a confrontation. The standoff continued until about 4 pm. when the parliamentary leaders sent a message by Lawrence Bull and William Long requiring to know why the royalists had come and if they had not come in peace, then the parliamentary party would judge the royalist action an insurrection and endeavour to suppress it. Just at that moment, Hopton received orders from the Marquis to retreat to Wells with his troops. This he did taking both Bull and Long with him to receive Hertford's reply. The Marquis replied: 'I understand there is a great assembly of armed men now at Shepton, which I conceive is unlawfull, and desire to know by what authority they are met; for that as yet it seems to me a great violation of the peace of this County, and the Kingdom, to appear so armed; and to receive their answer.' The parliamentarians swiftly replied that they considered the Commission of Array illegal and that they had come to Shepton Mallet to keep the peace. Thus with both parties considering themselves to be the lawful representatives of government, it was becoming inevitable that force would in the end decide the issue. As Sir Ralph Hopton put it: 'And thus innocentlie beganne this cursed warr in those parts.'

Meanwhile in Wells, the mayor, Robert Morgan, was pressurised by the Marquis into handing over the keys of the magazine in St Cuthbert's Church to Sir Francis Dodington. He was also ordered to confiscate any arms found in the houses of possible parliamentary sympathisers and to seize all the arms and horses of men who entered the town. Hertford then told Sir Edward Rodney to assemble the militia of the north-west of the county of which he was colonel. The Wells contingent normally made up of 23 pikemen and 21 musketeers was mobilised under its Captain, Thomas Coward of Chamberlain St, and other contingents from neighbouring parishes were sent for. The Marquis in order to raise more troops, made the decision to send the younger sons of Lord John Poulett and Sir John Stawell back to Hinton St George, Cothelstone and Low Ham to raise more men and arms on the following day. Meanwhile the parliamentary leaders ended the day by sending out warrants to muster men at Chewton (Mendip) for Friday 5 August and a message to supporters in Bristol for two cannon firing 6lb shot. They also composed their own version of the day's events at Shepton Mallet and sent it by messenger to parliament in London. The report reached London by Thursday and on Friday the 5 August, the MPs amongst the Somerset Royalists, Hopton, Smyth and Digby were declared by parliament to be unfit to serve as MPs (Sir Edward Rodney the other Wells MP was not included because he had not been involved in the events at Shepton Mallet). Parliament also ordered that Hopton, Smyth, Gorges and Dodington should be sent for as delinquents and the Shepton Mallet petitioners were also proscribed. The parliamentary letter on the affair at Shepton Mallet was then published by the clerk of the House of Commons on 8 August. [7]

TUESDAY 2 AUGUST

The Wells Corporation met but the meeting was also attended by three of the royalist gentlemen: the city's MP Sir Edward Rodney, John Coventry and Hertford's steward, Edward Kirton as observers. The corporation seems to have been in no particular hurry to accommodate the visiting royalists. Its authority had been impugned and the question of providing arms for the royalists was studiously avoided, the city's legal business taking up most of the corporation's attention. However the corporation did agree to present the Marquis with an ox to be bought at Lydford Fair for £10. The limited nature of the corporation finances was also referred to when it was pointed out in the minutes that there was only £5 6s 2d left in the chest plus 'an old Spurryull' (a gold coin of James I 1603-25 worth 15s).

WEDNESDAY 3 AUGUST

The royalists in Wells then decided to make a reconnaissance and show of force into the Mendips north and east of Shepton Mallet to attempt to deter gentlemen inclined to parliament from joining the Chewton Mendip muster. Messages were sent to Popham, Horner and Ashe warning them to desist from making the rendezvous. It was then decided that a show of force was necessary and Hopton returned to Shepton Mallet which he had vacated so rapidly on the previous Monday. His men refreshed themselves in the taverns, confiscated arms and behaved in a somewhat boorish manner. 100 were left in the town as a garrison and Hopton returned to Wells. His expedition was ineffective as Sir John Horner assembled his Mells tenants and set off to join Alexander Popham at Compton Dando, prior to marching to the parliamentary rendezvous at Chewton (Mendip). Much to the Marquis's relief, the sons of Stawell and Poulett returned late in the evening with about 40 horse, twenty dragoons and a wagon full of arms.

THURSDAY 4 AUGUST

Early in the morning, the Marquis in Wells was informed by some local village constables that Sir John Stawell's regiment of militia was ready to march from the Quantock area. They also asked the Marquis to send some horse and dragoons to Boroughbridge to secure the Parret river crossing which he duly did. Stawell then set out from Wells accompanied by John Digby, Sir Francis Hawley with part of their troops and Edmund Wyndham and some volunteers to meet the militia. Fortunately for Stawell, he was also accompanied by the experienced soldier, Henry Lunsford. The royalist force numbered some 80 men.

Outside Street on the ridge overlooking Compton Dundon at Marshals Elm, this force encountered 600 parliamentary foot drawn from Taunton and South Petherton commanded by John Pyne, Captain Preston and Captain Sands. This force was intent on advancing to Glastonbury to close the Marquis's escape route from Wells. At the sight of the superior parliamentary forces, Lunsford drew up his horse into a long straight line so that its inferiority in numbers would not be so exaggerated, while Stawell interrogated a local countryman as to the intentions of the parliamentary force. When he realised that this force was intent on closing Hertford's probable escape route to the south of Wells and that out of the 600 men there were only about 50 cavalry, he decided that an attack would indeed be possible. Stawell attempted to persuade Pyne and Preston not to advance realising that a military action there would indeed precipitate a civil war but they refused and Stawell returned to his troops. On his return he found that Lunsford had divided the cavalry into three squadrons with Stawell commanding the centre and Digby and Hawley the flanks; this cavalry was half hidden from the parliamentarians by the unevenness of the ground. Lunsford himself took command of the 14 dragoons whom he dismounted, and placed hidden in two quarry pits flanking the ground over which the parliamentary troops were to advance, 150 yards in front of the royalist line.

Seeing the royalist troops drawn up on the hill, Pyne lost his nerve. He ordered an advance and then countermanded the order. His men jeered him and believing that the royalists 'were but a few horse and would run away', they resumed their advance led by a junior captain Joseph Osmond with Pyne, a man not known for conspicuous bravery, staying well in the rear. The parliamentarians soon opened a desultory fire but Lunsford delayed return fire from his dragoons until the parliamentarians were within 120 yards. On the third royalist volley, Osmond was killed and some of his men suffered injuries causing the parliamentary line to falter. Lunsford then told Stawell to attack with all his cavalry. The parliamentarians were soon routed with Preston and Sands both being captured. Pyne fled. Seven parliamentary soldiers were killed and 18 were to die of their wounds – the first blood to be spilt in Somerset. Stawell forbade any further killing and gathering up his squadron, the prisoners and about 60 of his enemies' horses, started to return to Wells. He was however worried about the whereabouts of Sir Francis Hawley and his own son John who were nowhere to be seen. He need not have worried. Hawley and the younger Stawell had not, in the heat of battle, heard Sir John's order to disengage and had pursued the parliamentarians to Somerton, taking many horses, arms and prisoners. Much to Sir John's relief they arrived back in Wells that evening about an hour later than Sir John himself. The parliamentary threat from the south had been neutralised for the moment but the threat to the city from the north was growing more ominous by the hour. [9]

Meanwhile while the confrontation was taking place at Marshals Elm, the Wells Corporation had again convened at the request of the royalists. This time it was because Hertford needed war supplies from the city's magazine in St Cuthbert's church and in his usual courteous manner, he sent two men well known to the corporation, Sir Edward Rodney and William Walrond, to make what must have been a token request as he already had the keys. Rodney and Walrond asked the corporation to deliver 300lbs of powder and 300 dozen bullets and 600 yards of match for which Rodney and Walrond would pay 12d a lb for the powder, 2d a lb for the bullets a 1d a yard for the match. They deposited £30 in the mayor's hands promising to pay any more that might be due. The corporation was in no position to disagree, the city being full of armed men and so the arms were handed over. [10]

FRIDAY 5 AUGUST

This was the decisive day. Sir Edward Rodney's militia regiment had arrived in Wells and was being reviewed in the morning by the Marquis in a field outside the city when news was received that a large parliamentary force led by Popham and Horner of around 12,000 men (40,000 according to parliamentarian estimates) had arrived on the Mendip Hills overlooking the city. The number of parliamentarians had been swollen by the arrival of men from north-east Somerset, west Wilts, Bristol, Bath and south Gloucestershire. The Bristol men had even brought four small cannon with them instead of the two originally requested. Included in the parliamentary army, ominously for the royalists, were ' Master Smith's [Thomas Smyth's] Tennants, 40 yeomen well armed, and all the inhabitants in that quarter where Sir Ralph Hopton liveth unto his very gates.' The parliamentary army although large was disorganised and generally quite poorly equipped. Parliamentary sources admitted that some men were armed only with swords while royalist sources claimed, somewhat patronisingly, that some were armed only with 'pitchforks, dungpeeks and such like weapons, not knowing (poor souls) whom to fight against but afraid they were of the papists.' However there were some well-armed troops: Alexander Popham's regiment 'came well armed and were most ready in the use of their Armes;' the Bristol mounted contingent consisting of 300 men was also well armed 'with Swords, Pistolls or Carbines' as was a Gloucestershire company of foot 'under a valiant and expert Captaine' and Sir Edward Hungerford from Farleigh Castle brought enough arms to equip 150 – 200 of the volunteers. The parliamentarians also had two large wains loaded with powder, bullet and match. What the parliamentarians admitted they lacked were 'expert Souldiers and Commanders.' The troops, despite lack of equipment, were highly motivated and 'could not be stayed but would march over the Hill which was neer foure miles, until they came in sight of Wells, and there pitched upon a great Hill in view of the Town,' (probably Prior's Hill to the east of the modern A39 see Map 2). Many of these men on Mendip were Puritans, godly men, but it was not just anti-catholicism that motivated them. John Ashe, one of the parliamentary leaders, rightly saw that the countrymen were 'apprehensive and quite incensed by the late accidents occasioned since the bringing of these commissions into the county, by seizing arms, maiming some and murdering others, the report wherof hath spread far and nigh and hath brought many hither out of their counties to rescue this from their miseries and lest the same evils fall upon themselves afterwards.' This feeling was to grow as the war progressed leading to the neutralist Clubman movement in 1645 that aimed at driving out both warring parties. The final strand which motivated the parliamentarians was that 'the commission of array appeared as an instrument of class as well as of royal tyranny, and distrust and dislike of the king's actions merged into fear and hatred of the aristocracy's intentions.' Poulett's outburst as has been mentioned, was seen as an example of this arrogance. [11]

The Marquis on receipt of the news of the parliamentary army's approach, immediately sent out scouts who reported the large number of troops his parliamentary opponents had raised against him. What was he to do? Once again he was indecisive and called for advice. He was urged, probably by the professional soldiers, to send 500 horsemen up to the hill to charge the poorly organised and equipped parliamentary army and spread panic in its ranks. After all it had worked the day before at Marshals Elm. But the Marquis did not wish to shed any more blood. However he did take defensive measures in what was a fairly hopeless tactical situation. Hopton recalled: 'it was thought fit to draw all the foot presently upon the avenues of Wells which were immediately barrocadoed up as well as the time could afford as well as Sir Edward Rodney's militia regiment and Col Lunsford's new levied men which were about twelve score. The horse and the dragoons and the gentlemen that were volunteers were drawn out of the town towards the enemy, where they faced them upon a little hill at the foot of the great hill' (possibly at the northern end of what later became Stoberry Park or at Beryl. See map 2). This was a moment of acute danger for the citizens of Wells. Would the parliamentary army attack in the morning? Hertford decided to negotiate with his opponents. Just before midday he sent three JPs whom he had summoned to Wells, to take a letter containing his terms to the parliamentary commanders. Hertford required them to depart peacefully to their homes. If they refused to do this, they would be deemed responsible for any subsequent blood that might be shed. To back up his demand, he told them of the royalist victory at Marshals Elm the previous day of which they may have been unaware. The parliamentary commanders replied that they held the royalists responsible for the breach of the peace at Shepton Mallet on the previous Monday and desired to delay the negotiations until the next day (when they hoped that Pyne and Strode would have arrived). Thus the two sides confronted each other until the evening when Hertford sent a message saying that he would keep the peace until he received another letter from the parliamentarians. A truce was agreed until nine the following morning. All the royalist troops stayed at their posts except Sir Edward Rodney's militia regiment many of whom quietly slipped away, some men to their homes, others to join the parliamentarians on the hill.

On the top of Mendip, the parliamentarians spent an uncomfortable night. An attack by 500 trained royalist cavalry might have spread panic in their ranks and dispersed the army for some time. However the inevitable loss of life might have inflamed the parliamentary troops who would undoubtedly have returned to attack with possible dire consequences for the city. According to parliamentarian propagandists, the parliamentary army spent the night fasting in the cold (although it was only early August, Mendip mists can bring chilly conditions), the soldiers spending their time praying and singing psalms. Their commanders stayed with them, the elderly Sir John Horner remarking that his furze bed was 'the best that he ever lay upon.' In the morning, much to their relief, food and provisions were brought in by friendly countrymen from a ten mile radius. Suitably fortified, the parliamentarian soldiers were eager to go down to Wells to 'destroy the cavaliers and capture the incendiaries, those delinquent gentlemen then with the Marquess and carry them to the Parliament.'

In Wells meanwhile, the Royalists were busy making contingency plans for the morrow. Hertford had always wanted to avoid violence and now, seeing that the tactical situation was impossible and that he risked encirclement, decided to withdraw. Before retiring to bed, he ordered Hopton to plan a retreat.

SATURDAY 6 AUGUST.

The parliamentary commanders, aware that the morale of their troops was now high, sent their terms to Hertford at ten o clock in the morning. Hertford was immediately to disarm and disband his force, hand over the Somerset gentry leaders to the parliamentarians and return arms and prisoners. A distinction was thus made between the Marquis and his local supporters. The royalist Somerset gentry were seen as the real culprits because they had broken the peace of the county: the Marquis could go free, he was an outsider. The terms were backed up by a threat 'unless they [the terms] be forthwith yielded unto, we do much doubt whether it will be in our power to

William Piers 1580-1670. Bishop of Bath and Wells 1632-70.
(From a painting in the Bishop's Palace, Wells.) Photograph by Patrick Kirkby.

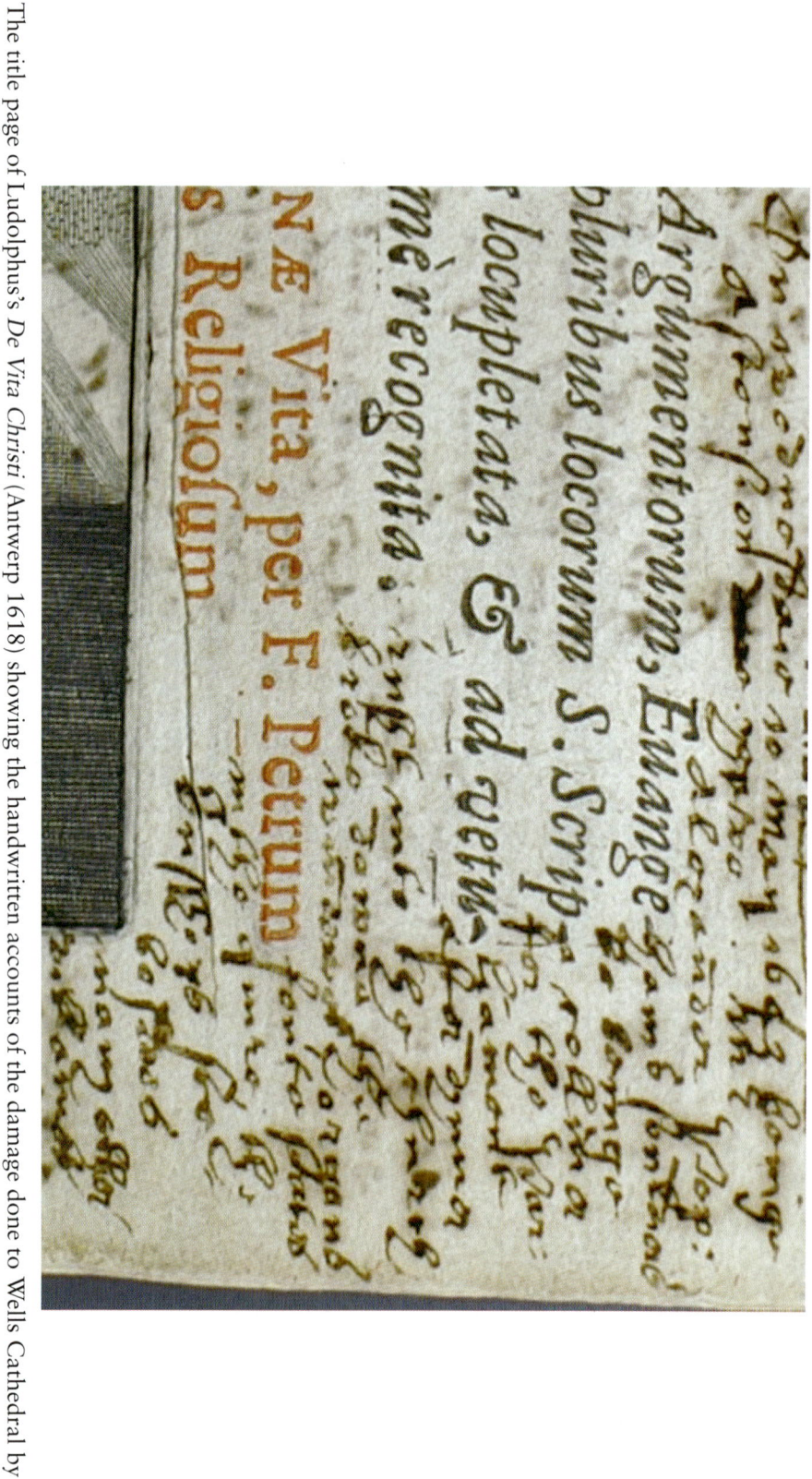

The title page of Ludolphus's *De Vita Christi* (Antwerp 1618) showing the handwritten accounts of the damage done to Wells Cathedral by parliamentary soldiers in 1643. (Wells Cathedral Library) Transcription: 'On Wednesdaie 10 May being Ascencion (daie – crossed through) yest[e]reve, Mr Alexander Popham's souldiers he being a coll[onel] in or for the Parliament after dynner rusht into the church broke downe the windows, organs f[r]onte seates in the quire the busshops see[t] besides many other villanies.'

Major Richard Atkyns, Prince Maurice's Regiment of Horse 1643. (Photograph of a model in the *Making of Britain Gallery* at The National Army Museum, Chelsea, London)

Prince Maurice 1621-52, Prince Palatine of the Rhine and nephew of Charles I. Lieutenant General in the south-west under the Marquis of Hertford 1643 (Contemporary print, National Portrait Gallery).

'THE COMBUSTION AT WELLS'

keep the Souldiers from assaulting the Town.' The Marquis, playing for time, was conciliatory in reply, offering to suspend the Commission of Array if the Somerset parliamentarians would suspend the Militia Ordinance locally; disband his troops if the parliamentarians did likewise and denied knowledge of any arms or goods taken. As for any prisoners, he had already released them!

While the messengers took his terms back, the plans for the royalist retreat were implemented. Fully aware that he was in danger of being surrounded, the Marquis got into his coach and escorted by Lunsford's foot soldiers, left the city through Southover on his way to Sherborne via Glastonbury. Hopton meanwhile sending off contingents of troops at regular intervals southwards, remained in Wells with his own troop accompanied by Lunsford and 40 musketeers. At 2 pm, hearing that Hertford had successfully reached Glastonbury, he retreated himself.

The parliamentarians, worried that the Marquis and his troops might slip away, had also divided their forces: one group moved on to the slope (probably Tor Hill) overlooking the town and opened fire on the Bishop's Palace with two of the small cannon causing some apprehension to the Marquis but no damage. Another group commanded by Pyne and Strode, which had just arrived from Glastonbury, also moved on to Tor Hill ready for an assault on the city while a small group of horse attempted to cut the Wells Glastonbury road just north of Coxley. Unfortunately for the parliamentarians, the cavalry failed to block the escape route. The excuse was given by a parliamentary eyewitness. Two of the royalist cavalry troops sent off by Hopton 'fronted us boldly being in number much greater and more experienced men, both in horsemanship and use of arms, our men being raw, untutored and inexperienced in the use of arms.' The parliamentarians fired on the royalists who returned fire stopping the parliamentarian advance. The royalists remained in position and the parliamentarians, afraid of being cut off from their main body of troops, retired to the ribald laughter of the royalists.

With Hertford's departure, Wells was now open to the parliamentarians. Robert Morgan, the mayor, on behalf of the citizens, immediately sent a message to the parliamentary commanders assuring them that the Marquis had left with all his troops and petitioned that the parliamentarian soldiers might not come down into the town nor 'attempt anything against them.' It is clear that the parliamentary commanders found it impossible to stop some of their men from entering Wells. These soldiers were determined to see the city 'the place where those lewd Cavalleers their enemies lay'. John Ashe rather disingenuously reported: 'some of us went down with them ...we left all in quiet and doe hope that those which remained there after our departure were not disorderly, unless they were provoked by the Cathedral Company.' One parliamentary source claimed that the citizens welcomed the parliamentarians. If this were so it was no doubt out of relief that a military confrontation had been avoided in the city. Whether they were provoked or not, a royalist account insisted that the parliamentary soldiers tore down the painted glass from the windows of the cathedral 'and in the height of their zeal gloried in that action more than in vanquishing of the Papists; and having found a picture that pleased them so wel that they placed it upon the point of a speare whether in admiration or derision I cannot tell.' The picture was of the Virgin Mary. For good measure, the bishop's palace was also looted. The city however, remained nervous but unscathed. [12] Parliamentary propaganda attempted to show that much damage had been done to the city during the royalist occupation. It was stated that 'the City of Wells hath been much rifled and racked, and the Cavaleers have poled and pinched the poor of the City, and hath made such an obstacle of the town, that it is not £10,000 will make satisfaction.' There may indeed have been costs to the citizens for the nine day occupation of the city: the assembled royalist troops would have been accommodated and fed by the citizens free of charge and no doubt there had been some damage to private property but £10,000 was probably a vastly inflated figure! Wells was now to be under parliamentary rule until the summer of 1643. [13]

NOTES

[1] Clarendon, Edward Earl of, Macray, D W, (ed), *The History of the Rebellion and Civil Wars in England,* Vol. 2, 1888, Oxford, pp 528-9: Dunning, R, *Somerset Families,* Tiverton 2002, p 114.

[2] Barnes, T G, *Somerset 1625-1640: A County's Government During the "Personal Rule,"* London, 1961, pp 37-39; Hembry, P, *The Bishops of Bath and Wells, 1540-1640: Social and Economic Problems,* pp 47-48, 213, 232, 240; *A Memento for Yeomen, Merchants, Citizens And all the Commons in England* , August 22 1642, BL E 113(13); Bettey, J H (ed), *Calendar of the Correspondence of the*

Smyth Family of Ashton Court, 1542-1642, BRS Vol XXXV, Bristol 1982, no 312 p 142, no 388 p 180; Clarendon, *A History of the Rebellion and Civil Wars in England op cit,* Vol 2, p 296.

[3] Barnes, T G, *Somerset 1625-1640, op cit,* p 36; Underdown, D, *Somerset in the Civil War and Interregnum,* Newton Abbot, 1973, p 75; Chadwyck Healey, C E H, (ed), *Bellum Civile: Hopton's Narrative of His Campaign in the West 1642-1644 and Other Papers,* SRS,Vol 18, 1902, pp 2-3.

[4] Wroughton, J, *The Civil War in Bath and North Somerset,* Bath 1973, pp 30-31; Barnes T G , *Somerset 1625-1640,* op cit, pp 24 & 30.

[5] Barnes, T G, *Somerset 1625-1640, op cit,* pp 26 & 135n; Wroughton, J, *The Civil War in Bath and North Somerset, op cit,* pp 26-28; Underdown, D, *Somerset in the Civil War and Interregnum, op cit,* p 20; Clarendon, *The History of the Rebellion and Civil Wars in England, op cit, Vol. II,* p 296.

[6] Chadwyck Healey, *Bellum Civile,* op cit, pp 2-3, *The Lord Marquesse of Hertford, His Letter, Sent to the Queen in Holland. Also a letter from the Committee in Sommersetshire, to the Houses of Parliament,* London, August 8 1642, BL, E109. (24), pp 5-6.

[7] Chadwick Healey, *Bellum Civile,* op cit, pp 4-5; *The Marquesse of Hertford, His Letter,* op cit, pp 6-8; *A True and Exact Relation of all the Proceedings of Marquesse Hartford, Lord Pawlet, Lord Seymor, Lord Coventry, Sir Ralph Hopton, and other His Maiesties Commissioners in the publishing of the Commission of Array in his Maiesties County of Somerset,* London 19 August 1642, (no BL reference or pagination).

[8] Nott & Hasler, SRS Vol 91, op cit, pp 830-831.

[9] Chadwyck Healey, *Bellum Civile* op cit, pp 7-9; *A True and Sad Relation Of divers passages in Somersetshire, between the Country and the Cavaleers concerning the Militia and the Commission of Array,* August 5 1642, p 5, BL E 109 (34.)

[10] Nott & Hasler, SRS Vol 91, op cit, p 831.

[11] *A True and Exact Relation,* op cit; Manning, B, *The English People and the English Revolution,* London 1976, p 200.

[12] *A Perfect Relation of All the passages and proceedings of the Marquesse Hartford, the Lord Paulet and the rest of the Cavelleers that were with them in Wels,* London, 12 August 1642, pp 3-8, BL E 111 (5); *Joyful Newes from Wells in Somerset-Shire,* London 12 August 1642 (no BL reference); *A Second Letter Sent from John Ashe Esquire ... ,* London, August 16 1642, pp 3-16, BL E 112 (13).

[13] *Exceeding Joyfull Newes from the Earl of Bedford ... , London August 23 1642, [no pagination]* BL E 113 (17).

CHAPTER 5

'THE DANGEROUSNESS OF THE TIMES': PARLIAMENTARY WELLS AUGUST 1642 – JUNE 1643

With the departure of the Marquis of Hertford and his men, the citizens of Wells found themselves under the control of parliamentary forces for the next eleven months. The threat of military violence was ever present. On 11 August the local parliamentary commissioners mustered the militia near Somerton. The meeting was infiltrated by some royalist gentry but the troops mostly held firm against the appeals of their erstwhile royalist commanders. The royalist gentry were forced to hurry away and Sir John Stawell was 'dangerously shot in the breech' during his escape. The parliamentary gentry were now able to enforce the Militia Ordinance in the central and northern areas of the county and under the leadership of Sheriff Sampford started a search for hidden caches of arms. A group of gentry including Popham and Strode and backed by a small force of militia and led by the sheriff arrived at the outskirts of Wells on Wednesday 16 August. They were met about a mile outside the city on the Glastonbury road by the mayor Robert Morgan and the masters of the corporation who accompanied them into the city. Allocating two men to each street a search was undertaken but no weapons were found. The bishop's palace was also searched but yielded nothing. The account sent to parliament by the sheriff claimed to have found caches of arms in several houses in Wells but the actual details which were entered as being found in Wells seem to refer to people and houses in the Bridgwater area. On the following day the soldiers went to Sir Edward Rodney's house at Pilton. Sir Edward was there – he had not accompanied Hertford in his flight but had returned to his house to await events. Sir Edward initially decided to cooperate and 'immediately sent warrants for the trained bands about them to give their attendance the day following.' On Friday 18 August the search party found at Farmer Twist's house near Glastonbury 100 suits of men's armour left behind by Sir John Stawell just under a fortnight previously. The unfortunate Twist although insisting that he was only Stawell's tenant and that the armour did not belong to him, was unceremoniously committed to Ilchester Gaol for not reporting the arms to the authorities. It was only at Lord Poulett's house at Hinton St George that the parliamentarians met with any resistance! [1]

The Marquis of Hertford after leaving Wells had taken refuge in Sherborne (old) Castle and the Earl of Bedford in command of a large parliamentary force of 7000 infantry, eight troops of cavalry and four cannon, soon arrived in the county on his way to attack Hertford at Sherborne. [2] On Saturday 19 August, the members of the Somerset parliamentary committee, Alexander Popham, Clement Walker, William Strode and John Ashe wrote to the Wells Corporation asking the city to entertain the Earl. They addressed their letter in particular to the mayor Robert Morgan, Stephen Haskett, and Thomas Salmon known supporters of theirs and to two pragmatic moderates, Bartholomew Cox and William Baron. The tone of the letter showed that although many of the national parliamentary leaders were suspicious of where the city's political loyalties lay, the local parliamentary gentry were concerned to take a conciliatory tone, no doubt anxious to support their friends who were leading the corporation and not to alienate the rest of the city in which royalist sentiment predominated. They wrote that the earl would indeed have come straight to the city had they 'been fully satisfied that there would have been fitting entertainment for him, which we conceive could not be without giving you notice of it. And although there be divers of opinion that your town is very ill affected to the peace of the kingdom ... yet we conceive otherwise of it and that all honest and good men will to their uttermost maintain the king, parliament and peace of the kingdom. We have therefore entreated his lordship not to desert you, assuring him that he shall find as faithful service among you as in any town in this county.' The corporation was to provide a fitting house for the Earl and the 20 people of his retinue and ensure that 'the stables in the inns and private stables [be] provided with store of litter, hay and oats for so great a retinue as will attend so noble a personage going about upon a business of public concern.' The corporation's reply was suitably diplomatic with the right amount of necessary humility: 'We do first render unto you our humble thanks for your favourable respect to us ... his Lordship and his retinue shall be very welcome to town which we will endeavour to express by the best entertainment we can get upon so short a warning.' The corporation proceeded to designate a house but did not specify which and provided a hogshead of claret for the earl and his retinue. The earl did not hurry and finally arrived on Sunday 25 August staying until Saturday 31, enjoying the corporation's hospitality slightly longer than expected. He then proceeded to Glastonbury where he rested until Tuesday 3 September not arriving to confront the Marquis of Hertford at Sherborne until Friday 6 September. [3]

The ensuing siege of Sherborne proved to be time consuming and unproductive for the parliamentarians and Bedford soon left enabling Hertford and the royalist army to slip away. Hertford made for Minehead and with Poulett, Smythe and Gorges sailed to Cardiff whilst Hopton with the other gentry rode over Exmoor into Devon and on into Cornwall. For Thomas Smythe it was the end of his war. On October 2 he died in Cardiff of smallpox and his stepfather Sir Ferdinando Gorges sorrowfully brought back his body to Long Ashton for burial. Smythe's widow Florence faithfully paid all the debts incurred by her husband's illness and death amounting to £137 17s; the melancholy list of payments included £1 16s 6d 'to a woman that tended him and washed his clothes,' 4s 'to the searcher, the poore, the watchmen at the boate side' and £1 1s 'to the boatman that brought the corpse over.' After her husband's death, her worries were now less about the war than the wardship of her underage son. [4]

Somerset was now in parliamentary hands: there was no organised royalist resistance and for the Wells citizens an anxious time began. Robert Morgan finished his year as mayor on 30 September 1642 and the new mayor was Robert Rowley with Morgan becoming the justice. A constant source of worry for the corporation was the billeting of 300 parliamentary troops in Glastonbury. On 4 October, the royalist Sir Edward Berkeley sent the corporation news that some parliamentary foot soldiers and cavalry were intending to march from Glastonbury to Wells to pillage the city. The corporation hastily convened and decided to send a delegation to negotiate with the soldiers. As the new mayor was ineligible because of his known royalist sympathies, Robert Morgan led a small deputation of parliamentary supporters that included Stephen Haskett, William Smith and Richard Fryer to Glastonbury to have 'some conference' with the local parliamentary commanders in order to avert the danger to the city. Fortunately they were successful and Wells was not troubled by marauding undisciplined soldiers during the winter of 1642/3. [5]

SIR EDWARD RODNEY

Within a week, the city heard of the capture and imprisonment of its MP, Sir Edward Rodney. After initially cooperating with the parliamentary forces, Rodney had retired to Sir Ralph Hopton's house at Witham with Sir Edward Berkeley and Dr James Dugdale of Evercreech, Hertford's chaplain. Rodney and Berkeley, according to their opponents, 'seducing and combining thereunto a large linke of power to knit against us, and with their friends, their Tenants and Freeholders did therewith fortify and strongly guard the house.' Consequently the parliamentarians under Captain Pym, attacked the house which was stoutly defended. After the defenders had used up their ammunition, Rodney, Berkeley and Dugdale attempted to escape but were intercepted by Lieutenant Hayward who according to his account exchanged pistol and carbine shots with them. Finally on seeing that the royalist troops in the house had surrendered and that parliamentary troops were approaching to assist Hayward, Rodney, Berkeley and Dugdale gave themselves up. Hayward then escorted Rodney and Berkeley to London where they were imprisoned in the Counter or Compter in Wood St in the City. After such a stirring encounter, Hayward's career ended in tragedy. He afterwards deserted to the king but was taken prisoner at Barnstaple in July 1644 by parliamentary forces and was tried and shot.

The Compter was a prison that normally catered for debtors or gentlemen who had disturbed the peace but was now used by parliament to incarcerate prisoners of war. It is most likely that as a man of means Sir Edward Rodney was imprisoned in the 'Masters' Side' rather than the meaner quarters of the 'Knights' Ward' or the aptly named 'the Hole.' On entering the prison his name would have been entered in the 'Black Book' and then he would have had to make the customary payments to the various officials: 12d to the gaoler for turning the key at the Masters' side door, 2s to the chamberlain, 12d for the compulsory 'garnish' of wine and 10d for dinner. Sir Edward stayed incarcerated in the Counter until the following January; a miserable and debilitating experience. In the prison he would no doubt have met Edmund Bower of New Street, Wells. Bower was probably one of the unnamed supporters of Hertford in early August and his capture was unrecorded. On 26 November 1642 he sent a petition to the House of Commons requesting his release but no further evidence on his case seems to survive and his release date is unknown.

By January 1642/3 Rodney's health was beginning to suffer and on Wednesday 18 January he petitioned the House of Lords stating that 'he hath lain Four Months in Prison, his health declining by reason of his Restraint' and asked to be allowed to have his place of confinement changed to the house of his friend Edward Stone in King Street, Westminster. Sir Edward also added that he had 'neither furnished Men, Horse, Plate, or other warlike Provision, neither [had] he acted any Thing tending to War;' It seems that Sir Edward was being somewhat economical with the truth! On 21 January the House of Lords agreed to Rodney's removal to King Street. Stone was not allowed to 'permit him to go abroad to any place without leave of this house [House of Lords] but only to St Margaret's Church in Westminster and that in his company and to return home with him back to his said House as soon as Church is done.' King Street was a more desirable place to stay than the Compter being on the main route from Charing Cross to the Houses of Parliament at Westminster. The House of Commons and the Somerset County Committee which was now ruling Somerset on behalf of parliament, were informed of Sir Edward's request and while the Commons agreed with the Lords' decision, the County Committee was most unhappy about Rodney's 'enlargement' and desired that their Lordships would bail no more prisoners from Somerset. The Lords replied tersely that Rodney had not been bailed and that only his prison had been changed. The conditions of Rodney's imprisonment were further eased on 1 March when he was given the liberty to visit his wife and family who had arrived from Somerset and were staying in the 'Ould Pallace at Westminster.' Sir Edward was also allowed to walk in the Dean's garden (the present College Garden) and the cloister for his health, provided that he was accompanied by Edward Stone. [6]

'FOR THE DEFENCE OF KING, PARLIAMENT AND THE KINGDOM'

Autumn and winter were to bring worrying times for the Wells citizens. In the autumn were the two major fairs of St Calixtus on 14 October and of St Andrew on 30 November, that could well be disrupted by political and military events. Traders from a wide area were accustomed to come to these fairs. An illustration of this is that in 1625 during a serious outbreak of the plague, the corporation had sent letters to the corporations of Lyme Regis, Bridgwater, Bath, Dorchester, Gloucester, Sherborne and Exeter informing them of the cancellation of a fair. While all these towns were under the control of parliament in the autumn of 1642, the parliamentary soldiers were not well disciplined at this stage and carriers and travellers could be molested on the highways. People were understandably nervous in what was for them an unprecedented situation. The Wells mercers who bought some of their more expensive fabrics from London to sell locally were also affected by the disruption of the carrier service between Wells and London due to military operations near Reading which the royal army reached on 6 November 1642. The military standoff in Reading meant that carriers were actually plundered by both sides. The Wells fairs took place but it is highly likely that not so many goods were on sale and that profits were also down due to a sparser attendance than usual. [7] The failure by the corporation to obtain the £20 left to the city in the will of Gabriel Johnson which was to be invested for charitable purposes, was another sign of the times. Jasper Dinham who was the executor was unable to make payment because of his incarceration in Taunton Castle as a 'suspicious delinquent' – a royalist supporter. [8]

The deputy lieutenants on behalf of the parliamentary county committee in the persons of William Strode and Clement Walker also put the city on a war footing. They had found the city militia defective in numbers and equipment and consequently on 21 November 1642, ordered the corporation to provide '20 good corslets with swords and pikes and as many muskets with bandaliers, rests, headpieces and swords' to equip the 40 men required. These men were to be ready 'to be mustered at 24 hours warning for the present service, which require great expedition in respect of the imminent dangers that threaten our peace.' The cost of this new equipment was to be borne by the citizens of Wells. [9]

January brought little relief. Hopton by this time had gathered his forces in Cornwall and moved them to the Devon border where he was opposed by the military governor of Plymouth, Colonel William Ruthin. Reinforcements for Ruthin commanded by Henry Grey, Earl of Stamford, reached Taunton on 2 January 1642/3 on their way west. From there Stamford wrote a threatening letter to the mayor of Wells, Robert Rowley: 'I expect you to send me on Wednesday being 4 January £50 to be employed for the defence of the king, parliament and kingdom; which money you are to levy of your city and if I receive it not, accordingly I shall have just cause to believe your town to be malignant and you must expect to be dealt with accordingly.' The corporation reacted speedily and on 4 January ordered that £13 taken from the chest should be sent immediately to mollify the Earl, the other £37 to be raised by a rate levied on the city. [10]

During the next two months, parliament gradually evolved a coherent system of regular taxation. On 27 January 1642/3, it decided to try to collect the money which was owed from previous parliamentary assessments, particularly those loans which had been authorised by parliament in the Propositions of 9 June 1642. The Propositions scheme had invited subscriptions of money, plate and offers to maintain horse, horsemen and arms to defend the kingdom against its enemies. Volunteers had been promised a high rate of interest of 8%. Many of the people who lent money were sceptical of the scheme and were doubtful that they would receive their money back. They were proved correct. William Strode who was the deputy lieutenant in charge of the eastern division of Somerset appointed George Milward of Shepton Mallet as the local collector and local parliamentary gentry subscribed generously. The response from the resident gentry of Wells is difficult to gauge because of the poor state of the existing records but the names are known of two gentlemen who gave: William Morgan, the brother of Robert Morgan, advanced £20 and Thomas Coward, £50. Others may well have followed suit. The money collected was to remain in Somerset to pay for the local parliamentary forces being raised to combat the threat of Sir Ralph Hopton's imminent advance from Cornwall towards Somerset. On the same day parliament also authorised further taxation. A county committee was formed to levy a tax of one twentieth on the value of their estates or one fifth of their yearly revenue on gentlemen who had supported the royalists. Again due to lack of surviving evidence it is not clear who in Wells paid. However by February a new centralised taxation system was introduced in the form of a weekly assessment on all landed property. Somerset had to raise £1050 a month or £12,600 a year, 50% more than the much resented ship money of the 1630s. The Wells records do not mention this assessment but the Wells contribution was probably at the rate of just under £10 a month, no doubt collected by the city receiver William Smith.[11]

Although Somerset was now at peace, public order could still be threatened by discharged soldiers passing through. One such incident occurred in early February 1642/3. Richard Hellyer, a discharged soldier from the royalist army, claiming that he had been briefly captured by the parliamentary defenders of Cirencester during the successful royalist assault on the town and transferred by them to a brief imprisonment in Gloucester which was still held by the parliamentarians, arrived in Wells on either the 8 or 9 February. His story must be treated with some suspicion. He had probably been a soldier in the Wells militia and as such would have accompanied the Marquis of Hertford on his retreat to Sherborne and from there to Wales and so to Cirencester. Prince Rupert took Cirencester by storm on 2 February 1643 and it is possible that Hellyer deserted before the battle because it is difficult to see how he might have been captured and moved out of the town during the successful royalist assault. On arrival in Wells, Hellyer, who had been an apprentice of Philip Bayley, a Southover blacksmith, became drunk and decided to visit his old master with whom he presumably had some old scores to settle. Wishing to rob the house, he attempted to break down the blacksmith's door with a sledgehammer and in his drunken frenzy threatened to extort £40 from the mayor and run the mayor through if the mayor decided to pursue him. When it was pointed out to him quite reasonably by John Symes, a blacksmith and friend of Bayley's, that as he did not have a sword he would find it difficult to carry out the deed, Hellyer was alleged to have replied that he would find one and said that 'the town would be fired before Easter next and being demanded who should fire the town he said that the king's troops should do it.' This touched a raw nerve amongst the witnesses who though they might welcome a royalist takeover of the city, were concerned about the possible violent behaviour of the troops. Hellyer of course denied that he had spoken these inflammatory words claiming that he had been 'overcome with drink' and the city JP was no doubt relieved when he went on his way to Salisbury to visit his friends. [12]

'HAVOCK'

At this time the cathedral clergy were also becoming increasingly worried for their own security. The damage done to the cathedral from undisciplined soldiers in the previous August and the threat of further violence only just averted in October, must have been exercising their minds. At the first chapter meeting in the New Year on 7 January 1642/3, the only recorded business was the appointment of the vicar of Dulverton but the meeting was noteworthy because of the unusually high attendance. The dean, Walter Raleigh, was present for the first time since 1 July 1642; also present were the treasurer, Robert Creighton a regular attender, the archdeacon of Taunton Gerard Wood who had missed two of the three previous meetings, the precentor Sebastian Smith who had only missed one and two resident prebendaries Thomas Walker and Robert Ashe (the master of the Cathedral Grammar School). An unrecorded discussion probably took place about the advisability of vacating Wells during the present unsettled times. Whereas chapter meetings had recently taken place at least every two months, there was to be no meeting of the cathedral chapter for nearly six months. By that time the political situation had radically altered. By 25 March 1643 the cathedral clergy were definitely absent being 'elsewhere inhabiting for certain causes best known to themselves, but chiefly by reason of the dangerousness of the times.' [13]

The fears of the cathedral clergy for their safety and for that of the cathedral fabric were soon realised by the events of April and May 1643. On 15 April some captains from Alexander Popham's regiment based in Glastonbury led their soldiers on a raid to Wells. One of the captains, possibly Captain Howard, had a list of the royalist supporters in the city and details of the size of their estates. There is an intriguing note in the Wells Corporation convocation book for 21 April 1643 where it is recorded 'that there was lent to Captain Howard £5, to be repaid by him within six days which is ordered to be paid by Mr William Smyth the receiver.' Was the captain extorting money? Did the corporation pay him for the list? The truth will probably never be known but it seems clear that Howard never repaid what may have been a bribe. The soldiers are not recorded as having damaged the city although it is likely that they were liberally supplied with food and drink by the inhabitants to avoid this. The cathedral precinct was not so fortunate. The soldiers caused serious damage in the cathedral by defacing pictures and destroying crucifixes. They also looted the bishop's palace destroying 'all such monuments or pictures they espied, either of religion, antiquity, or the kinges of England, and made such havock, and sold for little or nothing all the household stuffe.' No doubt some Wells citizens were eager to snap up bargains! Many important documents were also lost. Nathaniel Chyle who wrote a 'History of the Church of Wells' in 1680 commented: 'when the Bishopp's palace was plundered, the writings and Records of the Bishoprick, of noe advantage to Soldiers (got into the hands of the little) were seized on by some Attournies of the place and Neighbourhood, who having made some small Interest of them, as to theire practice, soe confounded and Embezild them and stifled, as impossible ever to be retrived.' [14]

Taking advantage of their commander Alexander Popham's absence in London, the soldiers returned on 10 May and 'after dynner rusht into the church, broke down the windowes, organs, fonte, seates in the quire, the busshops see[seat] besides many other villanies.' The events in April and May were witnessed and probably recorded by either Mark Tabor who was the registrar of the archdeaconry of Wells or his son-in-law Francis Keene, the keeper of the bishop's palace and park at Banwell. Tabor lived at what is now 21 Market Place and being so near the cathedral and working and worshipping there would have been in an excellent position to record what happened. Keene and his wife may well have been staying with Tabor at the time. One of them probably recorded the events of April and May 1643 at the top and down the right hand side of the title page of an early seventeeth century edition of a theological work entitled 'Vita Jesu Christi' by a fourteenth century theologian Ludolphus de Saxonia. The handwriting is diminutive and in a different hand from the account of the stone throwing incident in the cathedral on 8 April 1642 (already referred to) which is recorded at the foot of the left hand page opposite the title page. The book remained in the Tabor/Keene family until Tabor's granddaughter, and Keene's daughter, Sarah Westley, left it to the cathedral library in her will of 1701. [15]

THE ROYALIST VICTORY: JUNE 1643

Perhaps the parliamentary soldiers were motivated by the wish to gain loot knowing that they might soon have to retreat before the victorious Cornish army led by Sir Ralph Hopton and the troops of the Marquis of Hertford, which on 4 June began their advance into Somerset. The combined forces that Hopton and Hertford had under their command consisted of 4000 infantry, 2000 cavalry, 300 dragoons and 16 cannon. The royalists captured Taunton on 5 June 1643, Bridgwater on the sixth and Dunster Castle on the seventh. Worryingly for civilians in the path of the army, the cavalry under Prince Maurice of the Palatinate, the nephew of the king and brother of Prince Rupert, proved to be particularly ill-disciplined. Hopton although disapproving was 'never able to repress the extravagant disorder of the horse to the ruin and discomposure of all.' The cavalrymen for their part considered Hopton's Cornish infantry 'the best foot that they had seen for marching and fighting; but so mutinous withal, that nothing but an alarm could keep them from falling foul upon their officers.' After the taking of Taunton, Bridgewater and Dunster Castle, the royalist plan had been to return to capture Exeter where the parliamentary garrison was still holding out. On Friday 9 June as the royalists started to return to Exeter, these plans were abandoned when they learnt that the parliamentary general, Sir William Waller, was building up his forces at Bath and that 'the forces of Popham, Strode and their associates were at Wells and Glastonbury amounting to 3000 Horse and Foot, with intent to join with Waller and so make up a full and complete army.' The decision was then taken to deal with this threat before proceeding with the capture of Exeter. Consequently the royalist army returned to Taunton on Saturday 10 June and on the following day, the soldiers having rested, set off in the direction of Somerton. The parliamentary army at Wells and Glastonbury consisted of men drawn from Sir William Waller's troops at Bath and those soldiers who had fled from Taunton and Bridgwater but was only half the size of the royalist army. Alexander Popham realised that he had no alternative in the face of such superior numbers but to conduct an orderly retreat up on to the Mendip plateau where he would have the advantage of the ground. He no doubt hoped that the royalists would repeat their behaviour of August 1642 and not attempt an advance up on to the hill before he could join Waller.

Early on Monday 12 June about a mile outside Somerton in the direction of Glastonbury, dragoons forming the vanguard of the royalist army were attacked by a strong party of parliamentary cavalry in what was a delaying action. The attack was successfully beaten off with some casualties on both sides. The parliamentarians fought another minor rearguard action two miles south of Glastonbury to allow their infantry and carriages to vacate the town and retreat towards Wells. The royalists entered Glastonbury and then advanced on Wells. The parliamentary army continued to retreat in good order and mounted another successful rearguard action by lining the hedges along the Glastonbury/Wells road with dragoons (mounted infantry armed with carbines) who held off the royalist troops for an hour or more. By this time tension must have been high in Wells as the main body of the parliamentary troops hurried through. Fortunately for the citizens there seems to have been no actual fighting in the city only a short rearguard action on its northern outskirts that lasted about an hour allowing the main bulk of the parliamentarian infantry and carriages to get away. The parliamentary army took the (then) Bath road to the top of the Mendip ridge. (see Maps 1& 2)

Many in Wells must have been apprehensive that the events of the previous August might again be repeated but it was not to be. This time the 22 year old Prince Maurice was in charge of the cavalry. He was more aggressive and impetuous than Hopton and the sedentary Hertford, both of whom had to defer to his royal rank and the decision was taken to pursue the parliamentarians with the cavalry. The contemporary historian Clarendon comments on the arrogance of Prince Maurice who considered the parliamentary withdrawal a 'running away,' but the prince was brave and full of confidence. Arriving in England in August 1642 to support his uncle the king, he had had until now a successful war, defeating Sir William Waller three months previously on the Welsh border. With the departure of the cavalry under the prince and the Earl of Caernarvon with Hopton in attendance, Hertford set a rearguard in the northern part of the city and then allowed the infantry and some of his cavalry, tired from their 15 mile march from Somerton, to quarter in the city. No evidence survives as to how this was achieved but the arrival of over 4000 troops in a city of 2600 inhabitants must have caused many logistical problems. No doubt as at Taunton, the inhabitants of Wells were expected to provide free quarter which as it had been at Taunton was probably 'soberly taken.' The Marquis of Hertford remained in Wells, probably at the Bishop's Palace with which he was already familiar, while Prince Maurice and the Earl of Caernarvon with their cavalry regiments and young John Stawell (son of Sir John) with some of Hertford's cavalry, advanced up the hill following the Bath road, to confront the parliamentarians, capturing two of the enemy's wagons on the way.

On seeing the royalist cavalry, the parliamentarians following Waller's orders to avoid a pitched battle, retreated towards the village of Chewton (Mendip) screening their infantry and baggage train with their cavalry. The royalists followed the parliamentarians to within a mile of the entrance to the village but as the lane leading into the village was narrow and progress would be somewhat slow, the parliamentarian cavalry turned to face their royalist opponents. Prince Maurice decided to attack. Hopton immediately warned him of the dangers of pursuing too far should the attack be successful considering the proximity of Waller's army but little heed was taken of his advice. The Earl of Caernarvon, who himself was to die in battle three months later, immediately charged the parliamentarians 'with incomparable gallantry,' chased them into the lane, routed them and ignoring Hopton's advice pursued them for about five miles 'doing brave execution on them all the way, many of ther horse being slayn and taken, their foot entirely routed and dispersed; a great many killed, their carriages, ordnance and ammunition, all seized on by the noble victor, as the most memorable testimony of so brave a service.' Caernarvon pursued the parliamentarians as far as the High Littleton/ Farnborough/Timsbury area, five or six miles from Waller in Bath.

Hopton's fears were well founded. Unbeknown to the royalists, Waller had sent a 'fresh strong party' of horse and dragoons from Bath to assist the parliamentarians in their retreat. As it was now getting rather late in the evening, the royalists did not detect these troops and when Caernarvon stumbled upon them, he was immediately forced to retreat. He did however send a message to Prince Maurice warning him of the new danger. Unfortunately Prince Maurice had already ordered some of his cavalry to return to Wells due to the lateness of the day but when he learnt of the new parliamentarian threat, he retired from Chewton (Mendip) towards Wells and drew up his remaining cavalry on open ground probably at Nedge, a ridge just south of Chewton (Mendip). Meanwhile Caernarvon who had retreated in a disorderly fashion, reformed his troops and joined the Prince at Nedge to face the new danger.

The parliamentarians now had the advantage in numbers of horsed soldiers but Prince Maurice was undeterred and decided to attack. He charged the parliamentarians with the four troops of his regiment that remained and routed the troops opposite him. The parliamentary cavalry that was unengaged then outflanked the prince and attacked him in the rear, while Caernarvon not to be outdone outflanked the parliamentarians and attacked their rear. In the ensuing melee Prince Maurice was unhorsed, received two head wounds from a sword and was briefly captured. Fortunately two troops of horse commanded by Captain Richard Atkyns that had been on their way back to Wells, being informed of Prince Maurice's perilous situation, returned to the battle. The royalists, although outnumbered, were aided by a sudden Mendip mist that reduced visibility to ten yards. The parliamentary dragoons were reluctant to fire into the ensuing melee for fear of harming their own men and the prince's rescue was effected. Atkyns reported: 'my groom coming after us, espied the Prince, and all being in confusion, he alighted from his horse, and gave him to the Prince, which carried him off.' The royalists though still in danger having fired their pistols, renewed their attack and Caernarvon was able to drive the parliamentarians out of Chewton (Mendip) northwards. Because of the failing light, it being nearly 10 pm, Prince Maurice called off the pursuit and the royalists returned to Wells in the gathering darkness. In the action the royalists had lost about 30 men, the parliamentarian losses being somewhat higher. Hopton, now in his home country was concerned that the army's discipline should be maintained as far as was possible and was careful to point out in a dispatch to the king that the cavalry 'came orderly into this towne [Wells].' The parliamentary threat to Wells had been beaten off.

The royalists stayed in Wells for at least the next ten to twelve days. When the royalist troops had arrived in the city, the quartermasters assisted, probably unwillingly by the city's constables, were sent out immediately to find billets for the tired foot soldiers. For the Wells householders 'there was nothing more terrifying than the sudden knock on the door which heralded the arrival of soldiers in search of billets.' It is unlikely that the Wells householders were paid for providing food and shelter for the soldiers. Money was scarce. Atkyns reported that for the wounded men in his troop and of his division he received 20s a man from Sir Robert Long, the treasurer of the army, 'which was all the money I ever received for myself, or troops during the war.' At the end of the royalist army's stay in the city, the householders would have been presented with tickets signed by the quartering officers giving the number of men accommodated and the length of their stay. Theoretically these tickets were redeemable from the corporation but there is no evidence in the Wells Corporation records of this having been done.

On Tuesday 13 June, Hopton ordered a public thanksgiving in Wells for the victory and it is likely to have taken the form of a service in the cathedral. Clergy would have been available: the dean, Walter Raleigh and the treasurer Robert Creighton had both been present at a chapter meeting on 3 June, the first since 7 January 1643. The euphoria of victory was tempered by the melancholy succession of military burials which the parishioners of St Cuthbert's church witnessed: on 14 June – William Harris, 'a soldier slayn by his captayne', on 17 June – Samuel Tanner, on 21 June – James Sacah and John Tom, on 22 June – Bernard Jetson, on 23 June – John Estibrooke and William son of Captayne Henrie Kellow. Burials of those who succumbed to their wounds continued into July: Thomas Bull, a soldier, was buried on the sixth and on the twelfth three more soldiers whose names were unknown. John Perkins of Ottington in Devon was buried on the twentieth and two more soldiers were buried at the end of August. While the infantry remained quartered in the city, the cavalry were quartered in the neighbourhood, Atkyns himself being at Glastonbury. One of the Cornishmen left his mark because on 13 April 1644 Edward, a base child of Joane Wallbanck, was christened, the reputed father being Edward Baker a Cornish trooper. There is no evidence that the royalist troops did much damage to property in Wells but they had evidently pillaged property on their advance towards the city. Atkyns reported 'I went to my quarters at Glastonbury, where there was a handsome case of a house, but totally plundered, and neither bread not beer in it; but only part of a cheddar cheese, which looking blue, I found my foot-boy giving [some] to my greyhounds, and reproving him for it; he cried, saying there was nothing else to give them.' The royalist commanders however fared somewhat better. On Sunday 18 June Atkyns was invited to dine with Prince Maurice 'who had invited his officers to a buck.' Atkyns told the messenger, Major Thomas Sheldon, that he had arranged for Prince Maurice's chaplain to give him and his troop Holy Communion at that time. The worldly major replied 'Hang't, Hang't bully, thou may'st receive the sacrament at any time, but thou can'st not eat venison at any time.' Evidently the royalist commanders were helping themselves to game from the bishop's park! [16]

While in Wells, Hertford and Hopton decided to purge the city corporation of the two men who had been the most active supporters of parliament: Robert Morgan and Stephen Hasket. They met the mayor, Robert Rowley 'in conference' and ordered the arrest of Morgan and the expulsion of Haskett from the corporation. Morgan was arrested and imprisoned in Wells before being transferred to Taunton Castle. Morgan's crime, judging from his later career, was a too close relationship with the parliamentary county committee. His arrest by his local colleagues was effected without acrimony. Rowley visited Morgan in prison and stressed that it had been the Marquis of Hertford's decision that Morgan should be removed from the corporation. Rowley, who had had to execute Hertford's order was worried that Morgan might be offended with him for doing so 'whereupon Mr Morgan replied that he would not be offended with him but was contented to be put forth with all his heart.' The corporation recorded that 'Mr Morgan be removed both from his place of mastership and justice until *it be further considered* [author's italics].' In those dangerous times the corporation was keeping its options open – Robert Morgan was too well connected in parliamentary circles to be alienated!

The corporation proceeded in leisurely fashion against Haskett expelling him on 13 August 1643. Haskett, anticipating what was to happen to him, had already sent his goods out of the town in order to avoid confiscation. Also arrested was Robert Morgan's brother, William Morgan. He was charged with advancing money to parliament on the Propositions of 1642 and for receiving in his house in Wells Sir Francis Pile who had been excepted from a pardon in a royal proclamation. [17]

Hopton now had to consider the coming campaign against William Waller. He wrote from Wells to the parliamentary general in Bath proposing a conference between them to discuss exchange of prisoners and to try to avoid further bloodshed. Waller's reply showed the dilemma that members of the gentry class who had been friends in more peaceful times were in when they now found themselves on opposing sides. Waller wrote in reply 'Certainly my affections to you are so unchangeable, that hostility itself cannot violate my friendship to your person. But I must be true to the cause wherein I serve. ... I should most gladly wait upon you according to your desire but that I look upon you as engaged in that party beyond the possibility of a retreat and uncapable of being wrought upon by any persuasions. And I know the conference could never be so close between us but that it would take wind and receive a construction to my dishonour. That great God who is the searcher of my heart knows with what a sad sense I go upon this service and with what a perfect hatred I detest this war without an enemy ... We are both upon the stage, and must act such parts as are assigned us in this tragedy. Let us do it in a way of honour without personal animosities.' The war was thus to continue leading to Waller's defeat at the battle of Landsdown three weeks later. [18]

NOTES

[1] *Exceeding Joyfull Newes From the Earl of Bedford*, London, 23 August 1642 (no pagination), BL E 113(17); *A Coppie of a Letter, Read in the House of Commons: Sent from Master Sampford 26 August 1642*, BL E 114 (18).

[2] Underdown, D, *Somerset in the Civil War and Interregnum*, Newton Abbot, 1973, pp 40-41.

[3] Nott A & Hasler J, (eds), *Wells Convocation Acts Books 1589-1665, Part 1 1589-1629, Part 2 1629-44; 1662-5*, SRS Vols 90 & 91, 834-5; Chadwyck Healey, C E H, (ed) *Bellum Civile: Hopton's Narrative of the Campaign in the West (1642-1644) and other Papers*, SRS Vol 18, 1902, p 12 note 1.

[4] Underdown, D, *Somerset in the Civil War and Interregnum*, op cit, pp 41-43; Bettey, J H, (ed) *Calendar of the Correspondence of the Smythe Family*, BRS Vol XXXV, 1982, no 430 p 202.

[5] Nott & Hasler, SRS Vol 91, op cit, pp 839-840.

[6] *Certain and true News from Somerset-shire with the besieging of Sir Ralph Hopton's House ...*, London, October 15, 1642, BL E 122 (18); Thornbury, W, *Old and New London,* London 1878, Vol I, pp 364-374; *JHL Vol 5,* London 1802, pp 560,568,577, 628-9; for Bower see *JHC Vol 2,* London 1802, p 864; the Palace of Westminster was called 'the Ould Pallace' because it had been superceded by the Palace of Whitehall in King Street as the London residence of the king.

[7] Nott & Hasler, SRS Vol 90, op cit, pp 420-1; Underdown, D, *Somerset in the Civil War and Interregnum, op cit,* p 43.

[8] Nott & Hasler, SRS Vol 91, op cit, p 843.

[9] Nott & Hasler, SRS Vol 91, op cit, p 844; Nott & Hasler, SRS 90 pp 343-4 shows the depleted state of the armour stored in the Almshouse hall in 1621 which was still probably the case in 1642.

[10] Royle, T, *Civil War: The Wars of the Three Kingdoms 1638-1660,* London 2004, p 235; Nott & Hasler, SRS Vol 91,op cit, p 846.

[11] Wroughton, J, *An Unhappy Civil War: The Experiences of Ordinary People in Gloucestershire, Somerset and Wiltshire 1642-1646,* Bath, 1999, pp 73-81; Underdown, D, *Somerset in the Civil War and Interregnum,* opcit, p 46; Everett Green, M A, (ed), *Calendar of the Proceedings of the Committee for Compounding Vol. II 1643-46,* London 1890, p 1234.

[12] WTH *Wells Corporation Sessions Book 1625-50,* fo. 87.

[13] Bailey, D S, (ed) *Wells Cathedral Chapter Act Book 1666-1683,* London, 1973, pp 426-7; Nott & Hasler, SRS Vol 91,op cit, p 847.

[14] *Calendar of the Manuscripts of the Dean and Chapter of Wells, Vol. II,* HMC, 1914, p 427; Nott & Hasler, SRS Vol 91, op cit, p 848; Reynolds, H E, (ed), *Wells Cathedral: Its Foundation, Constitutional History and Statutes,* Wells, 1881, p cxlv.

[15] *Calendar of the Manuscripts of the Dean and Chapter of Wells Vol. II,* op cit, p 427; personal information from Anne Crawford, Wells Cathedral Archivist; Bailey, D S, *Wells Manor of Canon Grange,* Stroud, 1982, pp 66-67.

[16] The account of the Royalist campaign in June 1643 is taken from Chadwyck Healey, *Bellum Civile op cit,* pp 47-51; Young, P, (ed), *Military Memoirs: The Civil War: The Vindication of Richard Atkyns,* London 1967, pp 12-17; Trevelyan Sir W.C. & Trevelyan Sir C.E., *Trevelyan Papers 3,* Camden Series 105, London 1872, pp 235-8; Jeffs, R, (ed), *Mercurius Aulicus, The English Revolution III Newsbooks, Vol I,* London 1971, pp 317-8 & 341-3; the account of the billeting of troops and the quotations are taken from Wroughton, *The Unhappy Civil War op cit* pp 104-105 & Young, *The Vindication of Richard Atkins op cit,* p 15; the burials are listed in the *St Cuthbert Wells Parish Register 1609-1665,* SRO D/P/W St C 2/1/1.

[17] Nott & Hasler, SRS Vol 91,op cit, pp 850-2; CCC Vol. II *op cit, p 1380.*

[18] Underdown, D, *Somerset in the Civil War and Interregnum op cit,* pp 55-56.

CHAPTER 6

ROYALIST WELLS: JULY 1643-JULY 1645

To the gentry who ran the war, conscience and honour were most important considerations but the war had to be paid for with money and in human suffering; the people of Wells were to experience both in the next two years. No premonitions of what the future might bring were evident amongst the Wells householders at the time of the royalist victory. There must have been a sense of relief at the departure of the parliamentary army and the return to some kind of stability. The first priority for the majority of the corporation was to celebrate the royalist victory. On 27 July 1643 news came of the 'yielding up of Bristol to the use of the king's majesty.' A rather thinly attended corporation meeting (only 13 members out of a possible 24) voted 'that in token of their congratulation there shall be ringing of bells and bonfires within Wells and one bonfire to be made at the charge of the corporation.' Three days later the corporation still in celebratory mood agreed that there should be a dinner for the 24 members and their wives and the burgesses 'as it has been anciently accustomed.' Over 100 could have attended this unusual event – unusual because normally only the 24 members of the corporation attended civic dinners at this time of the year. The final cause for celebration was the receipt of the news that Sir Edward Rodney had been released from imprisonment in London and had returned home to Pilton Park. It was agreed that members of the corporation should ride to Sir Edward's home and present him with gifts of sugar and wine. However not all Wells burgesses were happy about the royalist victory. William Saunders, David Barrett and Anthony Taunton, three radical shoemakers, had left the city with the retreating parliamentary army having 'born arms and been in actual rebellion against his majesty.' The corporation called a general convocation (a meeting of all burgesses) to deal with their rebellion and it was generally agreed amongst those present that the three men should be disenfranchised from the privileges and liberties of the city and not readmitted until they had submitted themselves to the king. [1]

PAYING FOR THE WAR

Meanwhile the county had to be administered and the war had to be fought and paid for. The royal government of Somerset was re-established by the appointment of a new county committee among whose members were the Wells barrister Edward Wykes, the estranged city recorder John Baber, Sir Edward Rodney and William Walrond. The clerk to the committee was the diocesan registrar Alexander Jett. Other Wells gentlemen also worked for the royalist cause: Valentine Trym acted as under-sheriff to Sir Thomas Bridges while the lawyer William Morgan, the brother of the parliamentarian Robert, coordinated the supply of arms to the royalist forces. In early 1645 he wrote; 'there is never a day butt that I have commaunds from my Lord Hopton about match and Bullett to be sent to Taunton, Lamport, Sherborne & other places next the Enemy who is now in Dorsettshire & on our borders.' After the royalist victory at Chewton (Mendip) the pattern of normal life resumed; the quarter sessions were held and in late October 1643 the king ordered from Oxford that the assizes should be held in Wells in the following February. The news became known in Wells on 23 November 1643 causing a flurry of excitement. The royalists also initially imposed a weekly county contribution of £1500 which, after the fall of Bristol in July 1643, was raised to £2000. The collection was to be organised by the constables and paid to the officials of the hundred who would then distribute funds as necessary. Compared to the annual ship money total of £60 a year paid by Wells in the 1630s, the Wells tax burden had now risen considerably to nearly £800 per annum. Coupled with this was an extensive programme of impressment of soldiers initiated by Sir Ralph Hopton in October 1643. This was because the Cornish army which had been in Wells in June, had advanced into Dorset under Prince Maurice to drive out the parliamentary forces and Hopton needed an army to attack Sir William Waller in Hampshire. [2]

'ROYALIST WELLS: JULY 1643 – JULY 1645'

THE CASE OF THE POSTMASTER

The heavy hand of royalist government was also felt in Wells in October 1643. The Wells Corporation was extremely sensitive about the rights it had gained in the Elizabethan charter and resented any attempt to override them. However the case of the postmaster showed how the exigencies of war had rendered it impotent to influence events. Sir Ralph Hopton, regarded by the corporation as a sympathetic friend, had appointed Joseph Nurton, a Wells innkeeper, as his local postmaster, responsible for maintaining communications between him and the Wells area. It was possibly not the most diplomatic appointment as Nurton's relationship with the corporation had not been without tension. Nurton had become a burgess in 1636 appropriately enough on 5 November in line with his fiery temperament. He was in trouble with the corporation in September 1640 when he said to Thomas Salmon 'thou art a fool and so are all the rest of the 24.' He was fined 10s and subsequently disenfranchised when he refused to pay. Nurton evidently took to his new job with enthusiasm and little tact. According to the corporation he had been 'taking up any horses within three miles of Wells for which he does enforce the country here adjoining to contribute and pay him money to their great hurt and grievances'. To a husbandman, the loss of a horse could severely affect his livelihood and the demand for what was considered illegal taxation was an affront to the corporation. Nurton also insulted one of the constables Thomas Foster, who complained to the mayor who then issued a warrant ordering Nurton to appear before him to answer Foster's complaint. Nurton refused claiming that 'he had business to do for the king,' The confrontation was made worse by the abuse which Nurton's wife Ursula vented on the unfortunate constable, Robert Thomas, who had been sent to bring her husband to the mayor. Ursula said that Thomas Foster was a 'hoarse Whoremaster baggerlie rogue and that both his father (Henry Foster, a master on the corporation) and father in law (Richard Casbeard, a capital burgess) and all his generation were Baggers.' Nurton then went to the mayor, refused to give sureties for good behaviour and when the mayor committed him to the city gaol, assaulted the constable Robert Thomas with a knife in his hand and threatened to kill him. Nurton's wife Ursula not to be outdone stuck a burning candle in the face of one of the verderers (street wardens) who was assisting Robert Thomas. While this was happening Nurton was able to make his escape. On the same day, the mayor William West, a staunch royalist wrote to Hopton in Bristol complaining of Nurton's behaviour asking him to discharge Nurton from his post. Hopton's reply was received the following day. Hopton made no mention of Nurton and instead billeted Prince Maurice's regiment of about 800 men in the city: common soldiers were to be paid 2s 6d a week, ensigns and other inferior officers 3s 6d a week and superior officers 6s a week each to be paid for from the city's contibution to the weekly county assessment. Whether or not any of this money was actually paid to householders for board and lodging is unclear. Hopton signed himself rather ironically 'your very loving friend.' It seems likely that the regiment remained quartered in Wells throughout the winter until the campaigning season began in April 1644 when Prince Maurice led his troops against the parliamentary stronghold of Lyme Regis. [3]

THE THREAT TO THE CATHEDRAL ESTABLISHMENT

Wells was unaffected by opposing armies during the winter of 1643-4 and the city went about its usual business. The dean and chapter continued to make appointments to prebends and the members of the chapter argued about the election of canons residentiary and the allocation of canonical houses. There was even a quarrel between the wives of the vicars choral over who should sit in the two seats allocated in the cathedral 'quire' for vicars' wives. However outside the royalist enclave in the west, parliament in London was beginning to dismantle the church as the citizens of Wells knew it. Should the king be defeated, the organisation and worship of the church would be radically different from what had been experienced before. This must have worried the church hierarchy in Wells as the news filtered through from London. In early 1643 both Houses of Parliament approved a bill that abolished the archbishops, bishops and deans and chapters. This bill was not turned into an Ordinance of Parliament until 1646 but remained as a potent threat to the ecclesiastical establishment in Wells throughout the civil war. From early 1644 both houses of parliament ceased to use the Book of

Common Prayer. It was replaced in January 1645 by the Directory of Public Worship drawn up by the Westminster Assembly of Divines. This group had first met on 1 July 1643 and consisted of 121 ordained ministers with ten peers and twenty MPs as lay assessors. Also present were eight Presbyterian commissioners from Scotland. Monthly fasts became a regular feature and when it was realised in December 1644 that the next one would fall on Christmas Day, an ordinance was rushed through parliament with the title 'for better observance of the Monthly fast, and most especially next Wednesday, commonly called the Feast of the Nativity of Christ on which men took liberty to carnal and sensual delight contrary to the life which Christ himself led on earth.' The attack on the traditional Anglican calendar followed with a parliamentary ordinance that banned the observance of Christmas, Easter, Whit Sunday, holy days, saints' days and Rogation processions. Although these regulations had no force in Wells at the time, their existence must have been a further reminder of what might happen if the king were to be defeated.

The events in London during 1644 may well be the reason for the lack of formal recorded meetings of the cathedral chapter during most of 1644. The chapter may well have not wanted to leave any evidence of their business meetings if they were to be abolished. The last meetings of a rather depleted cathedral chapter took place on January 28 1644/5; it was not to meet again for over 15 years. Present at the initial morning meeting were only four men: Dean Raleigh, Dr Gerard Wood, the archdeacon of Wells, his brother Dr Roger Wood, a resident canon and official of the archdeaconry of Wells with Tristram Towse the elder, the deputy chapter clerk, taking the minutes. The record states 'yf it sholl heareafter happen that the corporacion of the deane and chapter to be dissolved by act of parliament or by any other lawful meanes then the caution money which each chapter member had paid should be returned to him from the debts due to the dean and chapter.' The last appointment made by the bishop, that of Arthur Mattock to be general receiver of the bishop's lordships, manor and lands was ratified. In the afternoon of that late January day, Dr Robert Creyghton, the treasurer, joined the group and the last lease of dean and chapter land, that of the rectory at Cheddar to Christoper Dodington, the Wells Corporation recorder, was sealed. Also ratified was the bishop's grant of the manor of Chard and lands in Banwell to the new receiver general and to Alexander Jett. The catalyst for the decision to plan for the possible demise of the chapter may well have been the public execution of William Laud, late Bishop of Bath and Wells and Archbishop of Canterbury, on Tower Hill on 10 January 1644/5. These particular members of the cathedral chapter then dispersed never to meet again.

Dean Raleigh went to his rectory at Chedzoy near Bridgwater where he remained until captured by parliamentary forces in July 1645. His tragic story is told in the next chapter. Of the other cathedral officers, the treasurer Robert Creighton made his way to the royalist headquarters at Oxford (leaving his wife in Wells), where he was made a doctor of divinity and appointed chaplain to the king. His wife Frances stayed in Wells near her father William Walrond and was still living at Creighton's canonical house (now 3 The Liberty) in 1649. When Oxford fell to parliament in 1646, Creighton escaped to Cornwall and, disguised as a labourer, took ship for France. There he joined the exiled Prince of Wales at the court of Queen Henrietta Maria at the old palace of St Germain en Laye near Paris. The diarist John Evelyn heard him preach there on 12 September 1649. From 1653-5 he lived in Utrecht in the Netherlands where he acted as tutor to Edmund Verney son of the Buckinghamshire gentleman Sir Ralph Verney. Verney's biographer describes Creighton as 'a humourless Laudian-in-exile ... an intellectual Scot [with a] rigid approach to life and learning.' Creighton continued to act as chaplain to Prince Charles at The Hague and 'preached liberally before him against the Presbyterians and murderers of King Charles I.' He called Presbyterianism 'the cursed Genevan tyranny' and edited a compilation of tracts attacking it. He remained in the Netherlands until 1660 when he returned with the new king.[4]

The chancellor John Young, also a royal chaplain, had not been resident in Wells since he had been made Dean of Winchester in 1634. He had family connections in Wells being the brother-in-law of Andrew Bowerman and had been chancellor of Wells Cathedral since 1611. He did not survive the Interregnum, dying at Wallop in Hampshire where he was rector in 1654. The third member of the chapter, the precentor Sebastian Smith, possibly retired to either of his Somerset benefices of Compton Dando or North Curry from where he was evicted during the Commonwealth period. He survived until the Restoration on an annuity of £60 granted to him for his life by the House of Commons in 1649.

'ROYALIST WELLS: JULY 1643 – JULY 1645'

The movements of the archdeacon of Taunton, William Piers the son of the bishop in 1645, are unknown at this time. He was also vicar of Kingsbury Episcopi in Somerset and may well have retired there or joined his father on his estate at Cuddesdon in Oxfordshire. After the parliamentary victory in Somerset in August 1645, Piers experienced severe problems. His position as the son of a disgraced bishop made his punishment more severe than many of his fellow churchmen. The seventeeth century apologist for the deprived royalist clergy, John Walker, paints a vivid if somewhat inaccurate picture of Piers's sufferings. Piers was forced because of lack of means to 'marry an ordinary woman with a very small estate.' Some confusion arises over the identification of this woman and the date of the marriage. After the Restoration Piers married, most probably in 1661, Mary Coward the daughter of Thomas Coward of Wells. Walker may well have become confused between Mary Coward's Wells family and other Cowards living in Ditcheat and West Pennard who may have helped Piers during his troubles during the Interregnum. During that period, he earned his living as a small farmer having to thresh his own grain and sell his own cheeses and apples at Taunton market. He also supplemented his income by selling tobacco. A witness reported that she had seen Piers and other sequestered clergymen 'sitting together eating bread and salt and drinking water, none of them having a penny to buy beer.' On one occasion he was imprisoned in Ilchester gaol for acting as godfather according to the rites of the abolished Church of England to the inappropriately named Charles, the son of John Tarleton, vicar of Ilminster. While incarcerated, 'he was forced to hang out a glove and beg the charity of the town for subsistence.' Piers was to be restored as archdeacon in 1660. [5]

The archdeacon of Wells Gerard Wood retired to his rectory at Child Okeford in Dorset where he died in October 1645. On Gerard Wood's death William Watts, prebendary of Henstridge was appointed archdeacon of Wells but never took up his post. His admission as a canon resident had been refused by the cathedral chapter because although recommended by the king in October 1643, he had not appeared in Wells to meet the chapter. This was not surprising because his goods had been seized by parliament in May 1643 and he was with the royal army as a chaplain to Prince Rupert during that year. After the end of the civil war in 1646 he left with the Prince and died at Kinsale in Ireland in 1649. The archdeacon of Bath

William Davis probably retired to his vicarage at Chard, Somerset whence he was ejected in 1648. He died before 1660. Of the resident canons, the elderly Paul Godwin, went either to Nettlebury near Beaminster Dorset or Kingweston near Glastonbury from both of which he was ejected in 1646. He died in 1654. Thomas Walker retired to the Oxford diocese to await events. Fortunately his wife and family were granted an allowance by the Barons of the Exchequer and Walker survived to return to Wells in 1660. Roger Wood, the brother of the archdeacon died in 1650. Robert Aish the master of the Cathedral Grammar School and prebendary of the cathedral remained in residence and the fortunes of the Vicars Choral who continued to live in Vicars Close will be covered later. The attacks by parliamentary soldiers had seriously damaged the cathedral fittings as has been seen and the organist John Oker had left Wells in either 1642 or more likely 1643 after the destruction of the organ and had taken up a post at Gloucester cathedral which still had its organ. Humphrey Marsh the sacrist and sexton appointed in 1624 remained in Wells and in 1649 was leasing the house east of the Lady Chapel (one of two small tenements since demolished). This was probably the tenement described in 1634 as 'lying upon the church Camery [the area of land to the south of the quire and Lady Chapel] of the west side next unto the canonicall howse [the Rib] where ... now Dr Wood archdeacon of Wells inhabiteth.' In 1649 Marsh was also leasing the Camery. He remained in office until his retirement on 2 January 1664/5. [6]

DEMANDS, THREATS AND MURDER

Meanwhile the Wells Corporation continued with routine business. However by February 1643/4 the outside world was again beginning to intrude. The assizes took place in Wells and thoughts turned to the new campaigning season that was soon to start; the royalists in the west had to be ready for any eventuality. On 12 February 1643/4 the corporation received a warrant from four royalist commissioners, two of whom were John Baber and William Walrond, to buy from Bristol 60 barrels of gunpowder costing £300 for the eastern division of the county to be placed in the Wells magazine in St Cuthbert's church known affectionately as 'the powder room.' The commissioners assessed the corporation with the other authorities in the hundred of

Wells Forum for their share of the costs that had to be collected and brought to the High Sheriff of the county in Bath by 8 March. In the same month Prince Maurice was appointed as lieutenant general of the West and very soon made his presence felt.[7] On 14 April 1644 by an order of the council of war held at Crewkerne on 9 April, Prince Maurice ordered the city and parish to raise a further £100 to supply his army. To back up this demand, John Baber, the recorder, who had not attended a convocation meeting for over three years, made an appearance. Baber had signed the demand with Edward Wykes and probably enjoyed being able to give orders to his erstwhile enemies the most bitter of whom, Bartholomew Cox, was present on that day. The language of the demand was peremptory: the money had to be found in six days and paid to Baber and Wykes at the Crown Inn in the Market Place, Wells 'and if any person shall refuse to pay his rate assessed on him we are to certify his highness of their contempt.' The corporation hastened to comply and the city's share came to £36 7s with the out parish paying £63 13s. The problem of having a absentee recalcitrant recorder was also solved at this time by the death of John Baber in early July. A united corporation moved quickly to appoint as his successor, Edward Wykes the barrister from the Liberty, whom it held in high esteem.[8]

Scandal also hit the city when in late May 1644 Thomas Brinte, the churchwarden of St Cuthbert's, murdered the constable, the tanner Thomas Foster, son of a senior master of the corporation Henry Foster. Brinte had a history of abusing the members of the corporation and in 1637 had petitioned to sue Henry Foster in Star Chamber so there may have been a serious feud between him and the Foster family. The war situation may have encouraged people to perpetrate acts of violence but the murder of an official of the corporation was unprecedented. Brinte was found guilty by the coroner's inquest and stripped of his office of churchwarden but his eventual fate is unknown.[9]

THE 1644 CAMPAIGN

The 1644 campaigning season started when the parliamentary general, the Earl of Essex, marched into the west, intent on relieving the siege of Lyme Regis, currently being undertaken by Prince Maurice, and of disrupting royalist recruitment. Prince Maurice retreated from Lyme to Exeter while Essex occupied Weymouth and Bridport arriving in Chard by the end of June. Volunteers flocked to his standard but were willing only to serve under Somerset officers and so were of little immediate use. Essex detached a small party of horse and foot to besiege Taunton Castle which was taken by the parliamentarians on July 10. One result of this may have been the release of Robert Morgan from captivity. But he may already have had his freedom because he had been appointed as a committee member for Somerset by parliament to execute a parliamentary ordinance of 1 July 1644. Although the bulk of the west was still in royalist hands, parliament, in the aftermath of its decisive victory over Prince Rupert at Marston Moor in Yorkshire on 2 July 1644, felt confident enough to create a Parliamentary Association of the Western Counties on 19 August to rival the Royalist Association. On 1 September 1644 Morgan was given a further task as a committee member of collecting money in Somerset by parliamentary ordinance to pay for the army in Ireland. Again it is clear that this was a token gesture in a predominately royalist county but the appointment shows that Morgan was well regarded by the leading parliamentary gentry in Somerset and in the event of a parliamentary victory could hope to play an important role in the future county government. [10]

To avoid a parliamentarian victory in the royalist heartland of the west, the king decided to come to the west himself to gain support and to direct military operations. He arrived in Bath on 15 July 1644 with 9000 horse and foot. The cavalry were 'hard put to it' for saddles and bridles and searched everywhere for extra horses, while the foot soldiers were poorly shod. News soon reached Wells of the king's arrival in the county. On 17 July the corporation wrote anxiously to Edward Wykes the new recorder who was with the king at Bath, to find out if the king wished to visit the city. Wykes was asked if he 'would certify us by the return of this messenger whether you do know of any certainty of his majesty's coming to this town and when it will be; and what present is fit to be presented.' It is doubtful if Wykes ever received this message for by 17 July the king was at Mells Court the home of Sir John Horner. It was soon clear that the king did not intend to visit Wells for on 18 July he wrote a flattering letter to the corporation from Mells with a sting in the tail. After taking 'particular notice of the constant readiness and affection of the corporation of the city of Wells to us and our cause,' he went

A page from the Wells Corporation Receiver's Book 1652-3 showing the signatures of some of the members of the Wells Corporation: Robert Hole, Samuel Reade, Thomas Nixon(s), James Hurman, John Standish T[own] Cl[erk], William Baron maior [mayor], Thomas Meade, Joseph Gallington, Stephen Haskett, Robert Hill, Hen[ry] Baron and Joseph Plum[m]er. (Wells City Archives, Wells Town Hall)

The Crown Inn in the Market Place, Wells, the usual meeting place of government commissioners. (Photograph Patrick Kirkby)

Wells Market place as it would have appeared in 1665 showing the Market/Town Hall, the High Cross and the Conduit. Detail from the plan of Wells by William Simes 1735. (British Library Board maps K, Top, 38.9)

Lechlade's House, now 17 The Liberty, Wells. A canonical house where William Walrond lived between c1640 and 1661; now part of Wells Cathedral School. (Photograph Patrick Kirkby)

The Rib, a canonical house, the residence of Samuel Ward, Archdeacon of Taunton until 1643. Taken over by Cornelius Burges, later acquired by the Corporation of Wells and leased to Robert Hole until 1661 when it was repossessed by Bishop Piers. (Photograph Patrick Kirkby)

The Deanery. Dean Raleigh, stabbed by David Barrett, died here in October 1646 and Cornelius Burges lived here from 1649–1661. (Photograph Patrick Kirkby)

on to ask the corporation 'speedily to furnish £500 with expedition and cheerfulness' to his treasurer at war John Ashburnham who was the bearer of the letter. He assured the corporation that he would repay the loan 'as soon as God shall enable us.' The response of the corporation was speedy and realistic but disappointing for the king; £63 in total was all that 22 of the leading capital burgesses were willing to lend to be recouped from corporation revenue; a further £20 was lent of the burgesses' money and £20 from the revenues of the corporation. £30 for 200 pairs of shoes for the poorly shod royalist troops was paid by the corporation to the shoemaker Richard Casbeard who supplied the shoes at £3 a score, while £1 was given to the trumpeter of the king's guard. The king, as the corporation probably suspected, was never able to repay the money sent. At the same time it seems clear that the general of the artillery, Lord Percy, had issued a warrant for the blacksmiths in the city to provide horseshoes for the use of the horses pulling the artillery train. These were duly sent. While this activity was taking place in Wells, the king dined with Lord Hopton at his newly fortified house at Witham and on 19 July rode from Mells to Bruton where he stayed with Sir Charles Berkeley. The following day the king was at Queen Camel and on 21 July he moved to Ilchester where he issued a summons for a general meeting of the county on the adjacent King's Moor on the 23rd. While at Ilchester the king wrote to the corporation commanding it to make an assessment rate in the city to reimburse the blacksmiths for the horsehoes so that 'satisfaction ... be given to the said poor smiths for their wares. This we doubt not but you will cheerfully and readily perform.' [11]

The king was well received by the countrymen who assembled on King's Moor on 23 July. Present was Sir Edward Rodney one of the four colonels appointed, with 1000 foot soldiers from the north of the county. Amongst them as officers were Lieutenant Colonel Thomas Coward, Major William Morgan and the mayor of Wells, the innkeeper William West, with a small contingent of men from the city. Despite the crowd, few men wished to enlist and a meeting held by Sir John Stawell at Bridgwater produced similarly disappointing results. With Rodney's men and 800 from Bristol, the king left the county and marched into Devon on 25 July in pursuit of the Earl of Essex who by this time had reached Cornwall. The royal army followed Essex into Cornwall and caught up with him at Lostwithiel.

Thomas Coward later claimed that he had been commanded by the Somerset *posse comitatus* (a body of men, distinct from the militia, summoned by the county sheriff to maintain law and order) to attend the king no further than the Devon border but was compelled by the royalist commanders to go as far as Exeter. William Morgan, also claimed that he was under duress to take up a commission in the same body and to march only as far as Exeter. As the law enforcement duties of the *posse comitatus* had largely been taken over by the militia in the period immediatiately before the civil war, both men's statements can be viewed with some suspicion. It is clear however from a letter that William West wrote to the Wells Corporation that the Wells contingent under West did march into Cornwall playing their part in the defeat of Essex at Lostwithiel. [12]

The king's departure for Cornwall with his army made Somerset vulnerable to a parliamentary attack and it was not slow in coming. In early August a force of 2000 parliamentary horse and dragoons entered the county from Hampshire under the command of the Scottish lieutenant general, John Middleton. On 14 August Middleton's force unsuccessfully attacked a royalist supply convoy at North Petherton. Two days later, Middleton wrote to the high constable of the hundred of Wells Forum demanding '60 sufficient horse, mare or geldings for saddle, together with 60 bridles and as many saddles, every horse or mare or gelding with the bridle and saddle to be of full value of £8.' These were to be brought to the general's headquarters at Milborne Port by the 20th at 10 am. The high constable, Benedick Clutterbuck immediately sent a copy of this warrant to the Wells Corporation. The language of the letter attempted to reassure the inhabitants of the hundred promising them that their horses would be protected and their houses 'kept from plundering if they complied with the warrant.' Middleton followed this request with a letter on 22 August to the Wells Corporation demanding £300 by 24 August with the similar offer of protection from plundering if the money were paid but with the threat that if it were refused, the inhabitants of the city would 'answer ... at your perils.' The members of the corporation were in a quandary. They knew that the king was far away but were hopeful that he might be victorious in Cornwall. If that were the case, he would then return with superior forces to drive Middleton away. On 23 August the corporation decided to play for time and composed a petition to

Middleton. The order that the hundred should provide 60 horses meant that the city and the Liberty would be liable for a quarter of the total. It acquainted him with the facts about what the city's share of the hundred tax burden should be i.e. that the city should only pay one quarter of the total for the whole hundred of which quarter the cathedral liberty paid a fifth and that that was all it should pay. In an attempt to avoid paying the exra £300, it then painted a pitiful picture of a city from which some of the chief inhabitants had departed 'by which means your petitioners lack both their assistance and sufficiency. Therefore they do desire your worship to consider the poor and desolate estate of the poor borough in these distracted times; and your petitioners as duty bindeth shall pray for the peace and quiet of this poor afflicted kingdom.' The corporation obviously decided to wait on events in a fluid political situation because the petition was never sent. [13]

The corporation was right to wait. The parliamentary threat was soon countered by royalist military success in Cornwall. The king then started his return eastwards with his army in time to save Wells from making the payment to Middleton. Edward Wykes the recorder had died in early August on the royalist march westwards and there were several candidates for his office. The corporation were kept well informed of the progress of the royal army towards Somerset in the letters it received from prominent gentlemen supporting the various candidates for the vacant post of recorder. Hopton wrote from Fowey on 1 September and again from Okehampton on the 5th. William West the mayor was given permission by the king on 4 September to return home and by 7th was at Tiverton. By the 26 September the Wells contingent had returned and William West was able to preside over a convocation meeting once more. However late in September the corporation received a letter from the king at Chard dated 26 September asking it to collect from the city 500 pairs of stockings and 500 pairs of shoes and have them ready for collection in the town hall on Wednesday 2 October. On this occasion although the king had ordered that the money for the shoes and stockings should be raised in the city, there was no attempt made by the corporation at the time to implement this as had been done with the 200 pairs of shoes provided in July. It is unlikely that the astute shoemaker Richard Casbeard would have arranged for the making of the shoes without a clear financial guarantee. In December 1644 the royalist commissioners in session at the Crown Inn at Wells were still unable to get Casbeard to produce the shoes. Undoubtedly the hardening of attitude in Wells against the continual royalist demands was caused by the attempts of the royalist officers to collect the excise earlier in the autumn. In May 1644, royalist MPs at Oxford had decided to follow the example of their parliamentary opponents and impose an excise tax on merchandise, the proceeds of which were to be sent to the central royalist treasury at Oxford. When the royalist officers arrived in Wells in November 1644, the new mayor, none other than the disgruntled Richard Casbeard, consulted the local county commissioners and in consequence refused to publish the royal proclamation for the excise and went into hiding. According to one of the royal officers, one of the masters on the corporation asserted 'that he would pay no excise, and another that we came to rob the people.' These recurring demands for money and supplies were too much for a member of the corporation who was a butcher: William Hiett who had been a member since 1639 refused to attend and did so only when threatened with a fine; Ralph Ciniox, also a capital burgess and butcher, had already left the city a year before for the village of Mark ten miles away where he set up his business afresh. [14]

THE END OF THE WAR

The adverse reaction to the imposition of the excise in the autumn of 1644 was a sign of the war weariness that was pervading the city. The 1645 campaigning season started with the arrival in Somerset in late February of the royalist commander Lord George Goring with an army comprised of horse, foot, dragoons and artillery. The main strategic problem for the royalists was the continued resistance of Taunton, taken by the parliamentarians in July 1644. Goring was soon followed by the 14 year old Prince of Wales who arrived in Bristol in early March 1645 with a council of his own and a commission from his father appointing him general of the Western Association. Advancing towards Taunton, Goring's troops soon caused outrage in the villages through which they passed particularly in the parishes of East Brent, Burnham, Berrow, Mark and Lympsham. Captain John Somerset of South Brent although a royalist, led the opposition to Goring's men and was arrested with a colleague for his actions. He wrote to William Morgan in Wells asking for help and advice. Morgan was able to reassure them: 'the Comissioners are all strong for you if you pr[o]ce[e]d to a tryale.' [15]

It was now time for the royalists to coordinate their attack on Taunton. Consequently on 24 March 1645, Goring met two of the prince's council, the Lords Capell and Culpepper at Wells, to determine strategy. Any plans they made had to be quickly shelved in order to drive off an attack by Sir William Waller and a parliamentary force advancing from Dorset. Goring was only partially successful and a further advance by Waller, this time reinforced by Cromwell, forced Goring to retreat via Glastonbury to Wells in late March or early April this time quartering horse and dragoons in the city. Some of Goring's men were killed in the skirmishes with the parliamentarians and were buried in Wells. Among them were: Richard Coulin a Cornish captain from Liskard, Edward Read another Cornishman and Captain John Marley the son of the mayor and governor of Newcastle. Goring also held a court martial in Wells for Christopher Daniell of Warminster Wilts ' who was tried here by a counsel of warr and found guiltie of bearinge armes ... against King Charles and soe condem'd, executed and buried.' As Goring's usual practice was to take free quarter wherever he was, the Wells householders must have suffered badly. Unfortunately the loss of the corporation convocation books and the general lack of records for this period make it difficult to assess any damage caused. It is not clear how long the troops stayed but it would not have been more than a month. The prince then ordered Goring to join another royalist force commanded by Sir Richard Grenville before Taunton and Goring sent his foot soldiers and cannon but not the mounted soldiers who presumably stayed on in Wells. Goring himself retired to Bath to take the waters and after a few days joined Prince Charles in Bristol.

Throughout April the royalists tried vainly to capture Taunton which held out under its commander Robert Blake until it was relieved by a parliamentary force under Col Ralph Weldon on 11 May 1645. During the winter and early spring, passing soldiers and possibly some of Goring's troops had formed liaisons with local Wells girls and Francis Standish, the curate of St Cuthbert Wells, faithfully set down the results of some of them. On 7 October 1645 he recorded the birth of William 'a base child of Elizabeth Lancaster reputed father a trooper – name not known;' Stephen a 'base child', parents unknown, was 'layd at Doctor Chrightones gate in the church liberty' on 9 November; on 21 November Thomizen Ozwell gave birth to a base child by a trooper; on 20 January 1645/6 Henry a base child was christened, the father thought to be Henry, a trooper. Sadly on 16 August 1645 an unnamed base child of Ellinor Bratton was buried, the reputed father being Nicholas Prince a trooper. Such were some of the results of war! [16]

May 1645 saw the development of the neutralist club movement in Somerset. Clubmen were usually yeomen or less affluent farmers who, weary of the armies' depredations on their land, banded together in a show of force to deter both royalist and parliamentary armies. Men armed with fowling pieces, pikes, halberds and 'great clubs' interposed themselves between royalist and parliamentary patrols and made them drink together instead of fighting. One of their banners proclaimed: 'if you offer to plunder or take our cattle, be assured we will bid you to battle.' On 2 June 5000 armed clubmen gathered at Castle Cary and adopted a petition denouncing the 'intolerable oppression, repine and violence' of the royalist soldiers and elected a delegation to present it to the Prince of Wales who was then in Wells. The royalists attempted to counter this and in July there was a royalist-engineered club meeting in Wells that blamed parliament for the failure of the peace talks with the king. The petition was condemned by the parliamentary press who said its wording was influenced 'by a malignant conjunction of the lawyer and the clergyman.' The petition it was alleged showed no more understanding of politics than 'ploughmen do Greek.' [17]

The final experience of military operations in the vicinity of Wells came with the arrival in Somerset on 5 July of the New Model Army under the command of Sir Thomas Fairfax fresh from its conclusive victory over the king's forces at Naseby on 14 June 1645. Goring was defeated at Langport on 10 July, The exemplary behaviour of the New Model Army in contrast to Goring's undisciplined troops and the conciliatory attitude adopted by Fairfax, won over most of the clubmen to the parliamentary side. An outlying detachment of the New Model Army reached Wells on 16 July where it dealt with an attack launched by a royalist force from Bristol sent by Prince Rupert. Bridgwater fell to Fairfax on 22 July and on Tuesday 28 Fairfax arrived in Wells with the main body of his army. On 29 July he detached two regiments of horse and some dragoons to reconnoitre Bath and on the following day left Wells and drew up his army on the Mendip Hills to the north of the city where much to his surprise, he learnt that the troops he had dispatched to Bath had easily taken it. Leading two regiments of foot to Bath to supplement the new garrison, Fairfax sent the remainder of his army back to Wells. He stayed in Bath overnight on the 30 July and on the afternoon of the 31st returned to Wells. After a day's rest, Fairfax and the rest of the New Model Army left Wells en route to attack Sherborne Castle and to deal with the clubmen at Shaftesbury.

In early September, parliament issued warrants to 'raise the power of the county' and Sir John Horner of Mells organised an assembly of troops on the hills to the north of Wells. At this meeting Oliver Cromwell was present but there is no evidence that he visited Wells on his way to the gathering. Finally Fairfax and Cromwell took Bristol by storm on 10 September 1645. For Wells the war was over although general hostilities did not cease until April 1646. [18]

THE EFFECTS OF WAR

Economic life in Wells was disrupted by the war but lack of hard evidence makes it difficult to be precise about the level of disruption. Only general suggestions can be made as to what may have happened. The high regular taxation assessments plus further continual demands for money were unwelcome to a population used to low taxation and tax avoidance. Armies passed through or near Wells on a number of occasions causing fear and uncertainty amongst the citizens. The stability of economic life was also threatened, especially during the parliamentary occupation of Wells in the first year of the war, by roving bands of undisciplined soldiers seeking loot, provisions and horses but Wells, because of its lack of fortifications, was never besieged as Taunton, Bridgwater and Bath were. Although Wells seems not to have been severely affected by troops looking for plunder during the two years of royalist occupation, the local country districts which provided provisions for the twice weekly markets were affected and this may have caused some temporary shortages. However the presence of troops in the city, particularly during the winter of 1643/4 with the consequent increased need for provisions, may have stimulated the food market that was also helped by a succession of good harvests from 1642-5. The inns and alehouses must have been well patronised and would have profited by the large numbers of visiting gentry for the various meetings, royalist quarter sessions and assizes and by the resident military. Ordinary people, to supplement their incomes, brewed and sold ale illegally without a licence as they had often done in the past but the lack of petty sessions records from 1643-6 makes it impossible to determine if there were an increase in this activity during the period of the war. The authorities attempted to stop this practice in the first winter of the war but their attitude to offenders was fairly lenient. On 21 January 1642/3 the mayor Robert Rowley and the justice Robert Morgan issued a series of fines to unlicensed alehouses. In one of the cases Henry Jones, a Wells glazier, denied that he sold and bought ale but claimed that it was his wife who did. The mayor and justice admonished him and told him to discipline his wife which he agreed to do. Jones and his wife evidently ignored the orders of the mayor and justice because on 9 February he sold a pot of ale to Robert Lightfoot for 2d who then reported him and he was again admonished. [19]

The clothiers of Wells, now mostly engaged in stocking making and worsted cloth manufacture, may have seen their regular sales decline through lower attendance at markets and fairs. They must however have benefited somewhat from war contracts for soldiers' clothing for which they were paid from the local rates as the shoemaker Richard Casbeard was. The mercers and woollen and linen drapers may have been hit quite hard by the decline in purchasing power of their wealthier clientele but most of them were fairly wealthy men with supplementary incomes from land. The disruption of the carrier service due to military operations would have often made it difficult for them to import from London luxury goods and the fashionable new draperies essential for the Wells tailoring industry. The poorer people whose incomes had been squeezed by the sharp rise in the cost of living from the 1630s also sometimes attempted to supplement their income illegally. The women hucksters who worked the twice-weekly markets could be tempted to indulge in illegal activities. In August 1643 Marie Batt was fined for engrossing and regrating of apples, plums and pears and other things in the market. Engrossing meant that she had been buying up large quantities of fruit in the market (cornering the market) and then in a monopoly situation reselling (regrating) them at a profit. [20]

Besides the small group of artisans who left the city because of political pressures during the civil war, the (admittedly partial) property records suggest that the war caused more mobility in the population than before; 45% of the lessees recorded in the 1649 parliamentary survey of the dean and chapter and vicars' property being newcomers to the city. Some of the properties they acquired were those left vacant by the departed clergy and ecclesiastical officials. For example, Tristram Towse the elder left Wells and lived in retirement at Weare 12 miles away. These newcomers, some of whom were from the rural areas outside the city, were particularly attracted, in an inflationary period, by the low rents of dean and chapter properties which in 1649 were reckoned to be 428% below current market values. In contrast, the lessees of corporation properties tended to stay in the city encouraged by the very modest rise in rents, only 6.3% between 1604 and 1642. Out of 26 High Street properties where the lessees are known, 17 were held by the same family in 1642 and 1662 and of the other nine, three of the 1642 lessees died during the 20 year period and death may have accounted for some of the other changes in lessees. The same pattern applies for other main streets of the city Chamberlain St, New St and Union St, St Cuthbert's St, Tucker Street and Southover. [21]

Most of the lawyers and gentlemen who lived in Wells were royalists and were able to secure employment in the Western Association between 1643-5. However they may have found difficulty in collecting their rents from land because of the disruption to communications caused by the war. Andrew Bowerman was forced in April 1644 to sell his plate in Bristol to provide himself with ready cash and altered his will accordingly. This may have been an expedient practised by others. [22]

The civil war caused much social disruption. There were many more strangers in the city than before the war. Whereas before 1642 only 10% of couples married in Wells were from outside the parish, in the three years between March 1643 and March 1646 of the 181 marriages solemnised in Wells, 43% were between non-residents most of whom came from Somerset, the highest number being from Glastonbury. Some of the young people left the city and joined opposing armies. A group of men went with William West as far as

UNDER GOD'S VISITATION

Cornwall in 1644 and others probably enlisted or were pressed at various times. Little is known of them but being a member of the army exposed them to new ideas in religion and politics. One young Wells man, Joshua Garment who signed the Protestation in Wells in 1642, served as a parliamentary soldier for three years during the civil war and after the war became a Ranter. His subsequent career will be discussed in a later chapter. David Barrett the Wells shoemaker and later Baptist, after leaving Wells with two other burgesses with the parliamentary army in the summer of 1643, was by 1644 living in Bristol where he lodged in Whitecross St with nine other families in the requisitioned house of Robert Foster, the 1642 assize judge. Stephen Haskett also removed his business to Bristol and the two may well have met there. Both were to play leading roles in Wells during the period of the Interregnum. [23]

The war also brought a rise in random acts of violence. The behaviour of Joseph Nurton and the murder of Thomas Foster have been mentioned but on 19 July 1645 John Hance a Dutch trumpeter was 'slayn in this city with a pistol' and an Irishman Gray Holliner Gorren was killed in mysterious circumstances in Dulcote near Wells. On 14 June 1643 a soldier called William Harris was killed by his captain. The sight of wounded and dying soldiers must have become part of the regular experience of Wells citizens. [19] For the citizens of Wells there was worse to come. On 3 August 1645 the churchwarden of St Cuthbert's entered the burial of Joan the wife of Richard Davis with the ominous comment 'the first that died of the sickness.' Richard's death was entered two days later. An enemy worse than the opposing armies had slipped into Wells unnoticed. [24]

NOTES

[1] Nott, A, & Hasler, J, (eds), *Wells Convocation Acts Books 1589-1665 Part 2 1629-44; 1662-65*, SRS 91, Taunton 2004, pp 848, 850, 853-4.

[2] Underdown, D, *Somerset in the Civil War and Interregnum*, Newton Abbot 1973, pp 67-73; Everett Green, M A, *Calendar of the Proceedings of the Committee for Compounding Vol. II 1643-46*, London 1890, p 963; for the letter from William Morgan see Symonds, H, *A Bypath of the Civil War*, SANHS 65, 1919, pp 57-8.

[3] Nott & Hasler, SRS Vol 91, op cit, pp 858-860.

[4] DNB, *Robert Creighton 1593-1672* by John S. Macauley 2004; Tinniswood, A, *The Verneys*, London, 2007, pp 273, 293-4.

[5] Walker John (abridged by R. Whittaker), *The Sufferings of the Clergy during the Great Rebellion*, London 1863, pp 69-70; Bailey, DS, (ed), *Wells Chapter Act*

Book 1666-83, HMSO Vol. 72, London, 1973, p xi; Nott & Hasler, SRS Vol 91, op cit, p 1025.
6. *Calendar of the Manuscripts of the Dean and Chapter of Wells Vol. II*, HMSO London, 1914, pp 427-30; Morrill, J, *The Church in England, 1642-9*, in Morrill, J, (ed), *Reactions To The English Civil War 1642-9*, London 1982, pp 89-94; Woolrych, A, *Britain in Revolution 1625-1660*, Oxford 2002, pp 270-1. For the fortunes of the cathedral clergy for the period immediately after January 1645 see Matthews, A G, (ed), *A Revision of John Walker's Sufferings of the Clergy during the Grand Rebellion, 1642-60*, Oxford 1948,, pp 31, 133, 317-319; DNB entries for Raleigh and Creyghton; Bailey, D S, (ed), *Wells Cathedral Chapter Act Book 1666-83*, HMSO London, 1973, pp ix-xii; Colchester, L S, *Wells Cathedral School: I – The First Thousand years c 909-1964*, Wells, (no date), pp 30-1; Archdeacon Wood's house "The Rib", still stands but Marsh's tenement has disappeared., see Bailey, D, *Canonical Houses of Wells*, Gloucester 1982, pp 138-9.
7. Nott & Hasler, SRS Vol 91, op cit, pp 863-4.
8. Nott & Hasler, SRS Vol 91, op cit, pp 864-5.
9. Nott & Hasler, SRS Vol 91, op cit, p 866.
10. Underdown, *Somerset in the Civil War and Interregnum op cit*, pp 73-74; Firth C.H. & Rait R.S. (eds.), *Acts and Ordinances of the Interregnum 1642-60*, London 1911, pp 459-61 & 531.
11. Green, E, *The King's March through Somerset*, SANHS 24, Part 2, 1878, pp 43-9; Nott & Hasler, SRS Vol 91, op cit, pp 869-874.
12. Everett Green, *CCC 1643-60 Vol. II 1643-6 op cit*, pp 1234, 1380; Underdown, D, *Somerset in the Civil War and Interregnum, op cit*, pp 76-7; for the *posse comitatus* see Barnes, T G, *Somerset 1625-1640: A County's Government During the 'Personal Rule,'* London, 1961, pp 127 & 130.
13. Nott & Hasler, SRS Vol 91, op cit, pp 875-6.
14. Nott & Hasler, SRS Vol 91, op cit, pp 878-80; BL WCL ADD/1406; for the excise see Hutton, R, *The Royalist War Effort 1642-1646, 2nd edition*, London, 2003, p 93 & Underdown, *Somerset in the Civil War and Interregnum,op citt*, p 81.
15. Green, SANHS 24 Part II, op cit, 56-58,
16. Underdown, D, *Somerset in the Civil War and Interregnum*, op cit, pp 88-95; SRO DP W St C. 2/1/1.
17. Underdown, D,*Somerset in the Civil War and Interregnum*,op cit, p 106.
18. Underdown, D, *Somerset in the Civil War and Interregnum*,op cit,, pp 108-115; a contemporary account of Fairfax's stay in the Wells area can be found in Sprigge, J, *Anglia Rediviva: England's Recovery*, London 1647, pp 82-6.
19. WTH. Wells Corporation Sessions Book 1625 – 50, folio 86.
20. WTH Wells Corporation Sessions Book 1625 – 50, folio 88.
21. Scrase, A J, *Wells: The Anatomy of a medieval and Early Modern Property Market Working Paper 30*, Faculty of the Built Environment, University of the West of England, 1993, pp 214, 217-221; Scrace, A J, *Wells: A Small City*, Stroud 2006, p 97; Scrase, A J, & Hasler, J, *Wells Corporation Properties*, SRS 87, Taunton 2002, pp169-219; Scrase, Tony, *The Inhabitants of Wells 1600-1649*, History Round Wells, Issue 7, 2003, pp. 14-19.

[22] Andrew Bowerman's will of 1647 can be found at NA Probate 11/200.
[23] SRO D/P/W/St. Cu. 2/1/1; *Joshua Garment,* Hessayon A., DNB 2004; Everett Green, M A, (ed), *Calendar of the Committee for the Advance of Money Part I 1642-45,* 1888, pp 377- 397.
[24] SRO D P W St. Cu. 2/1/1.

CHAPTER 7

THE AFTERMATH: 1645-49

'THE SICKNESS'

The nature of the illness of epidemic proportions which affected Wells in August 1645 is difficult to determine. The St Cuthbert's parish register describes it as 'the sickness' with the stress on the definite article, the common way of describing bubonic plague at the time but the disease may well have been typhus. The citizens of Wells in July 1645 must have been fearful of an outbreak of infectious disease because they knew that neighbouring villages and towns were already affected. The 'sickness' had broken out in Bristol in the autumn of 1644 and by the summer of 1645 was raging from Bristol to Frome. It was also present to the south of Wells at Taunton and its neighbouring villages and it would be only a matter of time before it reached Wells. The infection could have come from any of these places by the regular carrier service. The corporation however usually guarded against this by keeping carriers out of the city when there was fear of infection. It seems therefore more likely that it was the parliamentary army that was the main carrier.

The first death from 'the sickness' occurred in the city on 3 August so it is possible that the infection was brought by the army which had arrived on 28 July.[1] Medical knowledge at the time did not understand how disease was transmitted and could only suggest time-honoured methods to attempt to restrict the spread of infection.[2] The corporation used the Privy Council Orders of 1578/9 on the control of the plague as a guide on how to act. These orders had been reprinted by parliament in 1641 and the corporation would have had a copy. The orders stated that JPs were to meet every three weeks during plague epidemics to receive reports on the progress of the disease and to raise the necessary local taxation to pay for the relief of the sick. All clothing and bedding of plague victims had to be burnt and funerals had to take place at dusk to reduce the numbers of those attending. All infected houses had to be shut up for at least six weeks with all members of the family, whether sick or otherwise still inside them; the local watchmen under the constables were to enforce this. Draconian measures were to be taken against any infected person who was found wandering around in public; the punishment was usually whipping but persistent offenders could be hung. [3]

Unfortunately, owing to the lack of the corporation records for 1645, we do not know the precise measures which the corporation took to control infection and relieve suffering; those taken in previous years were the ones probably implemented in 1645. These included attempting to stop further infection from entering the city by banning innkeepers from receiving into their houses any inhabitants from plague-ridden areas; allowing merchants only to import goods under licence from the mayor and forbidding travel to and from infected areas. The punishments inflicted for breaking these rules were in the first instance a 40s fine and for any subsequent offence imprisonment. Infected households were put into quarantine and red crosses were painted on their doors. Any person leaving an infected house was imprisoned and if uninfected, placed in the stocks on the outskirts of the city. A 24 hour watch was also instituted outside infected houses to make sure nobody left. In the outbreak of plague in Tucker Street in 1603, all the residents of the street who were uninfected were forced to remain there and not allowed to 'repair and recourse up into the market, but what provision they want shall be provided by some persons appointed to do the same; and so that the charge of keeping in and maintaining of the said infected persons is great ... a rate [is to be] made through every street of the city or borough for the performing of the same.' Overseers were appointed to disburse the rate to provide the provisions for the sick. The same types of measures were almost certainly made in 1645. It is also likely that the two autumn fairs of St Calixtus (14 October) and St Andrew (30 November) were cancelled as had been the case before and the twice-weekly markets severely curtailed between August and November. Sir John Webb a recusant of Canford, Dorset who was residing in Wells at the time, wrote to the Committee for Compounding in London saying that he could not come to London to settle his affairs 'because of the great extremity of the plague in Wells.' [4]

The 'sickness' lasted for four months from August until the end of November. The average number of monthly deaths in the city from April to July 1645 before the onset of the 'sickness' was fourteen. In August 1645, 63 died: in September the death toll was 109. Thereafter there was a gradual decline: 89 in October, 58 in November and falling to 22 in December before levelling out at 19 each for January and February, the normal average for the winter months. There were some notable tragedies: on 24 August William Stone and Peternell his wife died on the same day as did Hugh and Alice Millard on 2 September. The worst tragedy of all was that which befell Captain Henry Kellow. He had already lost one son in the war and another son James died on 4 August; two other sons soon followed: Henry on 1 October and John on 3 October, His wife Ellinor died on 20 October, his daughter Elizabeth on 22 October and another daughter Margaret on 3 November. The final tragedy struck on 17 March 1645/6 when his daughter Ann died. Even in an age of high child mortality, Kellow's family loss was exceptional in the speed with which it occurred. The streets of Wells must have reverberated to the solemn tolling of the funeral knells for the dead, costing (in the laconic entries in the churchwardens' accounts), one shilling per hour. It is difficult to imagine the dejection felt by the people of Wells at this new affliction after three years of war. Perhaps the description of the scene at Bristol in September 1645 as witnessed by Joshua Sprigge, a chaplain of the New Model Army (which had so recently been in Wells), may give some feeling of what it was like to live in a disease ridden city. It was 'more like a prison than a city, and the people more like prisoners than citizens; being brought so low with taxations, so poor in habit, and so dejected in countenance; the streets so noisome, and the houses so nasty as that they were unfit to receive friends or freemen till they were cleansed.' [5]

THE ECONOMIC CRISIS

The ending of the epidemic did not bring an end to hardship. After a series of good harvests during the civil war years, the harvest of 1646 was disappointing and the three succeeding harvests were bad. The food supply was further affected by disease amongst cattle and sheep. Food prices rose by 47% between 1646 and 1650, The newspaper, *The Moderate Intelligencer,* reported in March 1649 from Somerset 'that things are very scarce here ... all things deare.' This harvest failure caused a crisis throughout the economy and would have affected Wells badly. 'Harvest failure meant that all those who had to buy food – landless artisans and labourers as well as townsmen – spent a higher proportion of their incomes on food and so had less to spend on other things.' Demand for consumer goods fell and 'wage cutting and unemployment spread through the textile and leather industries' that were so important to the success of the Wells economy. *The Moderate Intelligencer* again reported in April 1649 that the poor in Somerset were 'in a sad condition, no employment, or little, to what formerly, all things deare, and labour cheap ...', which was ' ... the worst condition that can befall this life ...' [6]

The Wells Corporation, although relatively powerless, did what it could to ameliorate the difficult economic situation but it could only implement the traditional measures it had always taken to safeguard the city's economy. The corporation discouraged illegal traders in the city's market who bought goods for resale elsewhere by carefully checking the activities of illegal hucksters most of whom were women. In May 1647, the Widow Gorway, a huckster, although she claimed that she had bought 'noethinge in this market but at Bristol,' was nevertheless admonished by the mayor and justice not to buy anything in the Wells market. Wells traders also took the initiative to defend their trading positions by banning outsiders from trading. In August 1649, George Baber, a woollen draper of Wells, informed the Wells justice that Timothy Player and John Meres of Shepton Mallet, hosiers 'did open their ware and sell their stockings unto Francis Sheares mother and to others which as he is informed is against the liberties and privileges of this city.' Carriers travelling through Wells were checked to make sure that their goods were destined for other markets and were not to be sold in Wells. John Parsons of Tetbury, Gloucestershire was viewed with suspicion when he arrived in Wells on 22 May 1647 with five horses laden with wool. He was allowed to proceed after paying a modest fine of 12d when it was clear that the wool was destined for Exeter market. Other carriers were treated with the same suspicion.

Another problem in a time of poor harvests was that the barley

'THE AFTERMATH: 1645-49'

used to make bread for the poor was bought up by maltsters for making into beer. [7] In January 1648/9 at the Wells quarter sessions the court received a petition claiming that the 'dearth of all sorts of graine and victuals' was caused by 'the multiplicity of Alehouwses both licensed and unlicensed and of the many Forestallers, Ingrossers, Hucksters and Maultsters.' In response, the JPs at the quarter sessions ordered that registration of alehouses should be strictly enforced. As in the past, measures were no doubt taken to buy in grain to distribute to the poor and poor children were put to work. In November 1648 a determined effort was made to bind poor children to apprenticeships. Most burgesses who were approached agreed to take one or contribute to the binding of one except Henry Baron who was 'not minded to take any.' [8]

'At a time of high food prices and unemployment, the unprecedented heavy burden of taxation became almost unbearable.' When Somerset fell to the parliamentarians in the late summer of 1645 a weekly assessment payable to London was levied to support the army. The county assessment was set at the very high rate of £1250 a week or £65,000 a year as compared with the annual county total of £8000 for the much disliked ship money of the government of Charles I in the late 1630s. If it were calculated at the same rate as ship money this would have meant that the annual amount levied for the borough of Wells and the Liberty had risen from £60 to £487 10s or a weekly rate of £9 7s 6d. To raise this sort of sum, the tax base was lowered to include everybody except the very poor. Added to this tax was the excise levied on goods needed by everybody such as beer, salt, soap, cloth and leather. It was paid by the producer who passed it on to consumers in the form of higher prices. No doubt the citizens during the period 1645-9 resented the collection of the excise by the parliamentarians as much as they had disliked that imposed by the royalists in December 1644. At Frome there was a riot in January 1648/9 'against the Excise men, and Souldiers that were come with them, to assist them in the levying thereof.' The rioters were the very men who had supported parliament in the civil war. The soldiers who accompanied the excise men were also to become a permanent feature of life in Wells which was forced to accommodate a troop of about 80 troopers paid for from the weekly assessment for the duration of the period 1645-1660. [9]

NATIONAL POLITICS 1645-9

As the people of Wells recovered from the trauma of epidemic disease in the spring of 1646, the civil war was moving to its conclusion and on 5 May 1646, Charles I surrendered to the Scottish army at Newark in Nottinghamshire. The next two and an half years were taken up by fruitless negotiations between the king and his erstwhile enemies. Charles despite making temporary concessions, refused to betray his core principles: the retention of episcopacy, sole power to appoint his ministers and control of the armed forces. Most of his opponents in parliament and the army genuinely wanted an agreement with him but Charles frustrated this by attempting to play one group off against another. He was able to do this because his opponents in parliament were roughly divided between the Presbyterians who wanted the abolition of episcopacy and the establishment of a Presbyterian system of church government and the Independents who wanted people to be able to worship as they wished. These differing opinions were mirrored at the local level in Wells where there were some ardent royalists who supported the retention of episcopacy, militant Presbyterians who wished to establish a new system of church government on the Scottish model and others of a more independent frame of mind desiring toleration of all religious groups. The various moves in the political game in London were followed in Wells and avidly discussed in the Wells inns.

The army was another player in the national drama. It was not disbanded at the end of the war and because its pay continually remained in arrears, its leaders and rank and file became more radical in their political and religious views putting forward their own manifesto and entering into their own negotiations with the king. The king's clandestine negotiations with the Scots led to the second civil war of 1648 in which although the city was not directly affected, royalist sympathisers came under suspicion once again. In the latter months of 1648 the political situation reached crisis point with the army determined to bring the king to trial as 'a man of blood.' The denouement and its repercussions for Wells will be discussed at the end of this chapter.

COUNTY POLITICS

With the parliamentary victory of 1645 the old county committee that had ruled Somerset in 1642/3 was reconstituted. Some of the older family names such as Popham, Horner, Hungerford and Pym were still represented; there were also lawyers like Lislebone Long of Stratton and William Prynne but the committee came to be dominated by John Pyne of Curry Mallet. Pyne was a supporter of godly reformation. He was energetic and ruthless and although probably a Presbyterian, was keen to encourage men with radical views such as Baptists and Independents. In 1645, Pyne outmanoeuvred his moderate gentry colleagues and recruited his own supporters on to the committee. One of these was Robert Morgan who before the war could not have hoped to aspire to such a role in county politics. Morgan brought David Barrett the Baptist shoemaker with him, and Barrett was appointed marshal to the county committee in charge of its prisoners. Regular meetings of the quarter sessions also resumed from October 1646 with the first meeting at Bridgwater and the second at Wells in January 1646/7. [10]

CITY POLITICS

The parliamentary victory in Somerset caused no immediate change in the political balance of the corporation. The recorder Christopher Dodington, appointed in September 1644 on the sudden death of Edward Wykes, was a royalist sympathiser and brother of the notoriously cruel royalist Sir Francis Dodington. He had been recommended to the corporation by, among others, Sir Ralph Hopton, Sir Edward Rodney and Edward Kirton the Marquis of Hertford's steward. He was to remain in office until removed in 1655.

Unfortunately there is no definitive list of corporation members between September 1644 and November 1647 owing to the loss of the corporation records. At the latter date it is clear that the corporation still contained men with a variety of political and religious views. Of the 24 members who attended in September 1644, 14 remained. These men represented a cross section of political and religious opinion. They ranged from strong Presbyterians such as Thomas Salmon, moderate pragmatists like William Baron mayor in 1639/40 and 1652/3 to a man who had fought for the king, William West. Of the ten who were no longer on the corporation the senior master Walter Brick had resigned due to age and ill health although he did not die until 1649. Ralph Ciniox had resigned from the corporation by November 1647 and had left the city to live in Mark although remaining a trustee of the Llewellyn's Almshouse. Henry Foster had died in October 1646, William Lewce in February 1644/5, John Hill in March 1644/5, the octogenarian William Taverner in June 1645, William Perry in October 1644 and John Loggins had succumbed to 'the sickness' in August 1645. Only two men cannot be accounted for: Robert Lane and Robert Phippen. Lane may have died outside the city but Phippen did not die until 1656 so he must have resigned for some reason.

The new men appointed to these vacancies again represented different shades of opinion with a slight strengthening of the parliamentary faction. Of the ten, four were probably men of moderate pragmatic views. Hugh Merefield a chandler, served through the Interregnum and survived the royalist purge of parliamentary supporters in 1662. Henry Baron a linen draper, whose father had been another long serving member also served throughout the same period and avoided the purge. Joseph Plummer served throughout the Interregnum. Of the opinions of Josiah Cooke who died in 1649, nothing is known. The group of more overt parliamentary supporters consisted of five men. Robert Morgan was re-instated as a master probably in place of Walter Brick and elected as mayor to succeed Henry Foster on 30 September 1646. Robert Hole, William Atwell, the Presbyterian Joseph Gallington (a former apprentice of Thomas Salmon) and John Cox were the other new members. Hole and Gallington were excluded from the corporation in the royalist purge of 1662 and the same possibly happened to Atwell. John Cox, the nephew of Bartholomew, was heavily involved in the purchase of the bishop's lands in 1647/8 being a close colleague of Robert Morgan and John Casbeard. Although still alive in 1663, he had left the corporation by September 1652 because his name is not included in the lists of corporation members found in the Wells Corporation Receiver's book which survives from that time. Nothing is known of the views of the final additional member, John Webb.

These were the men who had to support and in many cases carry through the policies of parliament and the county committee; they also had to safeguard the interests of the city in a rapidly changing situation. [11]

PUNISHING THE ROYALISTS

Immediately after the parliamentary victory, the new county committee under John Pyne got down to the business of punishing those men who had actively supported the royalist cause in Somerset. These men had often been the leaders of society acting as JPs, captains in the militia or holding other offices in the county before the war. Estates of known royalists were sequestrated or withheld from their owners until an assessed fine had been paid. The committee 'employed a tribe of sequestration officials,' of whom there were two or three in each hundred. One of the most assiduous was Edward Curll, a Puritan from Batcombe, who 'obviously enjoyed his work, hounding royalist landlords and uncovering attempted evasions by the uses of paid informers.' A rather extreme example of the way the process of sequestration could be carried out was in August 1649 when Curll was in Wells dealing with the case of Richard Mogge who had acted as deputy under-sheriff of the county under the Marquis of Hertford. Mogge was accused of 'being a captain of the trained bands, [and of] plundering and threatening rebels against the King;' consequently Curll sealed up Mogge's goods in a trunk in Mogge's study and locked the door. Mogge's reaction was explosive: he broke down the door and chased the constable left by Curle from the house shouting 'I care not a fart from the highest to the lowest of them all, nor for any man in England. Tis my house and my goods.' The following morning on returning, Curll found that the locks on the study door had been blocked and when he gained entry he found that the trunk had been opened by Mogge, the most valuable documents removed and the trunk resealed. Mogge's words, heard by Robert Hole, were reported by Curll to the London Committee for the Advance of Money which disbursed the fines collected by sequestration. Mogge claimed in his defence that he had removed only those documents that belonged to the High Sheriff. The resolution of the case is unknown. [12]

This policy had serious financial implications for some men resident or closely associated with Wells. The problem for the royalist gentlemen who suffered from sequestration and for the parliamentary Committee of Compounding which attempted to collect the fines, was that many of them were already heavily in debt. The man who faced the heaviest fines was William Walrond. He had left Wells on the arrival of the New Model Army on July 28 1645 and fled to Bristol where he surrendered to the parliamentary forces after the fall of that city in September. Walrond was dealt with quite severely by the county committee. His application for a pass to go to London to the Committee for Compounding to know the amount of his fine was refused and he was imprisoned by the county committee without a formal charge. In February 1645/6 he begged to know the charges against him and David Barrett, the county committee marshal, took him to Ilchester where he gave security for his good behaviour and was given a pass to go to London to compound. He finally arrived in London in May 1646 and on 25 June his fine was fixed at £630. Walrond claimed that he was unable to pay because of his poor financial position and his numerous responsibilities. He argued that he still had to maintain his children and grandchildren as well as his brother and his family who had been driven from Ireland by the Catholic rebellion there. He was also £1000 in debt, had paid £500 to the parliamentary army and had 'been damaged in £1200.' He begged leave to go into the country to raise the money for his fine or else he claimed that his lands would have to be sold which would yield little as he was 69 years of age and had only a life interest in them. The Committee for Compounding was sympathetic to Walrond's predicament and on 27 June 1646 granted him leave to return to Somerset. Before Walrond left he was able to include his son George in his composition. On 9 July 1647 the committee took another look at Walrond's finances and on 20 October 1647 reduced his fine to £150. Walrond was unable to pay this reduced sum and a further deposition made to the committee on 8 December 1647 revealed that he was now £2400 in debt. In consequence his fine was reduced to £40 which he was still unable to pay. In the end Walrond paid nothing and the committee, totally frustrated with his case, on 4 May 1649 granted him a full pardon and a discharge from sequestration. [13]

Valentine Trym of Wells and Wookey was fined £40 for acting as under-sheriff of Somerset to the royalist Sir Thomas Bridges of Keynsham in 1644. Thomas Coward the militia captain who was originally assessed at £160, had his assessment reduced to £45 because he was heavily in debt; he was unable to pay this reduced figure and his estate was initially sequestered for non-payment. Finally on 4 February 1648 he was discharged without payment. William Morgan's fine was assessed at £387: he paid in instalments and was finally able to secure his discharge by paying £20 in 1649, the committee noting, 'that he was before the wars and still is much in debt.' Morgan's family suffered as well: his nephew John Morgan of the hamlet of Worminster near Wells who had served as a major in the royal army, was fined £133 6s 8d but his other nephew William whose estate was valued at less than £200 only paid £5. Alexander Jett the former bishop's registrar was fined £33 for his work with the royalist administration as was Tristram Towse the former deputy chapter clerk who had probably assisted Jett, (Towse's son had married Jett's daughter.) Towse's claim for some mitigation of his fine because he had to support ten children, went unheeded and he was fined £50. William West for 'taking up arms for the defence of Wells' (his own words) was fined £40 while Henry Barlow because he assisted 'the late King against Parliament' was fined the munificent sum of 6s 8d! [14]

A PARLIAMENTARY BY-ELECTION

At the end of the civil war Wells had no MPs. Both Sir Edward Rodney and Sir Ralph Hopton had been impeached by parliament for supporting the king and faced heavy fines. Sir Edward Rodney had left Wells with Walrond on the arrival of the New Model Army on July 28 1645 and surrendered at Bristol on the fall of the city to Fairfax as Walrond had done. When interrogated, Sir Edward was again somewhat economical with the truth claiming that he had 'never borne arms and never fined, imprisoned nor sequestered any man for adherence to Parliament.' He was forced to submit details of his estate to the sequestrators appointed by the county committee who then sent the details to the Committee for Compounding in London. Rodney's fine was fixed at £1200 on 17 March 1646. However his financial position was dire: he was heavily in debt because of law suits against another section of his extended family concerning his inheritance and consequently was unable to pay the full amount. He had as he later said 'almost winded myself out of it [his family law suit], til these warres came which by sequestration plunderings, great taxes at Goldsmith's Hall, Haberdashers Hall and in the country cast me very far back again.' The proceedings dragged on for the next three years and finally on 4 May 1649, Sir Edward by settling annual incomes of £40 on the ministers at Westbury (sub Mendip) and Pilton where he owned the tithes, managed to get his fine reduced by £800. [15]

Hopton, who in 1646 had assumed full command of the royalist army in the West was defeated by Fairfax at Torrington on 16 February 1646. Hopton who had been wounded in the face with a pike and had had his horse killed under him, tried to make a stand at Bodmin and was finally forced to surrender to Fairfax at Truro on 14 March 1646. He then fled with the Prince of Wales first to the Isles of Scilly and then to Jersey. He never returned to England, dying in Bruges of an ague in September 1652 aged 56. [16]

The 1646 county and borough parliamentary by-elections were thus as eagerly awaited by the Wells burgesses as the elections of 1640 had been. The county committee led by John Pyne was outmanoeuvred by the high sheriff, Sir John Horner, and failed to get its candidate elected as the member for the county. It was successful at Bridgwater, Taunton and Minehead in securing the election of men who supported Pyne but Wells was to be a different matter. The committee attempted to interfere in Wells by launching an investigation in December 1645 into the role of the recorder, Christopher Dodington, during the late conflict. Although there is no evidence, this investigation is likely to have alienated the Wells Corporation which was always sensitive to outside interference in business it considered to be within its own prerogative. [17]

When the election was held in the late spring of 1646, the Wells Corporation chose as its two candidates the lawyers Clement Walker and Lislebone Long and both men were duly elected by the Wells burgesses. Their election was a setback for the Pyne interest: even the mayor of Wells, Robert Morgan, Pyne's supporter, was unable to influence the election. Walker a strong Presbyterian and able polemicist had always been an opponent of Pyne. A Dorset man, he had by 1640 bought an estate at Charterhouse on Mendip, seven miles north west of Wells, supported parliament in the civil war and in 1643 become a member of both the Somerset assessment and sequestration committees. He was a combative and aggressive man with a violent temper having seriously wounded his first wife when suspicious of her fidelity. He was intemperate in his language and had referred to Pyne disparagingly in his speeches. According to one hostile source he (Pyne) had 'curried favour with the local [Wells] Puritans to win the seat.' Lislebone Long from Stratton-on-the-Fosse, was a more moderate figure. He was held by his contemporaries to be 'a person of great integrity in the profession of law' and 'a very sober discrete gentleman.' Although a member of the county committee, he was always a moderate. The choice of these two men was astute: both were well known lawyers and the Wells Corporation had always been assiduous in retaining legal counsel. Walker was also a prominent Presbyterian elder in the county which would have appealed to the influential Presbyterian group on the corporation. Long's membership of the county committee would also be very useful in representing the city's interests there. [18]

CHURCH AFFAIRS: 'A PARISH OF ABOVE TEN THOUSAND SOULS'

Another of the immediate results in Wells of the parliamentary victory of July 1645 was the ousting of Thomas Westley from the vicarage of St Cuthbert's. The end of the civil war meant the end of episcopacy and an attempt to develop a new system of ecclesiastical organisation. The catalyst for Westley's dismissal was a circular letter sent by the Speaker of the House of Commons to the Somerset County Committee calling on it to divide the county into 'classical presbyteries and to appoint ministers and lay elders to serve them.' Westley, the friend of Bishop Piers, was removed from his position by the county committee probably in October 1645. He spent the next 15 years mostly in retirement at Chilcote, a hamlet two miles from Wells, having purchased a small estate which had formerly belonged to the small pre-reformation Chilcote Chapel, long since closed. His income was restricted to a grant of one fifth from the income of his former livings of St Cuthbert's Wells and East Brent. From the admittedly meagre evidence, it seems that Westley had never fully cooperated with the corporation and being a supporter of Bishop

Piers's policies, was not much liked by the Puritan members of the corporation who now had more influence. Much of the parish record keeping during the war had been done by the curate and Governor of the Almshouse in nearby Beggar Street, Francis Standish, and it is likely that Westley absented himself from his duties in May 1645 because until then Standish had signed himself as curate but from that time signed himself as 'clarcke' in the parish register. Westley was one among many royalist clergymen to be dispossessed in the county. During the following six months vacancy, Standish kept the records and probably took the services at the church until the appointment of the new ministers. After their appointment, although he no longer was responsible for keeping the register, he continued to collect records of baptisms until 1648 and later added them to the main register. He commented: 'Look in the last leafes of this booke for children baptised but not Registered from 1643-1648, the times being under God's visitation. But I have Registered their names, soe manie as came to my knowledge as faith fullie as if they were Registered in their owne Proper Place or yeare; and this I did for the content of the Parish, and the Good of their children for After times.'[19]

On 15 April 1646, William Thomas and Samuel Oliver 'two learned and godly Divines' were jointly appointed by parliament to the living of St Cuthbert, Wells because the parish was considered to 'be of vast Extent, comprehending within its Precincts above Ten Thousand Souls too great a charge for a single Pastor.' The appointment of these two men showed the religious temper of the corporation, the leaders of which were in favour of godly reformation. According to the parliamentary ordinance the desire to appoint these men was unanimous: the 'Corporation of the said City, and the other inhabitants of the said Parish [had] unanimously desired that [Thomas and Oliver might] be settled and appointed as joint Pastors, to undertake the Charge and Cure of the said Parish.' Their joint stipend was to be £300 (Westley's had been £50) with the basic money coming from the rents of the parsonage of Wells and extra money from the rents of the manors of North Curry, East Curry and Knapfee(in North Curry) in South Somerset which had been seized from the dean and chapter of Wells by the parliamentary sequestrators after the defeat of the royalists in 1645. Possibly the gaining of the extra endowment from the rents of the dean and chapter may also have been one of the incentives for the decision to appoint two ministers both of whom held other appointments. The hands of the wily shoemaker Richard Casbeard, mayor until 29 September 1645 and thereafter justice, and Robert Morgan newly returned to local politics may be seen in the gaining of the extra endowment. Both Robert Morgan and Richard Casbeard's son John were to be the prime movers in the purchase of many of the bishop's rights when they came up for sale in the following year. [20]

William Thomas, a Shropshire man educated at Brasenose College Oxford (M.A. in 1615), had been ordained in the Bath and Wells diocese and had become vicar of Ubley in the north of Somerset in 1618. A Presbyterian, he had been licensed to preach by Bishop Piers after the bishop's arrival in the diocese in 1633. Piers soon repented of his decision and suspended Thomas in 1635 because 'hee hath not published the King's Majesties declaration concerninge lawfull recreations to bee used on Sundaies after the ending of Eveninge prayer, [the Book of Sports].' The other charges against him were that he refused to subscribe to articles upholding the Prayer Book; that he refused to declare resistance to the king unlawful and that he refused to condemn the defacing of church ornaments. After a three-year suspension he was restored to his living in 1638. His supporters considered him a good scholar but only a useful preacher. According to a contemporary, he did not possess a constitution that could endure much hardship, nor did he have the courage and boldness of some of his fellow ministers. He was apt to be dejected by the appearance of evil and tended to be very solitary and serious. He was minister of St Cuthbert's for only two years and retired back to Ubley in 1648.

His fellow minister Samuel Oliver, a Cornishman, was another Presbyterian. Educated at Exeter College Oxford, he received his BA from the university in February 1622/3. He was then ordained in the Bath and Wells diocese in 1623 and appointed vicar of Camely near Bath in 1627. His career was not as controversial as Thomas's but he was well thought of by the powerful Westminster Assembly which appointed him in 1646 to officiate in Bath Abbey. [21]

The classical system of presbyteries to replace the diocese of Bath and Wells was not set up in Somerset until March 1648. The original idea of the county committee was to divide the county into nine distinct groups or *classes* 'but by reason of the scarcity of fitting ministers and elders to constitute so many classes,' it had been decided 'to reduce them for the present into four,' one of which was centred on Wells and Bruton. This *classis* was rather unwieldy containing 110 parishes with 14 ministers in overall charge supported by 30 elders, the main bulk of parish services still being taken by the remaining parish clergy. The ministers and lay elders met monthly to hear sermons, settle contentious issues and supervise parish affairs which included ordaining and appointing new ministers. These last two powers were necessary because about 100 Somerset clergy had been ejected in the years following the war with one fifth of parishes being affected. Wells as we have seen was one of them. The two newly appointed ministers in Wells, William Thomas and Samuel Oliver, were supported by three elders: Thomas Salmon, Joseph Gallington and Stephen Haskett. The first two were already members of the corporation and Haskett was soon to return to his mastership. Their position as elders enhanced the power and prestige of these three men in the community. Although the records of the Wells Bruton classis and the meetings of the four classes in the provincial assembly have not survived, it is likely that the three elders encouraged godly behaviour by catechising – providing 'the young and ignorant with the fundamentals of knowledge that seventeenth century reformed theology demanded.' They also, with the ministers, would have controlled access to the three services per year of Holy Communion because 'Presbyterians stressed the need for religious preparation before coming to the Lord's Table.' However in most other respects, the traditional parochial structure of St Cuthbert's was maintained. Two churchwardens were appointed, one by the corporation as before; the overseers of the poor were elected as usual; the registers were kept and the bell ringers employed for celebratory occasions and to ring the funeral knells. From the few references to the officiating ministers in the churchwardens' accounts it would seem that the majority of the services were in 1649 being taken by Samuel Oliver, with help from Francis Standish.

Inside the church there were changes: the Laudian altar was removed from the east end of the chancel and a long communion table was placed lengthways running from east to west in the middle of the chancel with six forms to provide seating for the communicants. During the communion service the table was covered by a diaper cloth, a white linen cloth covered with a diamond pattern, donated by the wealthy mercer George Bull. The minister was able to use the two silver flagons for the wine and the water recently bequeathed to the church by Ezekiel Barkham in 1639 and an Elizabethan gilt chalice with a cover. The communion bread was placed on a plate given by Cornelius Watts and his wife in 1644. There was one major change however in the form of worship: the Book of Common Prayer was no longer in use, its place being taken by the new Directory of Public Worship. The Directory was very different from the Prayer Book in that it contained only guidelines for the officiating minister who alone had a copy. Worship was now to become extempore at the discretion of the minister. The Books of Common Prayer were no longer needed and in 1649 only 'fower old prayer bookes called Comon prayer bookes' survived. It is unclear if services were embellished with music. The earliest inventory, that of 1649, mentions only an old organ case and 'two pair of billows' in the storehouse. Preaching the word of God was the most important priority and Oliver preached from what was described as the 'new Pulpitt' a fine wooden one in the Jacobean style erected in 1636 and still in use. To aid him there was a new bible donated by Ezekiel Barkham placed on the pulpit cushion and if he waxed too eloquent, an hour glass! [22]

Francis Standish kept his connection with St Cuthbert's church as Governor of the Almshouse and probably still acted as curate: it is likely that he is the 'Mr Standish' referred to in the churchwardens' accounts for 1649. He continued with his duties at the Almshouse and as Governor was continually faced with a shortage of money due to the sequestration of some of the lands of the dean and chapter which provided the funds necessary for the maintenance of the almshouse or as he described it, 'a difficulty as to the making of estates to the Hospital arising from the Great Rebellion.' [23]

SOCIAL PROBLEMS

The hard economic times after the civil war caused much social disruption. Society was under strain and the Wells Petty Sessions records provide some evidence of this. The strengthening of the Puritan group on the corporation, the Presbyterian takeover of the parish church and the re-emergence of Robert Morgan did lead to delinquents being pursued with more energy than in the past. The number of meetings of the petty sessions was increased: during the year of Robert Morgan's mayoralty 1646-7, there were eight meetings instead of the normal two and in the following three years there were on average five meetings a year. The main cases dealt with were the traditional ones e g: recusancy, unlicensed tipplers (a seller of beer), illicit card playing in alehouses, Sunday observance, drunkenness, violence, immorality and the new one of juvenile crime. However some of the crimes reported were more serious than heretofore. Some Wells residents were not over-impressed by the zeal for moral reformation of some of the corporation members. Higgins, a cook in the High Street, detected a certain amount of hypocrisy in the actions of some of the more godly members of the corporation when he was reported to have said in 1646: 'a Puritan would goe two myles to heare a sermon, nine myles to a whoare.' However despite the increase in religious zeal, religious deviancy was still dealt with leniently. The Wells authorities had always been fairly tolerant of Catholics and this policy did not change. When James Pearce in May 1647 confessed that he was a catholic who had not been to church for three years and maintained that he would live and die in the Catholic religion, he was only gently admonished to reform by the mayor Robert Morgan.[24]

The proliferation of inns and alehouses in seventeenth century Wells brought much business to the city. The corporation had always carefully checked inn licences and fined illegal tipplers but realising the economic importance of the inns to the city had pursued a moderate policy. During the years after the civil war, this policy did not change. However it was not enforced rigorously enough for the godly Edward Curll of Batcombe, the sequestrator of royalist estates for the county committee. He saw it as his duty to crusade against alehouses which he called 'the nurseries of hell' and attacked maltsters 'who for private gain care not to undo the kingdom.' This would have made him unpopular in Wells where the leading man, Robert Morgan, controlled three inns and had interests in the malting business. On 27 March 1648 Curll attempted to incriminate the mayor of Wells, Thomas Salmon a Presbyterian elder, before the quarter sessions alleging that the corporation had re-licensed suppressed alehouses and protected alehouse keepers in danger of suppression. After hearing from Salmon, the justices rejected Curll's accusations as 'frivolous and vain.' There may however have been some truth in these accusations because the town clerk Bartholomew Cox, still very active despite his 74 years, had nearly 20 years before been suspended by the corporation for issuing licences on his own initiative for money. It is possible that he might have exceeded his authority again. The constable Joseph Gallington, another Presbyterian elder, was active in attacking illicit card playing in alehouses but again this was nothing new. [25]

Drunkenness had always been a problem with so much ale being sold in the city. The petty sessions in February 1646/7 dealt with a number of drink related cases. Non-observance of the Sabbath was particularly frowned upon especially when due to drunkenness. John Adams of Dulcote near Wells was so overcome with drink when walking down the Wells High Street on a Sunday 'that he wayled in the street as he went.' In April of the same year George Creed confessed that he had been drunk 'and that he was not at the church neither in the forenoon or afternoon.' Other drink-induced confrontations often got out of hand. William Sadler, 'a worsted man,' when he saw the Mendip lead miner Edmund King urinating against a house wall in the High Street, 'bid the said King to have a care that he did not throw down the wall.' King responded by attacking Sadler with a furze hook nearly severing a finger from his hand. [26]

The permanent presence of soldiers in the city during and after the civil war was not conducive to morality. Elizabeth Alford a widow was accused of being a drunkard and of keeping a disorderly house for soldiers. Her friend Ann Morgan who also 'entertained' soldiers, was so notorious that seven of her more moral female neighbours complained vehemently against her behaviour. Ann evidently had a wide clientele and employed four other women to assist her when business was brisk. In June 1649, when Richard Marks approached her house around midnight, the watchmen was able to overhear his conversation with Ann: 'I shall lie with you and will give thee a shilling'. Ann always the businesswoman replied, 'No I will have 18d for thou hast hindered me [in] the knitting of half a hose.' Her accusers also informed the watch that 'about a month since, one Captain Somerset, a captain of ye King's army did offer also a crowne to the said Ann Morgan to lie with her and threw down the money on the table but she said Noe I will have a yellow peece and the said captain Somersett having a horse at the doore she caused the said horse to be brought into the house.' Captain Somerset was none other than the gallant gentleman from South Brent who had opposed the depredations of General Goring's men in 1645 and whose flamboyant funeral monument in Brent Knoll church depicts him standing boldly flanked on either side by his wives and (hopefully) rising from his tomb at the resurrection. In a patriarchal society where sexual offences were concerned, women were usually punished more severely than men. In this case however, Ann's male client also received a painful and humiliating punishment. He was to ride the wooden horse, a military punishment (see note 27). On 22 June 1649, Ann was sentenced by the mayor Bartholomew Cox and the justice Thomas Salmon to be imprisoned 'until the Saturday morning market' and then 'set in the stocks near the place where the wooden horse is to stand appointed to be at the upper end of the market ... a soldier shall ride the wooden horse ... and after that time [she was] to be washed in the Palace Moat and then to be brought down to the prison and there to remain during the pleasure of the mayor and justice.' [27]

There is also evidence of a possible rise in juvenile crime after the civil war. Bad behaviour amongst young people was usually punished by the father or the master if the young person were apprenticed. The stealing by a small gang of three young girls of two parcels of kersey (coarse narrow cloth) from a market stall was unusual. There is also evidence of a gang of boys in Skinners Close (near Tor Hill, Wells) led by John Downe whose activities led to violence. They threw stones at Edward Bush 'and did break ... [his] forehead and drew bloud of him.' When Bush asked them why they would not let him pass through the gate 'they without answering him still continued throwing of stones.' Bush's reaction was violent and he struck Downe with his stick 'atwart his right eye of which beating the said John Downe hath languished in his body until this day ... and shed much blood.' [28]

"VILLANOUSLY MURDERED"

The most serious act of violence committed during this period was without doubt the murder of the dean. Dean Raleigh had, after

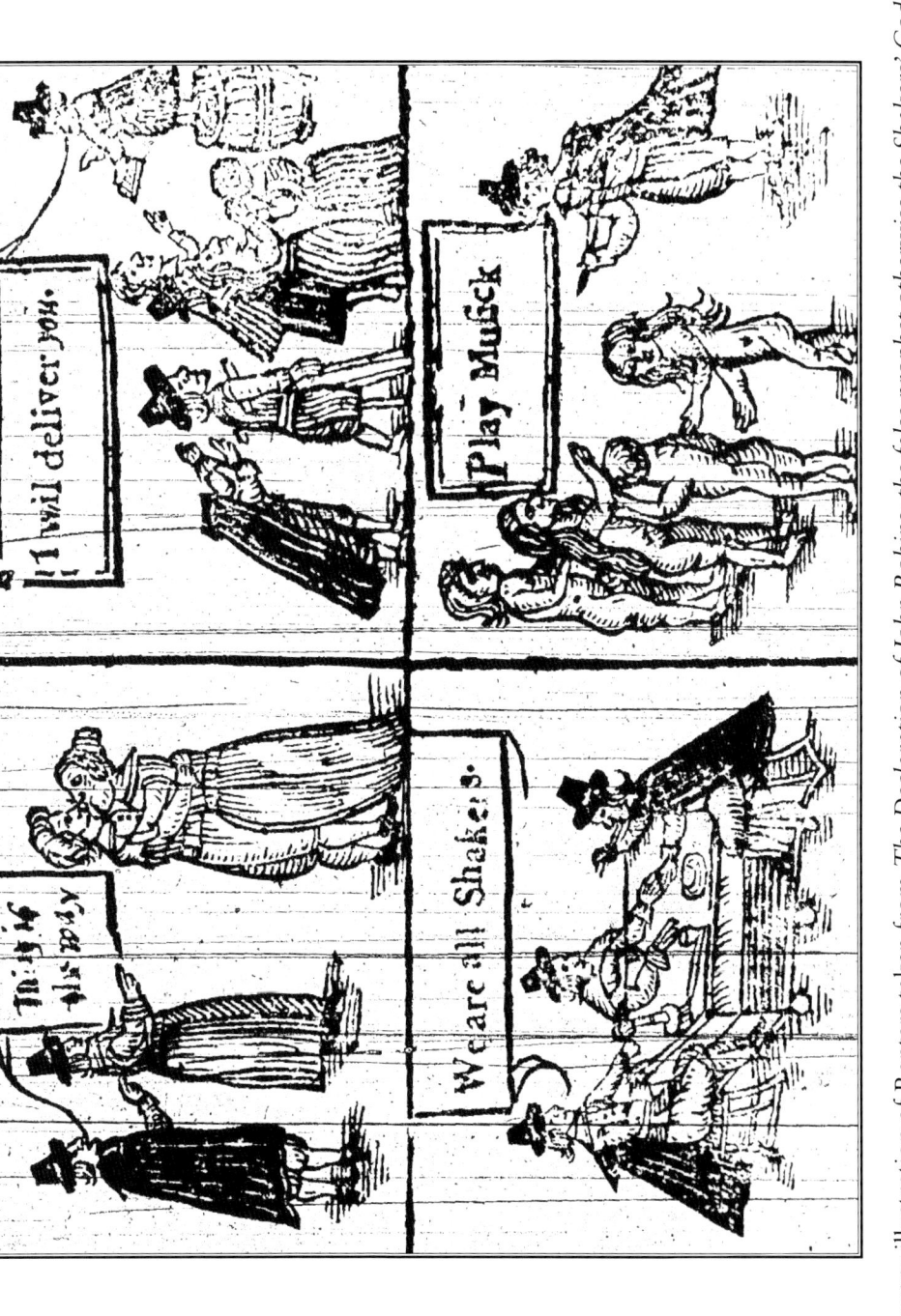

A contemporary illustration of Ranters taken from *The Declaration of John Robins: the false prophet otherwise the Shakers' God*, 1651. Reading clockwise the captions are: *This is the way; I will[l] deliver you; Play Musick; We are all Shakers*. (British Library)

A LOOKING-GLASSE FOR THE QUAKERS,

WHEREIN

They may behold themselves; and others also may behold their pernicious ways.

OR,

Deceit returned upon the Deceivers heads.

BEING AN

ANSWER

TO

James Naylor's pretended ANSWER to *Thomas Collier's* Book, called, *A Dialogue between a Minister and a Christian.*

Wherein the Truths asserted in that Dialogue are clearly proved; and *James Naylor* and the Quakers are proved to be the liers and deceivers; and so indeed they have made lies their refuge, and under falshood have they hid themselves.

Here is likewise a Relation of *James Naylor's* exaltation in the *West*, where the Quakers proclaimed him Christ; but have now found a CHRIST without them.

LONDON,
Printed for *Thomas Brewster*, at the Sign of the three Bibles at the West end of *Pauls*, 1657.

Title page of Thomas Collier's attack on the Quakers: *A Looking-Glasse for the Quakers*, 1657. (British Library)

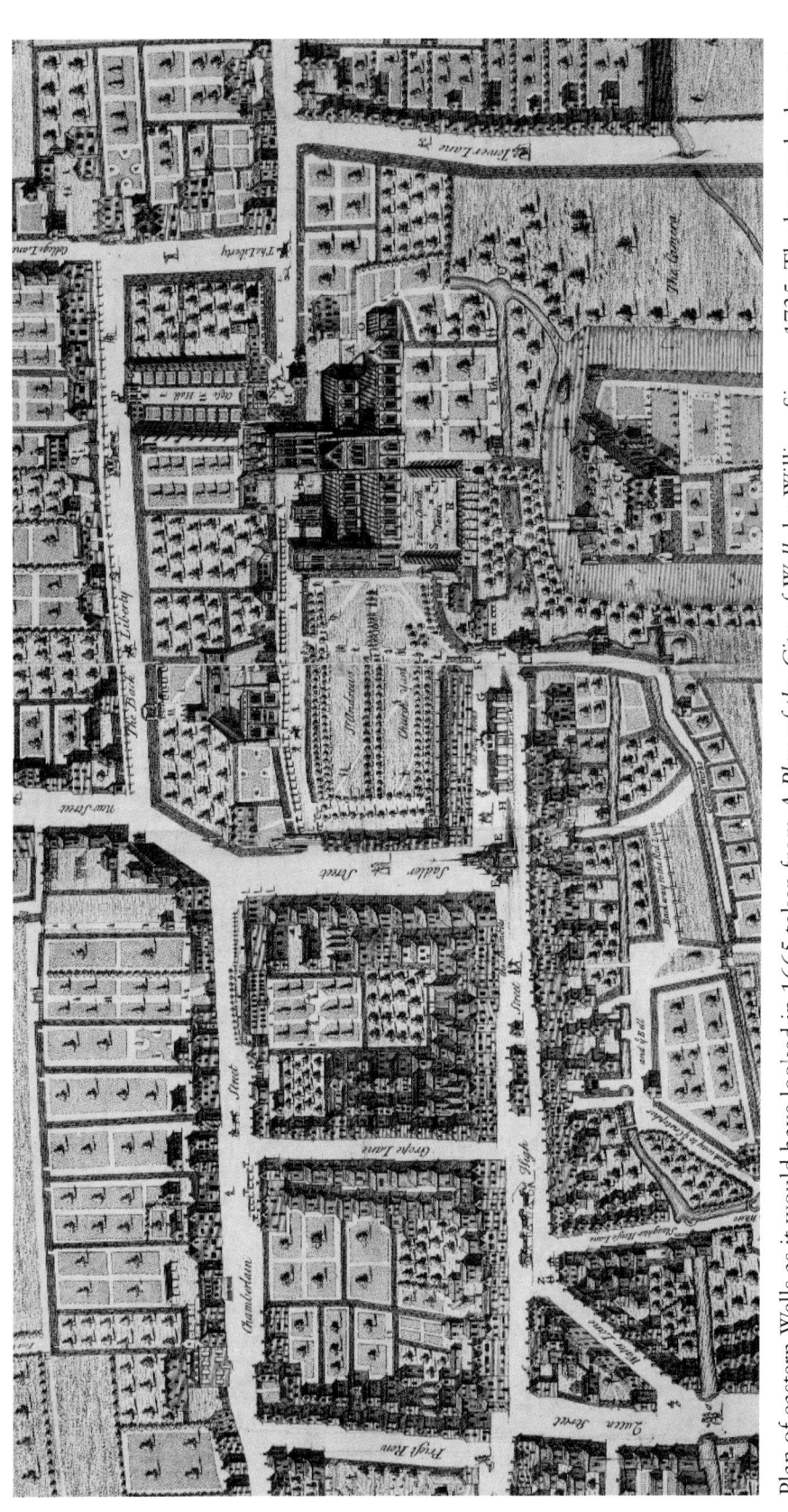

Plan of eastern Wells as it would have looked in 1665 taken from *A Plan of the City of Wells* by William Simes, 1735. The key to the letters on the map is as follows: A-The Cathedral of St Andrew; C- The Bishop's Palace; D-The Deanery; E-The High Cross; F-The Bekynton Conduit; H-The Market Place and Market House/Town Hall; I-The Palace Gate (now known as the Bishop's Eye); K-The Penniless Porch; M-the Chain Gate; N-The Vicars' Hall or Close Hall; O-The Cathedral Lady Chapel of St Mary; R-The Cathedral Cloister; S-The Cathedral Grammar School; T-The Cathedral Library. (The British Library Board, Maps K top 38.9)

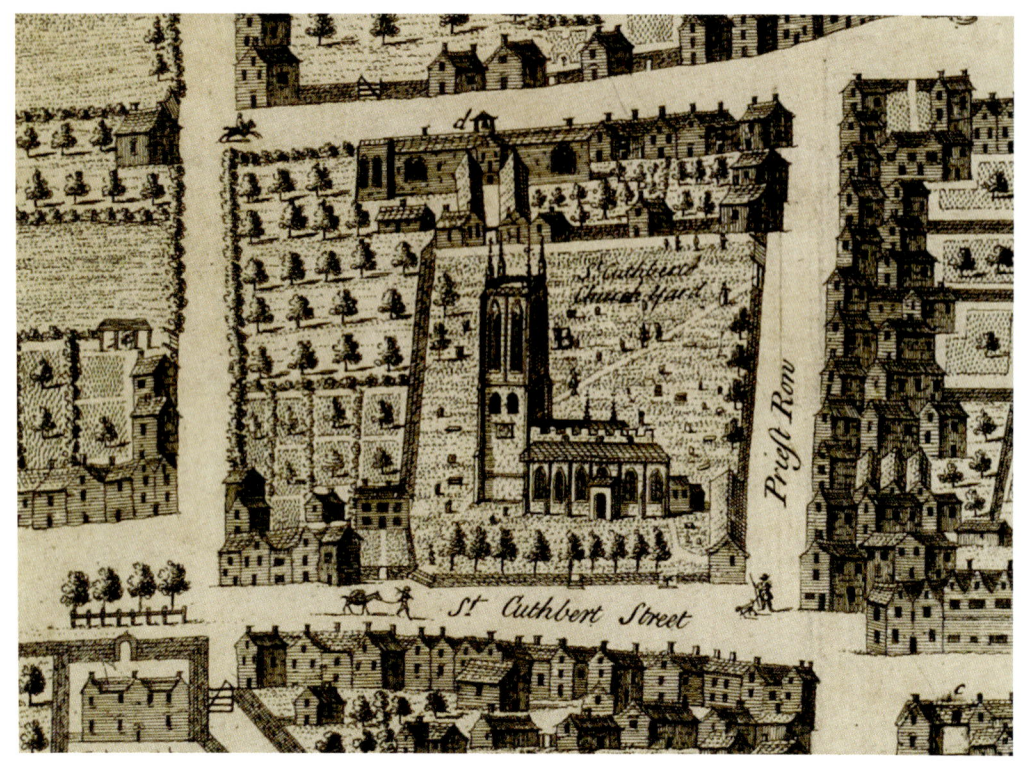

St Cuthbert's church, Wells from the plan by William Simes, 1735. The Almshouse is to the rear of the church (d). (The British Library Board, Maps K top 38.9)

The Royal Arms of Charles I in St Cuthbert's Church, Wells. Taken down in 1649 and re-erected in 1660. (Photograph Patrick Kirkby)

leaving Wells in January 1644/5, retired to his rectory at Chedzoy near Bridgwater where he lived until captured by the parliamentary army after the fall of Bridgwater on 21 July 1645. Initially placed under house arrest at Chedzoy, he was transferred to the county gaol at Ilchester and from there to the prison set up by the county committee at Banwell. In the late summer of 1646 he was removed to his own deanery on Cathedral Green at Wells where his gaoler was the county marshal David Barrett. Barrett described by his enemies as a 'renegade Welshman' and a bigamist, seems to have been corrupt in that he accepted bribes to free prisoners illegally on parole. Raleigh was annoyed when his request to visit his wife and children was refused by the county committee then sitting at Wells and informed the committee of Barrett's corruption. The committee disciplined Barrett, threatening him with dismissal if this practice were not stopped.

Barrett was furious with the dean and soon took out his anger on him in the most brutal way. Accounts differ as to what happened next but a pro-royalist account described it thus: 'This so incensed Barrett that, coming next morning into the Doctor's chamber, who happened then to be writing to his wife, he instantly laid his hand upon the letter to see it, but the dean utterly refused to permit him unless he had an order from the committee for that purpose, and so wrested the paper out of his hands; which being done, the fellow slipped back, drew his sword (a knife in other accounts), ran it immediately into the good man's belly home to his backbone, and gave him an incurable wound that he tumbled out of his chair apparently dead; but being brought to life ... he lingered on about six weeks and then died of his wound.' Whatever happened, Raleigh was mortally wounded by Barrett and on 10 October 1646 Raleigh was buried in the quire of Wells Cathedral before the dean's stall in an unmarked grave. The funeral service according to the now illegal Book of Common Prayer, was taken by Francis Standish who was promptly imprisoned for a short time by the county committee but was soon able to resume his duties at the Almshouse. Barrett was, according to the royalist account, taken into custody but was acquitted at the assizes and reinstated. However the assize orders make no mention of this and it is likely that the case never reached court. To further cover its tracks, the county committee even took out warrants to apprehend Raleigh's eldest son who had initiated the prosecution of Barrett. Barrett continued to thrive and remained county marshal for the next four years. In the following decade he was to play an important part in Wells politics and even escaped retribution when the monarchy was restored in 1660.[29]

CHURCH AFFAIRS: THE CATHEDRAL

The death of the dean in 1646 and the dispersal of the cathedral chapter in January 1644/5 caused a vacuum in the administration of the cathedral. It is probable that Humphrey Marsh the sacrist, responsible for keeping the sacred vessels of the cathedral, provided some continuity of administration. It was later alleged against him and his son-in-law John Edmunds by Dr Cornelius Burges, the presbyterian preacher in the cathedral from 1649-1660, that after Marsh's appointment as registrar by Burges in 1656, he and his son-in-law had taken 'all the large fees, burial dues and appropriated the cloisters and churchyard and sundry goods of the church.' They may well have done the same during the interim period between the departure of the cathedral clergy in 1645 and Burges's arrival in 1649. [30]

By 1649, the fabric of the cathedral was deteriorating. John Taylor, who visited Wells in 1649, while not giving specific details, commented: 'these blessed execrable times of troublesome tranquillity have spoiled and defaced one of the goodliest and [most] magnificent churches in the Christian world.' Taylor's somewhat generalised comments probably also referred to the damage to the cathedral inflicted by the parliamentary troops in 1643 that had not been repaired, as well as to the neglect of the fabric particularly since 1645. Another reason for the deterioration of the fabric can be found in the report of another visitor in 1649 who reported that 'thieves were stripping the lead from the roof with the consequence that the building was 'much ruined and leaky.' However a drawing of the west front of the cathedral in 1655 shows that the statues in the lowest tier had not been damaged.'[31]

It is likely that services in the cathedral continued in some form between 1645 and 1649. Francis Standish, who had officiated at Dean Raleigh's funeral in October 1646 and the remaining vicars choral may have continued to conduct some services on an individual basis until the arrival of Burges in 1649. For the vicars choral the future at the end of the civil war was initially bleak. As a body they petitioned the House of Lords stating that they and their families, some 60 poor persons in all, had always been bred in the service of music and were incapable of any gainful employment. They asked for the restoration of their stipends as had been granted to the petty clergy at St Paul's and Westminster Abbey. Unfortunately for them, their petition was turned down on 13 February 1645/6 by the Committee for Sequestrations in London. They were paid nothing and were forced to disband as a corporate body. However the 1649 parliamentary survey of the lands of the dean and chapter shows that there were twelve vicars choral (of the full complement of 14) still living in Vicars Close in that year. This survey brought some further hope of amelioration in their financial position and on 13 November 1649, the Barons of the Exchequer ordered further enquiries with a view to payment. The outcome is unknown but it would seem likely that some payment was made because evidence survives from 1658 to show that the surviving vicars were receiving small stipends from the Trustees for the Maintenance of Ministers and were still resident in Vicars Close. [32]

THE PURCHASE OF THE BISHOP'S RIGHTS AND LANDS

On 9 October 1646, an ordinance of both Houses of Parliament stated that the 'name, title, style and dignity of Archbishops and Bishops' should be 'wholly abolished and taken away that their 'charters, deeds, books and writings' should be vested in trustees 'for the payment of the just and necessary debts of the kingdom.' On 16 November 1646 a further ordinance was passed for the sale of the bishops' lands. [33]

This legislation posed a problem for the members of the Wells Corporation. Were they going to let the property and rights belonging to the bishop that they had always coveted fall into the hands of outside speculators? The answer was resoundingly in the negative. Fortunately two experienced men were at hand to give advice and to assist in the purchase of the former bishop's rights and property: these men were Robert Morgan and more importantly John Casbeard. The 29 year old Casbeard, the son of the wily shoemaker

Richard Casbeard, was in 1647 a Bristol attorney who early in that year was working as a surveyor in the Exeter diocese for the Trustees for the sale of Bishops' Lands. Ruthless and astute, he thrived 'on the fringes of parliamentary committees, knowing the right people, picking the best bargains from the confiscated property suddenly thrown on the market, speculating and making himself indispensable [for a consideration] to those less versed in the intricacies of the new bureaucracy.' He was also in business on his own account buying confiscated lands for himself and acting as an agent for others. [34]

During 1647, the former bishop's lands were surveyed and by the autumn, Casbeard, already knowing of the corporation's interest in any forthcoming sale, received from the parliamentary contractors a list of the former bishop's rights in the manor, borough and hundred of Wells. After taking advice from the city's two MPs, the lawyers Clement Walker and Lislebone Long, the corporation encouraged by Robert Morgan took action. On 28 November 1647, it met at the exchequer in the High St under the chairmanship of the mayor, Thomas Salmon. The corporation at this date still represented a range of political opinion but on such an issue concerning the future of the city, it could present a united front. In the words of the letter sent to Casbeard, the members 'did there unanimously consent that the purchase should be prosecuted with effect.' The corporation then set out that it wished to purchase a number of the former bishop's rights: these were those rights which had caused disputes between him and the city for more than 400 years. Summarised in the language of the time they were, 'the Royalty of the Town and Hundred of Wells and Wells Forum.' This included the bailiwick of the city, (the rights of the bishop's bailiff within the city boundaries and the hundred and the profits accruing from these rights); the borough courts (the three-weekly court of record for settling burgess disputes and the petty sessions dealing with minor breaches of the peace); the three weekly court or law day for the Forum; the four fairs in the city which belonged to the bishop; the annual Priddy and Binegar Fairs and the profits of the green wax (fines exacted by the bailiff on the authority of the green wax seal of the Exchequer in London). On 4 December 1647, the corporation followed up the initial letter with another authorising Robert Morgan, John Casbeard and John Cox to commence negotiations for the purchase of those rights outlined in the previous letter and on 15 December 1647 John Casbeard signed the contract on behalf of the corporation to purchase the royalties. [35]

The conveyance of purchase was not sealed until 22 March 1647/8 but in the interval between signing the contract and sealing the conveyance, the mayor Thomas Salmon revised the details of the original November letter. As Dr. Cornelius Burges, who was soon to enter into negotiations with the contractors for the sale of the bishop's lands in Wells, put it: 'this Contract lay (as the Contractors thought) sleeping, from the 15 of December, til the 15 of March following. In which time, the Agents of Wells slept not; for they being told by somebody, that if they could but get the first particular out of the Registers hands, and draw up and return another in the room, they might get much more into their Purchase and Conveyance, than they had indeed Contracted for.' It seems highly likely that the mayor Thomas Salmon then listened to Casbeard's and Morgan's advice and did exactly that. He now added to the original contract the two weekly markets in the city; the services of the market bailiff (who was actually paid from the income of the manor of Wells which was not included in the sale); the bishop's Guildhall in Wells Market Place where the manorial courts for the different hamlets in the manor of Wells were held as well as the hundred court and the three week courts for settling disputes, and some manorial rights such as impounding stray animals and confiscating the goods of felons. The corporation also claimed 'full Power and Authority to keep the aforesaid Courts and every one of them and the accustomed Writs and Process of the aforesaid Courts and Courts of Record, to be from time to time issued and awarded ... and also power to distrain for all sums of mony due and payable.' The corporation had now made a bid to take over all the former bishop's secular jurisdiction in the city/borough and in the hundred and had made an inroad into the late bishop's manorial rights that it was to exploit in the future including the valuable profits from Mendip lead. The sale price to the corporation of this package on 22 March 1648 was £412 13s 4d: a very good bargain! As well as the vague wording which could be exploited later, the corporation had managed to get the parliamentary contractors to accept a figure of £5 13s 4d for the bailiff's profits from the fairs when a more realistic figure would have been £40. [36]

The Wells Corporation could, by sealing this purchase, feel very pleased with itself. Any satisfaction felt locally was soon to be dissipated when the corporation learned in July 1648 that someone else was also interested in purchasing some of the former bishop's land in Wells together with those manorial rights which had not been sold to the corporation. That 'someone else' was Dr Cornelius Burges a Presbyterian clergyman from London. Burges had lent parliament a considerable sum of money during the civil war and afterwards and by 1648, the total owed him had risen to just over £4000. As it was clear to Burges that parliament was in no position to repay so large a loan, he decided to accept repayment in the form of bishops' lands and in July 1648 decided to embark on the purchase of some lands of the former Bishop of Bath and Wells. Burges soon discovered to his annoyance that the Wells Corporation was claiming some of the profits that he had expected to enjoy. His first act was to approach the mayor Thomas Salmon personally and ask him to give up those rights that had been inserted after the initial contract had been drawn up. This Salmon refused to do. In November 1648, Burges then went to the newly constituted Committee for Removing Obstructions in London with his complaint against the mayor. On 16 February 1648/9, the committee called Morgan and Casbeard before it to answer Burges's allegations. Casbeard claimed that he had another letter of attorney from the Wells Corporation empowering him to buy the extra items inserted into the original contract. However when the contractors for the committee issued a report agreeing with Burges's claims, Burges rather unwisely went ahead with his purchase. On 24 March 1648/9 for £4865, he bought what he considered were the unsold portions of the bishop's manor of Wells: these included the bishop's palace, the bishop's park and woods, the Mendip lead royalties and the Priddy minery plus other manorial rents.[37]

The Committee for Removing Obstructions however had not finished with the Wells Corporation and on 5 April 1649 it ordered Salmon and Casbeard to produce the original particular of 28 November 1647 and to indicate by what right they had substituted the second one. Salmon and Casbeard were unable to satisfy the committee which in May ordered them to convey to Burges what they had added illegally. Consequently in the same month Morgan and Salmon signed an agreement to re-convey to Burges any claim to the profits from Mendip lead, the former bishop's Guildhall in Wells and any other profits from the manor of Wells illegally taken by them. Burges then drew up an agreement to be signed by both parties containing what he thought had been agreed between him and the corporation. Much to his dismay and subsequent anger, the corporation then turned the tables on him, accusing him of misrepresenting what had been agreed. A stalemate ensued. By August 1649 when Casbeard had still not produced the original particular, the committee ordered his arrest. He was not actually imprisoned but was on bail for just over two years. The dispute however continued. A chancery suit brought by Burges against the corporation lasted from 1649-53. An attempt at arbitration between the parties failed when a preliminary agreement between the parties conveniently disappeared when Robert Morgan, who had it among his papers, died in October 1653. The agreement was never subsequently recovered.

In September 1649, parliament decided to sell the lands of the dean and chapter to help to pay army wages and so on 28 September 1649, perhaps unwisely seing that his dispute with corporation was still unresolved, Burges paid £1,069 10s 8d for the Wells deanery, the vicars' hall and an adjoining house, the chapter house and a field called Mundays Meadow lying on the northern side of the city. His third purchase effected on 28 May 1650, for which he paid £18 6s 8d, was the churchyard on the south side of the cathedral called the Camery. Burges had now spent nearly £2000 of his own money in addition to the £4000 he was owed by parliament. He then 'proceeded to follow the corporation's example in claiming more than he had paid for.' The inevitable conflict between Burges and the Corporation was to last for the next ten years and will be discussed in the following chapter. [38]

THE END OF THE DECADE

As the decade drew to a close, the rift between the army and the Presbyterians in parliament widened. The billeting of troops in Wells and the increased taxation required to pay for this had always been resented during the civil war and when the practice was continued in the years after the war, this resentment grew. The royalist insurrection in other parts of the country in 1648 caused the

Somerset County Committee to raise more troops for local defence. Clement Walker, the Wells MP was one of four local MPs who protested against this in parliament. 'We do not know any necessity of forces in the said county,' he argued. The Presbyterian majority in the House of Commons agreed with them and ordered the immediate disbandment of the extra forces in Somerset. [39]

Walker and the Presbyterians together with a group of moderate MPs were in favour of negotiations with the king but the army leaders had come to believe that the only solution to the country's constitutional problems was to get rid of a king who persistently refused to agree terms for a settlement. The failure of a moderate group of MPs in the autumn of 1648 to broker such a settlement with the king at Newport in the Isle of Wight and their consequent joining with the Presbyterian MPs led to the purge by the army of the more extreme Presbyterian MPs. On the morning of Wednesday 6 December 1648, 41 Presbyterian MPs of whom Walker was one (but not Lislebone Long the other Wells MP), were arrested at Westminster. They were taken to 'a common victualling house' nearby called 'Hell' and spent the day and night there. There were no beds and the prisoners were forced to sleep on the floor with most spending the night reading, talking and singing psalms. The following day was spent awaiting the pleasure of the Army Council, the only food provided for them being 'burnt wine and biscuits'. Finally on the Thursday evening they were forced to walk to two inns in the Strand where they were guarded by soldiers and given some sustenance. There they penned a protestation stating the 'the Army ... have not ... any power or jurisdiction to apprehend, secure, detain, imprison or remove our persons from place to place by any colour or authority whatsoever.' The army ignored the protest – such is the nature of military rule! [40]

Meanwhile in Somerset, Pyne's supporters were elated by the news of the arrest of Walker together with William Strode the Ilchester MP and William Prynne the Bath MP and of the destruction of the Presbyterian group in the House of Commons. Buoyed up with enthusiasm, they drew up a petition drafted by the ex-army preacher Thomas Collier, which asked that the army be 'encouraged, duly paid, not laid aside ... that justice be done on great offenders [the king] ... in satisfaction of the blood shed in your quarrel.' Collier who had recently moved to Wells and was living in the High Street had views that only a small minority of his fellow citizens shared. [41]

'THE AFTERMATH: 1645-49'

Clement Walker in the meanwhile continued under duress until late January 1648/9 being released just before the king's execution on 30 January 1648/9 which he may have witnessed. In March the House of Lords and the monarchy were abolished and in May 1649 the remaining members of the House of Commons, the Rump, declared themselves to be the governing body of a 'Commonwealth and free state of England.'

In Wells the political situation both local and national was discussed in the inns and alehouses. Although the majority of the citizens of Wells would have deplored the execution of the king, in the alehouses there were still those men, mostly it seems from outside the city, who were prepared to defend it. On 3 November 1649, Humfrie Butler urged the company in William Dericke's alehouse to drink to the king's health (the future Charles II), 'and because those present would not pledge the same, quarrelled with them, and did swear eight several oaths.' Leaving the alehouse and going into the Market Place he said loudly, 'all you that are Cavaliers come along with me.' In the same month on the 23rd, in the Flower de Luce inn kept by the ex royalist, William West, there was an argument concerning the late king's execution. Robert Allen (probably one of the Puritans from Batcombe), was reported to have said that the late king had had a fair trial whereupon the tailor Peter Sandford replied that Charles I had been tried by a company of rogues and 'so were all those that did take their part'. Allen and another man, John Gaik, argued on behalf of parliament and Sandford replied that 'he could find in his heart to throw a jug in their faces.' In St Cuthbert's church in 1649, the churchwardens authorised the taking down of the King's Arms as commanded by Act of Parliament and paid for the 'white lyming' of the stonework beneath. There was to be a delay of almost three years before the arms of the new state were displayed in the place of the former royal arms. [42]

NOTES
[1] Lynch, J, *For King & Parliament: Bristol and the Civil War,* Stroud 1999, p 94; Slack, P, *The Impact of Plague in Tudor and Stuart England,* Oxford, 1985, pp 7-17, 25, 65.

[2] Underdown, D, *Somerset in the Civil War and Interregnum,* Newton Abbot 1973, pp 122-3.

[3] Slack, P, *The Impact of Plague in Tudor and Stuart England, op cit,* p 210.

[4] *Nott, A & Hasler, J, Wells Convocation Acts Books 1589-1665 Part 1 1589-29*

Part 2 1629-44; 1662-65, SRS 90, pp 78,83-4, 157-61, 234-5, 413-15, 420-1; Everett Green, M A, (ed), *Calendar of the Proceedings of the Committee for Compounding Vol. II 1643-46*, London 1890, p 1038.

[5] SRO D P W St C 2/1/1; SRO D/P/W/St C 4/1/1; Sprigge's description of Bristol is quoted in Lynch, J, *For King & Parliament op cit*, p 163.

[6] Manning, B, *1649, The Crisis of the English Revolution*, London 1992, pp 79-82.

[7] WTH Wells Corporation Sessions Book 1625 – 50 folios 105, 158, 106.

[8] Bates Harbin, E H, (ed), *Quarter Sessions Records for the County of Somerset Vol. III Commonwealth 1646 – 1660*, SRS Vol. 28, Taunton 1912, p 83; WTH Wells Corporation Sessions Book 1625 – 50, folio 130.

[9] Manning, B, *1649, The crisis of the English Revolution op cit*, pp 84-89; Underdown, D, *Somerset in the Civil War and Interregnum op cit*, p 123.

[10] Underdown, D, *Somerset in the Civil War and Interregnum op cit* pp 121-7; Bates Harbin, SRO Vol 28 op cit, pp 1& 10.

[11] For Dodington see Nott & Hasler, SRS Vol 91 op cit, pp 877-880; for the corporation lists see Reynolds, H E, *Wells Cathedral: Its Foundation, Constitutional History and Statutes*, Wells 1887, pp cxlii-cxliii; Nott & Hasler, SRS Vol 91, op cit, p 877; SRO. D P W St C 2/1/1.

[12] Everett Green, M A, (ed), *Calendar of the Committee for the Advance of Money*, London 1888, p 981; WTH Corporation Sessions Book 1625-50 folio 160; Underdown, D, *Somerset in the Civil War and Interregnum op cit*, p 159.

[13] Everett Green, *CCC Vol. II, op cit*, p 963; Everett Green, *CAM op cit*, p 764.

[14] Everett Green, *CCC Vol II, op cit*, pp 754 (Coward), 1380 (Wm Morgan), 974 (Trym), 1191 (West), 1244 (John Morgan), 1333 (Jett); 1087 (Towse); Everett Green, *CCC Vol, III*, p 2099, (Barlow).

[15] Everett Green, *CCC Vol. II, op cit*, p 916; Underdown, D, *Somerset in the Civil War and Interregnum op cit*, p 127; Rodney's quotation is taken from his history of his family SRO DD/TB Box 20/1.

[16] DNB *Sir Ralph Hopton* by Ronald Hutton 2004.

[17] Underdown, D, *Somerset in the Civil War and Interregnum op cit*, p 131-132

[18] DNB *Clement Walker* by David Underdown, 2004; DNB *Lislebone Long* by John Wroughton, 2004.

[19] Standish's comments can be found in SRO D P W St C 2/1/1; for Westley see Matthews, A G (ed), *Walker Revised*, Oxford 1948, p 321; Underdown, D, *Somerset in the Civil War and Interregnum*, op cit, p 143; for the Chilcote Chapel see Serel,T, *Historical Notes on the Church of Saint Cuthbert in Wells*, Wells 1875, p 140.

[20] JHL Vol 8, London 1802, p 281.

[21] Foster, J, (ed), *Alumni Oxonienses 1500-1714, passim*; Steig, M, *Laud's Laboratory: The Diocese of Bath and Wells in the Early Seventeenth Century*, London 1982, pp 34, 293; Underdown, D, *Somerset in the Civil War and Interregnum*, op cit, pp 22, 68; for William Thomas see Calamy, E, *Account of the Ministers, Lecturers, Masters and Fellows of Colleges and Schoolmasters who were Ejected or Silenced after the Restoration in 1660*, 2nd ed., London, 1713, p 587.

[22] Shaw, W A, *A History of the English Church during the Civil Wars and under the*

'THE AFTERMATH: 1645-49'

Commonwealth 1640-1660, Vol. II, London, pp 31, 415-417; Underdown, D, *Somerset in the Civil War and Interregnum,* op cit, pp 143-146; Morrill, J, (ed), *Revolution and Restoration,* London 1992, p 73; *St Cuthbert's Churchwardens' Accounts 1649,* SRO D/P/W. St C 4/1/1; Serel, T, *Historical Notes on the Church of Saint Cuthbert in Wells,*op cit, pp 82-3; the quotations are from Vernon, E, *A Ministry of the Gospel: the Presbyterians during the English Revolution,* Durston, C,& Maltby, J, (eds), in *Religion in Revolutionary England,* Manchester, 2006, pp 115-132.

23 I am indebted to Jean Imray for information on the Almshouse in the 17th century.

24 For Higgins the cook see WTH Wells Corporation Sessions Book 1625-50, folio 134v; for Pearce see folio 105.

25 Curll's complaint is in Cockburn, J S, (ed), *Western Circuit Assize Orders 1629-1648,* Camden 4th Series, Vol. 17, London 1976, p 282.

26 WTH Wells Corporation Sessions Book 1625-50, folios 100, 104.

27 WTH Wells Corporation Sessions Book 1625-50 folio 155. The wooden horse was a cruel instrument in the form of a narrow bench raised too high off the ground for the soldier to rest his feet. This meant that as he sat astride it, his body weight bore down on his testicles causing him much discomfort. He would also have been dressed in women's clothing with a placard fastened to his back detailing his sins.

28 WTH Wells Corporation Sessions Book 1625-50 folios 118v, 119.

29 The main account of Dean Raleigh's career and death is taken from Walker Rev. J., (abridged by the Rev. R. Whittaker,) *The Sufferings of the Clergy of the Church of England during the Great Rebellion,* London 1863, pp 65-69 which contains some inaccuracies; for a corrective see the *DNB* entry for Raleigh by E.C. Marchant revised by David Underdown, 2004.

30 Burges in his petition of 29 April 1658 to be found in Everett Green, M A, (ed), *Calendar of State Papers Domestic Interregnum 1657-8,* HMSO 1884, no 167 refers to 'an old malignant and his son-in-law who had usurped the place,' (the cathedral). Matthews in *Walker Revised op cit* tentatively identifies the 'old malignant' as Thomas Westley, the former vicar of St Cuthbert's Wells. However Westley had no connection with the cathedral at this time and was living in retirement at Chilcote and did not have a son-in-law his only daughter dying unmarried. A more suitable candidate would be Humphrey Marsh, sacrist from 1624-1665. For Marsh see *Calendar of the Manuscripts of the Dean and Chapter of Wells Vol. II,* HMSO 1914, pp 382 & 435; for the identification of Marsh as the 'old malignant' see Underdown, D, *A Case Concerning Bishops' Lands: Cornelius Burges and the Corporation of Wells,* EHR 1963, p 36.

31 Colchester, LS, *Wells Cathedral: A History,* Wells 1982, p 160.

32 The lack of cathedral registers for this period makes any comment on activities in the cathedral tentative. I am grateful to A J Scrase for providing me with an annotated transcript of the 1649 Parliamentary Survey with property details. Ten vicars out of 14 petitioned in 1645/6 (see Mathews, *Walker Revised op cit,* p 16.) They were: Francis Standish, Arthur Alderley, William Atkins, Thomas Beaumont, Augustine Benford, Daniel Davis, James Dewbery, Anthony Mowrie, Henry Pope and Martin Symonds. By 1649 eight were still in the Close. Dewbery and Mowrie had died but their widows Mary Dewbery and Mary Mowrie were still living

there. The four missing vicars from the 1645/6 petition (John Bicknall, John Moss, John Oker and Anthony Walkley were also all living in Vicars Close. There was obviously considerable continuity of tenure here. By 1658 only Benford, Symonds (death reported 22 June 1658), Atkins, Beaumont, Standish, Davis and Alderley were in receipt of pensions from the Trustees for the Maintenance of Ministers. In the first list of vicars after the Restoration, that of 1664, only Beaumont, F. Standish, Davis and Alderley plus Moss of the original group were listed, Atkins having probably died. They were the only survivors of the original 14 of 1645. (see *Calendar of the manuscripts of the Dean and Chapter of Wells op cit* p 433 & Bailey, S, (ed), *Wells Cathedral Chapter Act Book 1666-83*, H.M.S.O. 1973, p 1.

[33] Matthews, *Walker Revised*, op cit, p xxviii.

[34] This quotation is taken from: Underdown, D, *A Case Concerning Bishop's Lands: Cornelius Burges and the Corporation of Wells*, E.H.R. New Series 78, 1963, p 24. The whole section on the purchase of the bishop's rights and property which follows is taken from Professor Underdown's authoritative account.

[35] Reynolds, H E, *Wells Cathedral: Its History and Statutes op cit*, pp cxlii – cxliii.

[36] Underdown, D, *A Case Concerning Bishops' Lands op cit*, p 26; Burges, C, *A case concerning the Buying of Bishops Lands with the Lawfulness thereof and the Difference between the Contractors for sale of those lands and the Corporation of Wells*, London 1659, pp 38-40.

[37] Underdown, D, *A Case Concerning Bishops' Lands*, op cit, pp 26-28.

[38] Underdown, D, *A Case Concerning Bishops' Lands*, op cit, p 27-8.

[39] Underdown, D, *Somerset in the Civil War and Interregnum*, op cit, p 148-9

[40] Underdown, D, *Pride's Purge: Politics in the Puritan Revolution*, Oxford 1972, pp 143-162.

[41] Underdown, D, *Somerset in the Civil War and Interregnum op cit*, p 153.

[42] DNB, *Clement Walker* Underdown, D. 2004: Bates Harbin, E H, (ed), *Quarter Sessions Records for the County of Somerset, Vol. III, Commonwealth 1646-60*, op cit, pp xxxii – xxxiii; SRO DPWStC 2/1/1.

CHAPTER 8

'BROYLES AND SHARP CONTENTIONS': 1649-59

As the year 1649 ended, the people of Wells still faced an uncertain future. The monarchy had been abolished, as had been the authority and jurisdictions of the bishop and of the dean and chapter. The new incumbent in the cathedral, Cornelius Burges had arrived and established himself in the deanery on Cathedral Green. In his wake came the parliamentary commissioners inquiring into the property and rental of the lands of the dean and chapter; it seemed inevitable that after their deliberations rents would rise. Troops were still quartered in the city and there was no sign that they would be removed.

The composition of the corporation was changing too. Some of the long-serving members either resigned or were removed by death and a small group of eight men who had consistently supported parliament during the civil war, began to dominate. This group consisted of Robert Morgan (died 1653), Stephen Haskett, Thomas Mead, William Whiting, Thomas Salmon (died 1658), Joseph Gallington, William Smith and William Baron. Hasket was able to return to the corporation and Whiting and Mead also joined. The aged survivor Bartholomew Cox took no further part in corporation affairs after 1650 and was succeeded as town clerk by John Standish, a supporter of the dominant group. The royalist William West, died in 1652. It is likely that he was expelled from the corporation after the second civil war in 1648 because in his will he does not refer to any of his colleagues on the corporation as his friends. Instead he chose as his executors James Clutterbuck, a friend of the ex-royalists Valentine Trym and Alexander Jett, and John Burges, the son of Cornelius Burges, the inveterate enemy of the corporation. The other notable royalist supporter, the haberdasher John Niblett, was forced to leave the corporation in January 1648/9 because he had been 'in arms against parliament.' This reference may refer to the civil war but it is more than likely that he may have become involved in the local unrest in 1648 due to the second civil war when the Scots unsuccessfully attempted by force of arms to coerce parliament and the army into making a settlement with the late king. [1]

'THOUGH THE CROWN SHOULD HANG ON A BUSH, I CHARGE YOU FORSAKE IT NOT'

The first danger that the newly constituted county regime of John Pyne had to confront in 1649 was the possibility of a royalist revolt. During the winter of 1649/50 royalist plotting began. The Commonwealth Council of State had in July 1649 vested the sole responsibility for collecting any evidence about clandestine royalist activity in the regicide Thomas Scot and according to the Wells MP Clement Walker, Scot's agents were 'swarming over England as lice and Frogs did in Egypt.' Initially few men in Somerset wished to get involved in the royalist plots but in April 1650, the royalist agent Alexander Keynes visited the West Country and persuaded some of the gentry to form a Western Association under the leadership of Lord Beauchamp the son of the now elderly Marquis of Hertford. The forming of the association was the catalyst for inflammatory talk in a Wells inn about an imminent royalist rising in early May 1650 by 'five men of lesser stamp.' Evidently these unnamed men denounced those who supported the Commonwealth as rogues and traitors, drank healths to their confusion and talked happily of cutting their throats. The news came to the Wells constable, David Barrett who promptly arrested them and sent them to Exeter gaol. Despite these ominous signs of the vigilance of the authorities, the Marquis of Hertford himself was soon able to rekindle some of the enthusiasm of July 1642 and persuaded Sir Charles Berkeley and Sir Edward Rodney to join the conspiracy. Rodney, a little later, sent his brother to the exiled Prince Charles at Breda in the Netherlands with details of the royalists' plans. However Pyne was quickly on the scent and in August arrested Rodney and imprisoned him in Taunton Castle. [2]

Meanwhile in June 1650 Prince Charles had arrived in Scotland and the Scots army entered the fray on his side. Cromwell hurried to Scotland and decisively defeated the Scots at the battle of Dunbar on 3 September 1650. The bells of St Cuthbert's rang to celebrate the victory; the churchwardens' accounts noted ' 5s to the ringers for the overthrow of the Scotts.' However the danger from Charles and the Scottish army would not be over until their defeat by Cromwell at the battle of Worcester on 3 September 1651. The victory at Dunbar emboldened Sir Edward Rodney to seek his release from prison. On 5 October 1650, the Council of State wrote to Colonel Desborough, the commander of its forces in the west, that it had received a 'desire from Sir Edward Rodney for his liberty and that if it will not be prejudicial to the peace of the country he is to release him on recognizances of £2000 with two sureties not to do anything prejudicial to the peace of the Commonwealth.' With the end of the immediate threat from the Scots, Rodney was released. He was not at liberty for long. In April 1651 one of the principal royalist agents was captured in London and in his interrogation revealed information concerning the Western Association. Lord Beauchamp was sent to the Tower of London and Rodney and another co-conspirator, Sir Edward Berkeley, were imprisoned in Taunton. Their case was reviewed by the Committee of Examinations in London which ordered Desborough and Pyne to give them bail. This was done on 3 June 1651, Rodney having to find a further £100 for himself and two sureties for £500 each. This last imprisonment marked the end of Rodney's involvement in local politics and at the age of 61 he was forced into retirement. To add to Sir Edward's sorrow his only son George, (his last surviving son of five) who had conducted negotiations for his father's release in London, died on his return home aged 21. Sir Edward was devastated. He wrote 'Many things have made me weary of the world ... if God had blessed my son with long life, I make no question but he would have recovered and kept it [the Rodney estate] up longer. But I conclude with Job. The Lord giveth and the Lord taketh away; blessed be the name of the Lord.' Sir Edward was not to see the king's restoration in 1660: he died in 1657. [3]

NATIONAL AND LOCAL GOVERNMENT 1649-59

The Long Parliament elected in late 1640 and purged in December 1648 continued to sit until the spring of 1653, increasingly at odds with the army. Wells had from December 1648 been served only by one MP, Lislebone Long. Clement Walker the other MP purged in 1648 had been re-arrested in October 1649 for his attack on the religious Independents in his 'History of Independency' and had been committed to the Tower of London on a charge of treason. He was never brought to trial and remained in the Tower dying there in October 1651. It is likely that he was not mourned by the political radicals who were ruling Wells at the time.

On 20 April 1653, Cromwell, now back in politics after his successful if bloody campaigns in Scotland and Ireland, finally put an end to the 1640 Long Parliament, known from 1648 as the Rump. The next seven years witnessed a series of constitutional experiments none of which lasted very long. The assembly which Cromwell and the army called next in 1653, a nominated assembly of only 140 members and known to history as the Barebone's Parliament, contained no representative from Wells and although it passed some useful reforms it was soon riven with disagreement and consented to its own dissolution in December 1653. Cromwell was then appointed Lord Protector on 16 December 1653 and the bells of St Cuthbert's were dutifully rung 'for the choice of the Lord Protector.' The Wells Corporation spent £1 on wine and cakes, 16d for pipes and tobacco and even engaged a trumpeter for 10s to celebrate the occasion. [5] A new national constitution based on a document drawn up by army officers called the Instrument of Government, was then inaugurated allowing Wells only one representative instead of the normal two and when a parliament was called for September 1654, the Wells burgesses again chose Lislebone Long. [6]

The small dominant group on the corporation led by Robert Morgan supported John Pyne who, until Cromwell became Lord Protector in December 1653, rewarded the most radical members of the corporation with minor roles in the government of the county. Although Pyne's authority in the county had seemed under threat when parliament abolished the county committee in early 1650, he was soon able to dominate the new sub committee for sequestrations, the commissioners for the county militia established in July 1650 and the tax assessment commissioners by filling them with his own nominees as he also did with the justice commission. Pyne's influence ended on Cromwell's elevation. The 'gallant' colonel felt that it was against his republican principles to serve a quasi-monarch.[7] During the period 1649-53, Robert Morgan served as a county JP and held other minor administrative offices such as treasurer for maimed soldiers in the east division of Somerset until his death in either late October or November 1653; Haskett served as tax commissioner for Somerset in 1649 and Mead did also in 1649 and 1650. [8]

These political events did not much affect the fabric of the ordinary citizens' lives but it is likely that the lack of stability in the national government did encourage the members of the ruling Wells elite to gain as many extra rights and as much extra property for the city and for themselves as they could before a more settled national political regime, possibly a reformed royalist one, were established which might want to return to the situation that had existed on the eve of the civil war in 1642.

For the citizens of Wells, harvests improved during the early 1650s bringing down the price of grain and trade flourished as civil order improved. The corporation's ownership of the fairs and the twice-weekly market brought it more income and enabled it to control access to the fairs and market more closely. On the negative side, taxes remained at a much higher level than before and the government survey of dean and chapter properties in 1649 brought the prospect of higher property prices when the freeholds were sold.

However, for the ruling radical elite of Wells, Pyne's declining influence after December 1653 meant that the leading Wells burgesses had to look elsewhere for a political patron to safeguard the interests of the city and its inhabitants. With Pyne's departure, more moderate men began to become JPs. Where else could the Wells radicals look but to the 'military overlord' of the southwest, John Desborough and his representative in Wells, Major John Jenkins? It is significant that the Wells Corporation Receiver's book lists among its expenses for the year 1652-3: 'Major Jenkins entertainment several times 23s 6,' and again in 1653-4: 25s 11d spent on 'wine and tobacco with Major Jenkins.' [9]

The military connection became more important in 1655. Unfortunately for Cromwell, the parliament of the Instrument of Government proved no less turbulent than the others he had had to deal with. When it attempted to amend the new constitution, he had no option but to dissolve it and on 22 January 1654/5 he duly did so. The spring of 1655 was again a time of tension with more royalist unrest. The revolt when it occurred started in Salisbury under John

Penruddock but was quickly quelled and the ringleaders executed. The Wells royalists did not become involved and the city was not affected. This uprising was one of the reasons for the next constitutional experiment – the military rule of the Major Generals established by Cromwell between August and October 1655. The constitutional experiment of the Major Generals was also designed to save money by reducing the size of the army and to pursue in a more determined fashion the reformation of manners because of the generally perceived moral degeneracy of the nation. The Major General in charge of the west was John Desborough, Cromwell's brother–in-law, and the status of Major John Jenkins, the commander of the troop of horse stationed in Wells, was further enhanced because of his close connections with Desborough.

Jenkins, a Welshman had, during the civil war, fought in the army of the Eastern Association, incorporated into the New Model Army in June 1645. He had been at the battle of Naseby on 14 June 1645 and had been a cavalry officer in the New Model Army that had entered Wells on 28 July 1645. In 1648 he had been with the regiment that had subdued the royalist insurrection in Wales and had been present at the battle of Preston which ended the second civil war in 1648. Jenkins was a Baptist with radical Leveller sympathies and refused to join the army that was gathering for the campaign against the Irish rebels in 1649. This show of defiance did not affect his career because he was well thought of by Desborough. Jenkins was certainly in Wells in August 1649 when he neglected to pay for 'meat' for his horse and some of his goods were distrained by the city constable. On 9 September 1650 Jenkins was appointed to command a troop of cavalry in Colonel Alexander Popham's regiment of horse to be stationed in Wells. Desborough in a letter to Cromwell dated 30 September 1650 gave Jenkins a valuable testimonial: 'Sir, Major Jenkins intending to waite on you, gave me this opertunity to troble you, truly he hath carried himself in all his bussines since I came to the regiment exceeding well; he ... hath much respect from all the well-affected gentlemen in the county.' Between 1649 and 1652 Jenkins, his cornet Samuel Bridger and another junior officer (possibly the Captain Smith buried in St Cuthbert's church in September 1650) became burgesses of the city and Bridger married Robert Morgan's daughter. [10]

Jenkins soon became a familiar figure in Wells and his troop integrated with the population, some of them marrying local girls. Although a Baptist, Jenkins marked his social position by purchasing a seat in the parish church where he worshipped with the dominant Presbyterian group on the corporation. In August 1656 when Cromwell decided to end the rule of the Major Generals and to call another parliament under the Instrument of Government, the corporation, in deference to Desborough's wishes, chose Jenkins to represent Wells, Lislebone Long taking one of the 11 county seats. The mayor, Stephen Haskett, had been required by the Lord Protector's warrant to elect a 'pious, sober, prudent person' to represent Wells. The indenture for Jenkins to represent Wells in the forthcoming parliament was made on 7 August 1656 and signed by Haskett, Gallington, Baron, Salmon, Smith and Mead, the men who controlled the Wells Corporation. Further local excitement was caused when it was learnt that the county election of eleven knights of the shire for Somerset was to be held at Wells on 'Wenseday 20 August ... between nyne and tenn of the clock in the foarnoon.' It is likely that some of the more prosperous burgesses were able to vote because under the terms of the Instrument of Government the vote was given to any man who was worth £200 either in real or personal property instead of just to holders of freehold land. Many poor freeholders therefore lost the vote and were replaced by townsmen of moderate wealth. The elections took place as designated 'in as fayer and peaceable manner as could bee desired or imagined' and lasted for six hours. The bags of votes were opened at mid-day and the new MPs were declared by the sheriff at 3 pm. Jenkins attended parliament and interestingly, in the spring of 1657, was in favour of Cromwell becoming king despite Desborough's opposition. Parliament adjourned in June 1657 and Jenkins returned to Wells. It briefly reconvened in January 1657/8 but was dissolved by Cromwell on 4 February 1657/8. Jenkins's political career was now at an end and he returned to his military duties once again. At the end of March 1658 he left Wells for the north east never to return, having been ordered to raise two companies of foot besides officers for the defence of Hartlepool in County Durham.

Oliver Cromwell died on 3 September 1658 and was succeeded by his son Richard as Lord Protector. He called a parliament in January 1658/1659 on the traditional pre-war franchise whereby Wells had two MPs. The Wells representatives chosen by the corporation and burgesses were the long-serving Lislebone Long and Thomas White the young city recorder. Long died on 16 March and although a writ for a replacement was issued, nobody was chosen for Wells before parliament was dissolved on 22 April 1659. Richard Cromwell resigned the protectorship in May 1659 and the Rump of the old Long Parliament of 1640 now consisting only of 43 members was restored. As both the MPs who had formerly sat in it were dead, Wells was not represented. [11]

'EVERY RAYLING SHIMEI'

As the Army was important politically, it was realistic of the corporation to cultivate its local representatives particularly as the dispute with Cornelius Burges over the bishop's rights and property continued uninterrupted throughout the 1650s.

Speculation about what plans Dr. Cornelius Burges might have for the bishop's and the dean and chapter's property was rife in Wells in the autumn of 1649. In the Flower de Luce inn on 23 November 1649, the assembled drinkers wondered if he would demolish the cathedral chapter house. Any fears they may have had about that eventuality were unfounded because on his arrival in Wells, Burges turned his attention to the bishop's palace and the deanery. Having no doubt looked over the palace, he decided to live in the deanery and to use material from the palace to refurbish the deanery to suit his domestic arrangements. Nathaniel Chyle, secretary to a later seventeenth century bishop considered Burges to have been a vandal and in his *History of Wells* written in 1680, the main contemporary source for Burges's structural changes, he denounced the alterations Burges had made. He alleged that Burges had stripped the lead from the roofs of the palace and removed timbers and other materials 'leaving only bare Walls, excepting the Gate Houses, which he tenanted out to some inferior people.' The palace then lay 'in Rubbish for some yeares.' On the ground floor of the deanery was a large hall. This was not to Burges's taste and by turning 'that noble Hall by making of a low roof, into Chambers, or rather Cabins, and by contracting these Rooms of State and making such dwindling alterations, spoild the whole house.' Chyle probably exaggerated the extent of the damage to the palace but it was considerable. When Bishop Piers was restored in 1660, he spent the enormous sum of £5000 on restoring the palace and his house at

Banwell. In contrast only £3000 was needed to be spent on refurbishing the cathedral. Burges evidently also built extra rooms in the deanery courtyard and 'one little thatcht house ... upon the north wall of the said deanery by the lane commonly called College Lane (now the North Liberty).' This house was demolished in 1683/4. The alterations to the deanery although unpopular with royalist contemporaries were 'solidly, if unhandsomely done' in the opinion of Dean Armitage Robinson writing in 1913 and Burges's changes remain largely unaltered at the time of writing. [12]

Once Burges was established in Wells, the corporation soon made it clear to him that his presence was unwelcome and did all it could to harass him and ostracise him socially. Although Burges claimed the right to collect the profits from the fairs, these were collected by the corporation. The corporation also took some of the profits from the manor of Wells which were Burges's by right, by seizing the animal pound in Southover, erecting further sheep pens, discharging Burges's hayward and appointing its own and collecting the profits from stray animals there. It also appropriated some chambers above the bishop's prison in the bishop's palace and raided the bishop's decoy pool at Westbury (sub Mendip) taking about a hundred wildfowl.

The social ostracism of the Doctor in the city proceeded apace. Burges reported: 'Then Belly-gods and every rayling Shimei gladly made it their business to run up and down to Gentlemens' Houses; yea anywhither, where any good chear was to be had, to make the Doctor odious by false reports ... Yea so far did some proud Wifelings of the faction proceed, that if any friend were but in a neighbourly manner familiar with the Doctor, or invited any of his to their Houses, they would take occasion to quarrel with them for entertaining their enemies: insomuch that scarce any person of quality durst to own the Doctor, or to come near his house, much more to own his cause. All which the Doctor bore, with what patience he could; knowing that nothing but nettles and Bryers can be expected of Dunghills.' [13]

'A VEXATIOUS, FRIVOLOUS AND CONTENTIOUS JAR'

While Burges was being harassed by his enemies on the corporation, the battle between him and them over the former bishop's rights and lands continued unabated. In October 1654, Burges, worried by thought of his own mortality (he was around 60 years old), tried a conciliatory approach and wrote directly to Thomas Salmon, of whom he seems to have had a good opinion, in an attempt to get the 1649 agreement between himself and the corporation sealed. Robert Morgan who had led the negotiations on behalf of the corporation had died in the previous year, and Burges thought he saw a chance of a settlement now that Morgan had left the scene. Surely Salmon would agree! Time was running out because as Burges put it: 'you [Salmon] and I be ancient men'. Burges was to be disappointed. The corporation's reply when it came contained no mollifying language. The dispute between Burges and the corporation had been 'causlesly started by him;' it was ' a vexatious, frivolous and contentious jar.' [14]

In June 1655 Burges then decided to petition the Committee for the Removal of Obstructions in London to resolve the issue. The corporation whilst outwardly cooperating with the new enquiry had no intention of agreeing to anything and when it seemed that the city recorder, Christopher Dodington, was near to an agreement with Burges involving major concessions by the corporation, the corporation dismissed him and appointed the young barrister Thomas White in his place. In December 1655, the corporation delivered the *coup de grace*. John Standish and David Barrett journeyed to London and on 22 December 1655 agreed with the Contractors for the Sale of Bishops' Lands to buy most of the disputed property i.e. the baileywicks of the city of Wells and the Hundred of Wells Forum, the former bishop's guildhall in the Market Place and his prison in the bishop's palace, the former bishop's borough rents and most importantly six canonical houses in the Liberty and one adjacent to the Market Place (all of which Burges claimed to have already bought) for the princely sum of £1,161. 5s. 7d.

Unfortunately for Burges, he had assumed when he made his first purchase in 1648 that he had bought these houses, even though they had not been specifically named in the contract of sale. The fact that he later offered to pay for them but in the end did not, suggests sharp practice on his part. Even more unfortunately he had sold the leases of three of them to his enemies. In June 1650 he had leased the canonical house in the Market Place (on the site of the present town hall) to Colonel John Dove of Salisbury for £120 through Dove's local agent, none other than John Casbeard. The house had then been subleased by Dove to John Standish the town clerk and to Robert Hole a member of the ruling Presbyterian group on the corporation. In July 1651 Burges had leased what had been Dr Walker's house in East Wells (on the site of the present 5-7 St Thomas St) to Robert Morgan and his stepson the woollen draper and innkeeper Humphrey Cordwent for £90. Finally he had leased (with right of entry) the precentor's house (now known as the Tower House and east of Vicars Close) to Cornet Samuel Bridger for £150. Both Cordwent and Bridger soon became suspicious of Burges's right of freehold title to these properties: Cordwent returned the house to Burges who repaid the purchase price of the lease but Burges refused to pay back Bridger who then lobbied the corporation to buy the freehold of the house possibly in the hope of extracting a better bargain from the corporation than he had got from Burges. He aimed to win back his payment to Burges by going to law. Once the corporation had bought the freehold of the houses from the Contractors on the 22 December 1655, it now had to gain possession of them from Burges. Legal action against him in the Court of Chancery ensued in the autumn of 1656. To facilitate the case, the corporation leased the three houses at issue to Thomas Mead who, assisted by John Standish as his counsel, was successful in his court action against Burges for trespass and illegal ejectment and succeeded on 30 June 1657 in gaining entry by evicting Burges from the three properties. Mead and Standish were handsomely rewarded by the corporation: Mead received property worth £200, £140 in cash as well as lavish expenses and Standish received £150. [15]

The corporation then set about turning the canonical house in the Market Place into 'a public room and house for reception of the country at the time of the assize and sessions.' This was a much-needed amenity. The town community had in 1572 built a town hall over part of the fish shambles in the middle of the High Street accessed by two flights of stairs on the eastern side. In 1599 the newly established corporation had moved its council office or exchequer from Priest Row, opposite the parish church of St Cuthbert, to rooms above the Ash and Well inn near the town hall on the north side of the High Street (now 28 High Street). It was here that an outer room was provided for the town clerk's office in 1605. It is likely that the new town hall proved to be unsuitable for corporation meetings possibly because of the odours rising from the fish shambles beneath and it is clear that by the 1630 some of the corporation meetings were taking place in the hall of the Bubwith Almshouse in Beggar St. It is also likely that some meetings were held in the exchequer with the town hall let to a member of the corporation. The January quarter sessions and the periodic assizes especially those of 1654 were probably held in the Almshouse Hall because the Corporation Receiver's accounts for 1654 when listing the gifts to the sheriff's butler and porter on that occasion, also mention the 15s spent on a cover for the table in the Almshouse Hall. The acquisition of the canonical house in the Market Place was therefore something to be welcomed because it provided a suitably spacious meeting place in the most prestigious part of the city. David Barrett, the corporation receiver, took charge of the restoration of the house. In the year 1657-8, he paid £46 5s 5d for repairs and in the following year the roof and floor were mended 'against the [quarter] sessions.' Barrett's supplementary account for 1659-60 shows that the walls of the house were re-limed, the roof again repaired and the stable partitioned to increase its capacity. Finally, for the comfort of the magistrates, 8d was paid to a workman for laying the 'Barkham Carpett' in the hall and for the better security of the prisoners, workmen were paid to 'mend the coope at [the] sessions.'

The corporation on acquiring the canonical house in East Wells which had been Dr Walker's, embarked on a modest programme of refurbishment: in the year 1657-8, it paid for repairs to the roof buying 200 lasts (laths), nails and pins to secure the tiles and paid the tilers 12s 11d. The hall window was also repaired and protected by four iron bars. Unfortunately for Cordwent, his influential stepfather was dead so he had to pay £111 to regain the lease and right of entry to the property from the corporation, £21 more than he had paid Burges. Bridger did not profit from the corporation's purchase either, he had to pay £150, the same amount as he had paid Burges. He was in no position to argue because he too had lost Morgan's influence and needed the house for his business interests having already converted part of it into a malt-house with 'some jerry-built additions' and installed a 'new-fashioned malt drying kiln.' To improve his finances, he soon sublet part of it to William Whiting the Croscombe clothier and corporation member between 1657 and 1660. However his financial position was soon to improve dramatically (see below). [16]

Of the four other properties bought by the corporation, two can be positively identified both being on the south side of modern St Andrew's street immediately to the east of the cathedral. The first was 'The Rib' where Dr Samuel Ward, archdeacon of Taunton had lived until his death in 1643, and which still stands. Between 1657 and 1660 Robert Hole, dispossessed of the canonical house in the Market Place, was able to lease the Rib from the corporation. The only repairs required here were to the windows. The other was a house that no longer exists which became known as the 'West Ruin.' Doctor Paul Godwin had lived here until 1645 but according to a report of 1689 it had been 'utterly ruined in the time of the late civill warres.' The state of decay referred to was probably not due to any military action but just to simple neglect. It was in good enough repair to be let to an unknown tenant by David Barrett the corporation receiver in 1657/8. Barrett records in his accounts that he paid 2s 11d for a new door lock for Doctor Godwin's house. The identities of the other two houses purchased by the corporation are unclear. The most likely candidates are: 'The East Ruin' which lay to the east of 'The Rib' but which no longer exists; a canonical house on the site of 6 and 7 Cathedral Green adjacent to Brown's Gate and the house on Cathedral Green which is now Wells Museum but no records of any property transactions survive at this date for these houses. It was in one of these houses that the archdeacon of Taunton, Dr Gerard Wood had lived until 1645. In the year 1657-8, the corporation repaired 'the leads at Dr Woods' and re-glazed some of the windows in the dining room there. Burges was also infuriated by the corporation's decision to sell the lease of the former bishop's guildhall in the Market Place and his prison with the rooms over it in the bishop's palace to the carpenter John Amor for £50. Burges described Amor as 'a young fellow of very mean condition ... newly set up [in] the trade of a carpenter, or mungrel-Joyner.' Amor having promised Burges not to make the purchase, had then gone back on his word and added to Burges's sense of victimisation in that 'he did affront the Doctor [Burges] both in words and deeds.' [17]

Burges had thus been outmanoeuvred by the corporation and incurred considerable damages from the civil lawsuits brought by his enemies. He was forced in 1657 to pay Mead £80, and Bridger £700 for refusing to pay back the purchase money on the Tower House. Burges reactivated the dispute in 1658 but with no success and an appeal to Major General Desborough brought no further progress. Mediators appointed by Desborough met the opposing parties at the Crown Inn in the Market Place but the corporation refused to budge. A 'festive' meeting between Burges and the corporation at the Christopher Inn in the High St on 23 December 1658 resolved nothing and meetings of the arbitrators continued fruitlessly during the summer of 1659. Burges published a long vindication of his claims in a pamphlet in 1659 but the fall of the Protectorate in May 1659 signalled the death knell of Burges's hopes of success.

DISSENSION IN THE CATHEDRAL

Burges's woes were not confined to his unpopularity in the city and his disastrous legal affairs. His enemies even mounted a campaign against him inside the cathedral where he had felt his position secure. His appointment as the official preacher in the cathedral had been ratified by parliament in January 1652/3 but despite this, Burges soon ran into trouble. In early 1653 he reported that he was being subjected to 'annoyance and interruption' from the local Baptists (see below) led by David Barrett and Cornet Samuel Bridger who tormented him with their 'perpetual scorns, derisions and raylings.' On 30 May 1653, the Council of State granted David Barrett's petition on behalf of 'the congregated church in Wells' to have the chapter house allowed to them 'to meet in for the exercise of religion unless good cause be shown to the contrary by the magistrate of Wells within 14 days.' As 'the magistrate of Wells' was a leading member of the corporation there was no objection and Burges had to bow to the inevitable and the Baptists were accommodated in the chapter house. [18]

A small group of ex-royalists in the Liberty and the city, led by William Walrond, however rallied to Burges's support and with their households formed the core of his congregation in the cathedral. This did not endear them to the ruling group on the corporation, still locked in dispute with Burges over the ownership of the former bishop's rights and property. In March 1655, Burges with the support of the Walrond group, appointed Humphrey Marsh the sexton, as registrar of the cathedral. (Marsh had been appointed sacrist in 1624 and his appointment as sexton had been confirmed in 1649 by the county committee.) From the certificate signed at the time the most important members of Walrond's group who signed it were: his great nephew Humphrey Walrond; George Bampfield, Walrond's son-in-law, another royalist; Thomas Coward the former royalist officer and Roger Bourne of Gothelney, the brother of Jane Wykes, the widow of the former royalist recorder of Wells, Edward Wykes. The names of some ex-royalists were conspicuously absent from the petition such as Alexander Jett the former bishop's registrar, and Valentyne Trym (buried in St Cuthbert's in 1660), both of whom were intent on coming to terms with the Protector's regime. Jett and his son-in-law, Tristram Towse the younger, indeed probably worshipped in the parish church because in 1654 Jett's daughter Margaret, the wife of Towse, purchased a seat there for 5s for the life of Jett's wife. Also some of the new residents in the Liberty such as the Thomas Whites, father and son, Jett's other son-in-law the London merchant John Prickman and John Blinman, keeper of the House of Correction at Shepton Mallet kept their distance.[19]

The corporation's response to Burges's regime in the cathedral was not slow in coming. In the early autumn of 1655, a group of St Cuthbert's parishioners, led by the town clerk, John Standish and with the obvious connivance of the city corporation, raided the cathedral library and took away over 200 books. 226 books were placed in the vestry house of St Cuthbert's church with an unspecified number remaining with Standish. The St Cuthbert churchwardens' accounts show payments for 'a frame for ye table of the library' and flour to make paste to fasten the titles to the books. The aim may well have been to give the citizens of Wells a public lending library but the action of removing the books was undoubtedly another move by the corporation to escalate the conflict between it and Burges.[20]

In 1656 Burges fell foul of the Protector's Council and the Trustees for the Maintenance of Ministers because he was a pluralist – holding more than one living. Burges also quarrelled with his new registrar, Humphrey Marsh over repairs to the cathedral. The Wells Corporation decided to exploit this situation by attempting to take over the cathedral. It did not act as the corporation but used the stratagem of a general petition from the inhabitants of 'Wells and St Cuthbert's parish' to the Lord Protector Cromwell, although the leading members of the corporation and the town clerk John Standish were undoubtedly the authors of this petition. The petition was dated

July 1656 and cited familiar arguments: the parish was a large one comprising 5,000 souls (not the 10,000 of the 1646 petition); the parish church of St Cuthbert could not hold all the people, consequently many had to worship in the cathedral; there was 'much decay in the covering, windows and other parts [of the cathedral]' that 'if not repaired, will be ruined and many pious people are disposed to contribute to the repairs.' The petition ended with the words: 'we therefore beg your order to continue the cathedral to us.' The petition was discussed by the Protector's Council and on 17 July 1656 the Council ordered that the parishioners of St Cuthbert's 'be allowed the use of the said cathedral, they setting and keeping it in good repair.'

Burges could do little but obey the order and handed over the keys of the cathedral to the St Cuthbert's parishioners who then recruited Humphrey Marsh to their side and confirmed him as sexton. Burges however continued to preach in the cathedral and, perhaps emboldened in June 1657 by the renewal of his £200 yearly stipend for preaching in the cathedral twice on Sunday by the Trustees for the Maintenance of Ministers, moved again to assert his rights in the cathedral. According to a second petition from the parishioners of St Cuthbert's dated 23 March 1657/8, Burges had retaken possession of the cathedral and kept it locked, threatening those sent into repair it, 'and admits none save at his pleasure.' The consequence of this was that people refused to subscribe to the repair of the cathedral. The petitioners asked the Council to confirm the order of July 1656 and order Burges to deliver the keys of the cathedral to them and to permit them to enjoy it for public worship. This the Council did. It is clear that the cathedral fabric suffered at this time. There were many broken windows although some repairs had been done and so many draughts that Burges was forced to preach from a lectern and not the pulpit. Consequently most of his sermons, no doubt to the delight of his enemies, were rendered inaudible. Burges however soon counterattacked and in a petition denied most of the parishioners' complaints, blaming them for the poor state of the cathedral fabric. He was particularly annoyed by Humphrey Marsh's desertion calling him 'an old malignant' who 'of late usurped the place and took all the large fees, burial dues, and has appropriated the cloisters and churchyard and sundry goods of the church … he is an old extortioner and has made disturbance in the church for his own gain.'

Burges's petition was, in April 1658, backed by one from the Walrond group who claimed that they had had 'free use of St Andrew's church, that it has been as much open as before, and that he [Burges] has in his preaching disclaimed all private interest therein.' Jett and Trym with the others however remained silent: they continued to cultivate their own interests. For example on April 1659, the Protector's council wrote to amongst others, Trym and Jett ordering them 'diligently to examine' a bill of complaint over a property transaction posted by none other than John Casbeard 'much trusting in your fidelities and care since given you.' On 29 April 1658, the Protector's Council ordered Burges to deliver up the keys of the cathedral to the parishioners. This he did but remained as preacher in the cathedral with an increase of £80 in his salary; no doubt the Council's way of trying to placate both sides. This final judgement meant that Burges had lost control of the cathedral for the time being, Marsh resumed his post and Burges, shorn of power, was only allowed to preach on sufferance in the cathedral under the watchful eyes of Marsh and the leaders of the corporation. [21]

These public quarrels over property and rights between warring Presbyterians were unedifying. Burges could be seen by royalists as aping the former bishop's role while his Presbyterian opponents on the corporation gave ammunition to their radical religious opponents by benefiting financially from the corporation's property transactions. Unfortunately no comments from the citizens of Wells on the contest between the two parties have survived but it is likely that they were glad to see the back of Burges in 1661 and did not mourn the removal of the Presbyterian leaders of the corporation when they were purged in 1662.

NOTES

[1] Underdown, D, *Somerset in the Civil War and Interregnum,* Newton Abbot, 1973, pp 163-169; William West's will can be found at NA PROB 11/221; The full list of corporation members who served at some period between the death of Robert Morgan in October/November 1653 and September 1662 is as follows: William Andrews, William Atwell, Henry Baron, William Baron, David Barrett, Richard Casbeard, Humphrey Cordwent, John Davidge, Richard Fryer, Joseph Gallington, Stephen Haskett, Robert Hill, Robert Hole, James Hurman, Thomas Meade, Hugh Merefield, James Middleham, Thomas Nixon, Joseph Plummer, Samuel Read, Thomas Salmon, William Smith, Robert Thomas, Henry Webster, William Whiting. Their biographies can be found in Nott A, & Hasler, J, (eds), *Wells Convocation Acts Books, Part 2 1629-44; 1662-65,* SRS Taunton 2004, pp 937-1024.

2. The quotation at the head of the paragraph is taken from Underdown, D, *Somerset in the Civil War and Interregnum, op cit,* p 160; Underdown, D, *Royalist Conspiracy in England 1649-60,* Newhaven, 1960, pp 20-48.

3. *Wells St Cuthbert, Churchwardens' Accounts 1649-65,* SRO D/P/WStC 4/1/1/; Everett Green, M A E, (ed), *CSPD 1650,* HMSO London 1873, pp 338 & 371; Underdown, D., *Somerset in the Civil War and Interregnum,* op cit, pp 160-2; Everett Green, M A E, (ed), *CSPD 1651,* HMSO 1877, pp 169, 174 & 234; Sir Edward Rodney's comment is taken from his account of his family S.R.O., DD/TB Box 20/1.

4. DNB *Clement Walker,* Underdown, D, 2004.

5. *Wells St Cuthbert, Churchwardens' Accounts 1649-65, op cit;* WTH *Receiver's Book,1652-65,* fo. 3.

6. DNB *Lislebone Long,* Wroughton, J, 2004.

7. Underdown, D, *Somerset in the Civil War and Interregnum,* op cit, pp 163-170 & 173-4.

8. Nott & Hasler, *Wells Convocation Act Books 1589-1665: Part 2 1629-44; 1662-65,* SRS 91, op cit, pp 974, 991, 993-4.

9. Underdown, D, *Somerset in the Civil War and Interregnum,* op cit, p 176; WTH *Wells Corporation Receiver's Book 1652-65,* fo 5v.

10. Nott & Hasler, SRS Vol 91, op cit, p 981; Firth C, & Davies G, *A Regimental History of Cromwell's Army Vol 1,* Oxford 1940, pp 200-209. For Bridger see Underdown, D, *A Case Concerning Bishops' Lands: Cornelius Burges and the Corporation of Wells,* EHR 1963, p 32; the three officers must have become burgesses between Jenkins's appointment in September 1650 and the commencement of the Wells Corporation Receiver's Book at the end of September 1652.

11. For the voting franchise see Underdown, D, *Somerset in the Civil War and Interregnum,* op cit, p 176; some examples of soldiers marrying local girls can be found in *Wells St Cuthbert Parish Register 1609-1665,* SRO D/P/WStC 2/1/1, e.g. 5 October 1650 Thomas Harperly of Stockton, Durham a soldier in Capt. Jenkins's troop married Alice Crane, widow; 2 January 1651/2 Robert Curse a trumpeter of Major Jenkins's troop married Dorothey Salmon; 26 June 1652 David Mercer a soldier of Major Jenkins's troop married Dorothey Hole; 21 April 1657 Samuel Robinson a soldier in Major Jenkins's troop married Ursula Nurton; Cockburn, J S, (ed), *Somerset Assize orders 1640-1659,* SRS Vol. 71, Taunton, 1971, nos. 185 & 186 pp 74-75.

12. Bates Harbin, E H, (ed), *Quarter Sessions Records of the County of Somerset Vol. III: Commonwealth 1646-60,* SRS Vol. 28, Taunton 1912, pp xxxii/iii; for the Bishop's Palace see Dunning, R W, *The Bishop's Palace,* in Colchester, L S, (ed), *Wells Cathedral: A History,* Wells 1982, p 241; Underdown, D, *A Case Concerning Bishops' Lands,* op cit, p 29; Bailey, D S, *Canonical Houses of Wells,* Gloucester 1982, pp 107-109; for Chyle's comments see Reynolds, E H, (ed), *Wells Cathedral: its Foundation, Constitutional History and Statutes,* 1881, pp lii & lvii.

13. Underdown, D, *A Case Concerning Bishops' Lands,* op cit, p 26, 29-32; Burges, C, *A case concerning the Buying of Bishops Lands with the Lawfulness thereof and*

'BROYLES AND SHARP CONTENTIONS'

the Difference between the Contractors for sale of those lands and the Corporation of Wells, London 1659 BL 108. g.33, p 61; Burges's reference to Shimei comes from *2 Samuel, Ch. 16:* Shimei met King David when he was fleeing from his son Absalom who had usurped the throne. Shimei cursed David and threw stones at him. David forgave Shimei when he was restored to the throne after Absalom's death, but David's successor Solomon put Shimei to death.

[14] Burges, C, *A case concerning the Buying of Bishops Lands*, op cit, pp 63-64.
[15] Underdown, D, *A Case Concerning Bishops' Lands*, op cit, pp 37-39.
[16] Underdown, D, *A Case Concerning Bishops' Lands*, op cit, pp 40-41; Bailey, D S, *The Canonical Houses of Wells op cit*, pp 131-2, 151, 161; WTH *Wells Corporation Receiver's Book,1652-81,* fos. 19-30 passim.
[17] Underdown, D, *A Case* Concerning *Bishops' Lands*, pp 38-39; Bailey, D S, *The Canonical Houses of Wells,* op cit, pp 113-4, 131, 137-147, 151, 161; Burges, C, *A case concerning the Buying of Bishops Lands,*op cit, pp 71-2; the details of the repairs to the houses can be found in WTH *Wells Corporation Receiver's Book 1652-81,* fos 19-30 passim. The bishop's prison was a freestanding building standing on the south side of the Horse Pool, a stream which now runs underground between the bishop's moat and the south cathedral cloister, Scrase A & Dunning R *The Bishop's Palace, Wells* , SDNQ Vol xxxv, Part 354, Sept 2001.
[18] Everett Green, CSPD 1652-3, op cit, p 360.
[19] Underdown, D, *A Case Concerning Bishops' Lands,*op cit, p 34; *Wells St Cuthbert Churchwardens' Accounts 1649-65,* SRO D/P/WStC 4/1/1; Bailey, D S, *Wells Manor of Canon Grange,* Bailey, Gloucester, 1985, pp 186-9.
[20] *Wells St Cuthbert Churchwardens' Accounts 1649-65,* op cit, *Wells Cathedral Library,* Wells Cathedral Publications, 2006, p 4.
[21] Underdown, D, *A Case Concerning Bishops' Lands,* op cit, pp 34-36; NA C/437/62.

CHAPTER 9

SOCIETY AND RELIGION: 1649-59

SOCIETY AND THE CHURCH

The hard-headed local politicians who resisted Cornelius Burges so successfully also kept a tight hold on local society through the punishments meted out by the petty sessions court which now, with the closure of the church courts, dealt with all moral offences. Their control of the parish church, attended by most of the population, gave them an oversight of the religious teaching there and control over the disbursement of poor law funds. Social control over young people was also increased by the threat of removal to either the West Indies or Virginia by the indentured servants system operated through the port of Bristol.

Moral reformation of society was a theme running through the 1650s. One of the main reasons why Cromwell suspended parliament and initiated military rule in the form of the major generals in 1655 was to accelerate the campaign for moral regeneration. There is however no evidence to suggest that the Wells Corporation embarked on any similar crusade. Although parliament had passed an act in 1650 stipulating the death penalty for adultery, this was ignored in Wells as in most other towns. Instead, in moral offences, the traditional punishments were applied. Adultery was punished by either a period in the stocks in the Market Place (newly repaired in 1654-5 for 4s 10d), by whipping or, for persistent offenders, by incarceration in the House of Correction at Shepton Mallet. The Wells beadle was paid 4d for 'whipping Derek's daughter' and 3s for carrying Duke's daughter to the House of Correction and bringing back Duke's daughter's child. The corporation receiver also paid 12d for the loan of a horse to draw the cart for the whipping of Mary Lay in 1655-6.

Moral pressure was also exerted through the parish church. The leading members of the corporation were now able to scrutinise the running of the parish church more closely than during the pre-war period. The dean and chapter who had been responsible for appointing the vicar no longer existed and the new Presbyterian system of church government placed power firmly in the hands of the three elders all of whom were members of the corporation. Thus the annual churchwardens' accounts were regularly signed by the mayor and the leading Presbyterian members of the corporation. Parochial life however continued much as before at St Cuthbert's church. Although attendance at church was no longer compulsory, evidence from the parish registers shows that the majority of the population still attended. Wells citizens were baptised, married and buried there; the registers were kept, the tithes and the poor rate collected and the bells rung for the dead, on the 5 November and on days of thanksgiving. The church fabric was maintained: the interior of the church was white limed, old lead was taken from the roof and replaced with new, windows were re-glazed and a settle provided before the 1636 pulpit possibly for the exhausted preacher. In November 1656, the vestry house in Priest Row as we have seen, was turned into a library to receive 226 books from the cathedral library. The aim of the library was to provide the literate members of the Wells public with educational reading matter.

Ministers came and went. William Thomas returned to Ubley in 1648 and was replaced by John Chetwynd a young 25-year-old Oxford graduate from Exeter College who had been a vicar for only one year at Stanton Drew. Chetwynd was the son of Edward Chetwynd formerly dean of Bristol Cathedral. From his later career it can be deduced that Chetwynd was a moderate who after the Restoration adapted himself to the new order. Samuel Oliver, minister since 1646, died aged around 50 in 1652 and was replaced by Henry Stubbes, a Gloucestershire man. Born probably in 1605, he was a man of varied experience. Oxford educated, he had been rector of Partney in Lincolnshire but because of his Puritan opinions – he was alleged to have been anabaptistically inclined – had been forced into exile in Ireland. After the victory of parliament, he returned and was appointed minister at St Phillips, Bristol, and at Chew Magna. In 1654 he was appointed by parliament to the committee responsible for ejecting 'ignorant and scandalous ministers.' Stubbes was an effective minister. He was remembered by those favourable to him as a man of calm temper, a 'grave divine [and a] plain, moving and fervent preacher.' He set a good example and was noted for his humility which was apparent in his dress, discourse and preaching. Most importantly he was strongly in favour of a programme of moral regeneration of the young and spent time catechising and instructing young people. During his ministry the church seems to have been quite generous in helping indigent people travelling through the city. In 1654 for example, an Irishman and his wife and children were given 5s, a seafaring man 9s, a minister's wife and children en route for Ireland 1s, a minister's wife recommended to Mr Stubbes by the minister in Bath 5s, an aged man from Germany and his wife, 2s 6d and a poor man who had been a slave under the Turks, 1s.[1]

INDENTURED SERVANTS

The future however was somewhat bleak for those young people living in the city who had been orphaned, who had failed to find a master or who were troublesome. The corporation's attitude to them was less benevolent than the church's attitude to outsiders. They could now be sent to the colonies. Besides opening up new opportunities for the city to acquire more rights and privileges, the 1650s had also given Wells merchants and artisans increased economic opportunities. The development of new colonies, especially Barbados and Virginia served from the port of Bristol, provided the popular imports of sugar and tobacco and export opportunities for local traders and artisans because the colonists were eager to buy the consumer goods which they were unable to manufacture for themselves. A contemporary wrote of Bristol that 'all men that are dealers in shop trades, launch into adventures by sea ... a poor shopkeeper that sells candles will have a bale of stockings, or piece of stuff for Nevis or Virginia.' The indications are that some Wells merchants and artisans did send goods to the new colonies. James Clutterbuck had a son and brother in Barbados and it is highly likely that the Wells Corporation used existing trading links to get rid of unwanted young people.. The *Bristol Registers of Servants Sent to Foreign Plantations: 1654-86*' besides giving the names of the indentured servants shipped to the colonies from Bristol, gave the names of the people to whom they were bound. Amongst the latter was a local man Richard Stacie of Wells, merchant. Stacie was an important local property owner having 13 urban properties in the city and some rural land as well as leasing one tenement from the corporation. He obviously had trading connections with Virginia because he contracted with the corporation to send two young people, Mary and Thomas Weiting there as indentured servants in 1659: Mary for five years and Thomas for eight. Two other local men with connections in Virginia are mentioned as involved in the indentured trade, Matthew Bendle of Wells and Thomas Hardwich of Westbury(sub Mendip) whose son Joseph emigrated to Virginia and established himself as a plantation owner. The other people involved were all from Bristol and were obviously well known to Wells traders. The most important of these were Robert Yeamans of Redland Court, knighted after the Restoration, who had extensive interests in the colonial trades, Robert Culme, a merchant with interests in Barbados and John Tailor and Stephen Walot both merchants with West Indian connections. It is clear that the leading members of the Wells community also had connections with the mariners who plied the Barbados and Virginia trades and these contacts were used. On 11 August 1656 Susan Thwaites of Wells was bound to the Bristol mariner Thomas Pearse for three years and carried by him to Barbados; and in 1659 Elizabeth Councell of Wells was bound to John Lane, mariner for four years bound for Virginia.

The arrangements for the sending of 22 young able bodied young people (13 women and nine men between 1656-60) from Wells to the colonies, were made by the corporation through these economic contacts. It seems that the young people had little choice in the matter and the colonial indenture system was the corporation's rather heartless way of solving a social problem. Sending these young people to the new colonies meant also that they would not become a charge on the poor rate. They were given free ocean passage and food, clothing and shelter during their period of service which could be anything from three to eight years and if they survived to return, a freedom bonus of £12. Sadly families could be split: of the three House sisters sent abroad, Elizabeth and Hester were sent to Barbados to the same master while their sister Mary went to Virginia. What happened to these young people in their new 'homes' in not known but they would have been totally under the authority of their new masters who had the right to whip them for any misdemeanours. In Barbados one extreme method of punishment was to string up offending servants by their hands and light matches between their fingers: it is to be hoped that none of the young people suffered that punishment. Life for the indentured servants was hard. If they endured the lengthy sea voyage they had to survive the tropical diseases and hard living conditions on the plantations. [2]

'READING, WRITING AND CASTING ACCOUNTS'

There was a somewhat more altruistic social concern in the founding of the charity school, later known as the Blue School, by Margaret Barkham in 1654. She was the widow of Ezekiel Barkham (died 1641) who had been appointed receiver general to Bishop Lake in 1621. In his will of 22 September 1641, Barkham had ordered that £800 from the proceeds of some land sales should be invested to provide income to finance a charity school. His widow Margaret did not act on his instructions until 1654 when, with the help of Thomas Coward and others, she used the money to set up a trust to buy land to provide a yearly income of £20 for the payment of 'an honest and religious schoolmaster conformable to the Church of England' who was to teach the boys a severely practical curriculum: to read, write and 'cast accounts'. The rest of the money from the endowment was to be spent in binding boys as apprentices to some trade with the proviso that the boys of New Street, Wells (where the Barkhams no doubt had lived), should be chosen as recipients of this charity before others. The school opened in the chapel of the Bubwith Almshouse and the teacher appointed was Francis Standish, former vicar choral of the cathedral and master of the almshouse. [3]

Times were hard for the one long established school in the city – the Cathedral 'Free Grammar School' in the room above the west cloister of the cathedral. The curriculum for the boys drawn from the city and the old diocese, who had to be respectable with 'appropriate clothes and manners', was different from that of the new school founded by Margaret Barkham in that as well as being taught reading and writing the boys were taught grammar (Latin). It is difficult to measure the effectiveness of the school. Archbishop Laud's visitation of 1634 had produced a response from the dean and chapter that showed that the supervision of the choristers at the school had been rather lax. John Oker the organist and Robert Aishe, one of the cathedral prebendaries who was the schoolmaster, were in charge of 'catechising and instructing' the six choristers. Evidently these six boys according to the report were 'not soe well ordered by the said Mr Oker as they ought to be.' Aishe, an Oxford MA, was paid £10 a year and for 'ought we [the dean and chapter] know is diligent in attending his place and performing his duty' of teaching the other boys (number unknown).

Robert Aishe was a Wells man, the son of John Aishe a chandler and former mayor of the city who had died in 1610. Although a supporter of the Puritan John Hole in 1607, John Aishe's desire for gentility and advancement for his children outweighed his faith when he arranged the marriage of his daughter Mary to the much older Catholic and genteel William Evans, the master of the Grammar School from 1592-1622, enabling his son Robert Aishe to succeed to this post on Evans's retirement in 1622. After the dean and chapter left in 1645, there was no music in the cathedral and the choir was disbanded but the elderly Aishe continued to preside over the school, being paid from the rents and profits of the manor of Congresbury by the Treasurers for the Lands of Deans and Chapters in London. By November 1655 it was clear that he was unable to fulfil his duties adequately if at all. His health had deteriorated and he made his will being 'weake of body but of perfect minde and memory.' Cornelius Burges later reported in 1658 that Aishe had been bedridden in his last years. It seems likely however that the members of the corporation were favourable to the school's continuing existence. Aishe had maintained links with the corporation through James Middleham, a corporation member who was his tenant in the house Aishe owned in Sadler Street, Wells and who provided Aishe with his meals – 'with whom I now table' as Aishe put it in his will. Aishe's other link with the corporation was through his good friend Thomas White of the Liberty, who was the executor of his will and whose son of the same name was recorder of Wells from 1656-1662. Aishe died in early 1657 aged around 70 and his will was proved in February 1657/8. The new master (appointed possibly by the same trustees) was no improvement: Burges again reported on 10 November 1657: 'that Mr Ash, the schoolmaster in Wells, is dead and one Sampson succeeded, that hath spoiled the Schoole, and is not approved.' He reported again on 4 February 1657/8 that the present schoolmaster Sampson was 'very unable [and] cannot give account of his grammer.' The school was not to receive a suitable schoolmaster until Charles Thirlby became master in 1663. [4]

'VERY AGED AND IMPOTENT AND LIKE TO PERISH'

Besides the young, the corporation was very concerned with provision for the elderly. The confiscation of the property of the dean and chapter in 1649, some of which provided the endowment income for the Bubwith almshouse, was very worrying to Francis Standish, the master of the almshouse. Three drafts of petitions to the central government from this almshouse survive from this time and although they no doubt exaggerate the plight of the residents 'who are very aged and impotent ... in great misery and like to perish,' they do encapsulate the worries Standish almost certainly had at the time. The Wells almshouses of Bubwith,(24 places), Still (six places), Brick (four places) were all on the same site adjacent to St Cuthbert's church but had different endowments. The Llewellyn almshouse in nearby Priest Row contained at this time six places. This last almshouse had always been under corporation control and during the 1650s the corporation in the absence of its erstwhile partner, the dean and chapter, assumed full responsibility for the Bubwith and Still almshouses. Income from the section of the almshouse founded by the will of Bishop Still (1608) came in regularly during the Interregnum and the Brick payments probably also, but income from the Bubwith endowed properties was continually in arrears despite orders from the Standing Committee of the County to the Wells sequestrator that it should be paid. An example of the difficulties which arose was the case of Sir Thomas Wroth of Petherton Park who had acquired the former dean and chapter manor of Newton Plecy in 1649-50. He should have paid a third of the rents from it to the Bubwith almshouse from the time of his purchase but he proved very difficult to deal with. He did not start regular payments until 1653 and never paid the arrears he owed from 1650. Wroth also demanded proper-signed receipts from Standish and if he did not receive them declared that he 'would pay the poor people no money at all.'

Francis Standish looked after his old people well. Basic food for the 30 residents of Bubwith and Still cost £52 per year and there were additional payments for oatmeal, salt, wood, coal, milk porridge rather than pease porridge on Tuesdays and Fridays, and extra meat at the main church festivals. The corporation paid for minor repairs to the almshouse structure and the stewards of the Still foundation paid for new gowns for all thirty residents. The corporation also gave some financial help towards the food. In 1655/6 it also gave the almshouse residents 10s 'which was accustomed to be given at the Renters' feast but was not now because there was no feast,' and in 1658-9 paid for extra meat for the residents. Standish worked hard to maintain the status quo and declared 'I look for nothing but as my Predecessors had before me and I hope it will not be denied me more than it was considering the time is poorer with me than it was for them.' [5]

'PROUD WIFELINGS'

Cornelius Burges's description of the wives of the leading burgesses (in the sub-title to this section,) leads to a discussion of the position of women in seventeenth century Wells society. Women so far have been marginal to this study, making occasional appearances mostly in a sensational way such as Ann Morgan and Ursula Nurton. The revolutionary years of 1642-1660 did little to enhance the status of women. Society remained patriarchal: 'the belief that God had ordained this rule of male over female was fundamental to social organisation.' In an age of high infant mortality the married woman's main role was to produce and rear children. No reliable contraceptives were known and 'folk remedies' were ineffective. Consequently women continued to bear children about every two years from marriage to menopause. Those who were sexually active outside marriage were punished more severely than men. There were however many spirited women in Wells who did not suffer impudent or rude men: Elizabeth Whiting beat Richard Atwell and called him an 'old toade' while Katherine Jones and her servant Marie Perry thrust John Horler into a boiling furnace 'by which his arme [was] scolded from the hand unto the shoulder.'

Women still remained barred from voting and consequently were unable to participate in government; they forfeited all property to their husbands on marriage and as this study has shown by inference, their educational opportunities were inferior to those of men. However they could exert some political influence in local politics. The 'proud wifelings' whom Burges so loathed were the wives of members of the corporation. These women had an important social position in the city: they were invited to the main civic banquet on 29 September each year and had special pews assigned them in St Cuthbert's church and the cathedral. As Burges's comment shows they also supported their husbands unofficially by attacking their enemies with gossip and innuendo. Women could also exert social pressure as in the case of the prostitute Ann Morgan. She was denounced by her respectable female neighbours who successfully pressurised the corporation into punishing her publicly.

Women also played an important economic role by working in the markets and fairs as hucksters and in the inns. They also controlled the extended households of the period having an important role in supervising servants and apprentices. In addition to their responsibilities in child rearing and running the household, women spun wool, bought goods for resale, made clothes and often produced butter and cheese which they sold at the market or made beer in their houses which they often sold illegally as tipplers. In 1647, Florence Millard the widow of William Millard who had kept the Ash and the Well inn in the High Street, was referred to as an illegal tippler and another widow Elizabeth Alford in April 1649 was described as a common drunkard who kept a disorderly house for soldiers. In January 1642/3 Grace Thomas was also accused of the same offence 'that she doth harbour and keepe men apprentices in her house all night.' Grace had her licence to sell ale taken away. Some women, such as the wife of Henry Jones (see above), seem to have been outside their husband's control.

The corporation property records also indicate that by the mid seventeenth century there were increasing numbers of women who were heads of households. Changing social conventions lessened the pressure on widows to re-marry and it became more socially acceptable for widows to be heads of single households. Few women's wills have survived but the 1655 will of Sarah Tabor the elderly widow of Mark Tabor, the former registrar of the archdeaconry of Wells, shows that Sarah although very ill, was a woman of spirit, very clear headed and eminently practical in the way she demised her property and possessions. She showed a complete command of detail especially where her house in the New Works in the Market Place was concerned, 'all other things affixed to the freehold leaden cisterns and conditt pipes as well underground as above ground' also mentioning such fittings as 'wainscott and glasse doores.' She needed no man to advise her and certainly not her son-in-law Francis Keene. They had been in obvious disagreement about a business matter and Sarah attempted in her will to force her son-in-law to do her bidding. She left him £60 (the exact sum he owed her) on the condition 'that he shall settle his son Walter Keene [with] his [the elder Keene's] life [interest] in the farm at Shipham which I hope accordingly.' She made her daughter Jane her executrix and appointed her two friends Alexander Jett and Nicholas Niblett as overseers of her will to make sure that the clauses in it were carried out. Her son-in-law was not included in the group of overseers. Most men on the other hand, still held the opinion that their wives were not really fit to handle matters on their own. One such was William Morgan, the brother of Robert, who wrote in his 1654 will that he desired his friends 'to advise my said lovinge wife in the performance of this my will.' From the evidence of wills however because of the inferior legal position of women, most men expected their wives to remarry and made provision accordingly. Wealthy widows were snapped up by ambitious men: in 1639 Robert Morgan quickly married Frances Cordwent, the executrix of her husband Humphrey's will after his death in 1638, to gain control of the leases of the inns her deceased husband had left her. However it was becoming increasingly the case that where women continued alone, they usually did not hold leaseholds in their own right but only as assignees. This situation had arisen because of the worsening legal position of women in the property market. Most of the property in Wells was owned by the corporation, the church or wealthy individual landowners so individuals leased property from them and the type of lease granted by these property owners was changing. Joint leases to husbands and wives or to women alone were in decline and were being replaced by leases of three lives granted solely to the husband with the wife being only one of the lives.

For those women who were unmarried and were not part of a household with a master, the future could be bleak. The prospect of indentured servitude in the new colonies was an ever-present threat.

It was only in some of the newly gathered churches that women were able to play an equal role with men being often allowed to debate, vote and preach within their congregations but it was only the Quakers who allowed women complete equality at meetings, half of the members of the sect being women. [6]

As 1659 drew to a close, the time was rapidly coming when the traditional ruling pattern of king and bishops and traditionally elected parliament would be restored; under these circumstances the general social position of women was unlikely to improve. Like Presbyterianism, the newly restored Anglican Church would afford no opportunities for women to participate in the running of religious affairs as the Baptists, Ranters and Quakers in the Wells area were beginning to do in the 1650s and it is to these last three groups that this study must now turn.

TOLERATION

There was after 1648 a small minority of people which forsook the Presbyterian system established in the parish church and set up its own independent churches. The army coup of December 1648 and the resultant purging of the leading Presbyterians in parliament had meant the end of the policy of religious uniformity and brought new opportunities for freedom of worship that could be exploited.

Although there had been since 1644 a movement by a minority group of Independent clergy in the Westminster Assembly to press for limited toleration for Congregational churches, this had been opposed by the Presbyterians who argued that religious unity encouraged the cohesiveness of the nation. In May 1648 the Presbyterian majority in parliament had passed 'An ordinance for the Punishing of Blasphemies and Heresies' the clauses of which threatened imprisonment for Baptists but this ordinance lapsed when the army took over in December 1648. The Independent clergy supported by Cromwell were now in the ascendant and demanded limited toleration for what was termed 'gathered congregations' such as the Baptists. A subsequent parliamentary act of 1650 repealed the penalties which had traditionally been imposed for not attending the established church and granted independent religious groups freedom to worship and disseminate their beliefs.

Those in Wells who benefited most from this new legislation were the Particular Baptists. They constituted a group that had broken away from the General Baptists believing that only an elect group could achieve salvation rather than that salvation should be open to all. A small group of Particular Baptists had grown up during the civil war in Wells and there were other small congregations in Wedmore, Axbridge and Cheddar. It is difficult to assess the number of Particular Baptists in Wells. Nationally it has been suggested that they made up only .025% of the national population but when considering their later behaviour in Wells, it would be reasonable to assume that the Particular Baptists in Wells had possibly 40/50 adherents.

The freedom of worship granted by parliament in 1650 meant that these small groups of Particular Baptists could now be organised into a coherent organisation. It was difficult to find a leader in Wells to achieve this because as has been noted, the radical members of the corporation were Presbyterians who had committed themselves to the new Presbyterian order at St Cuthbert's church. A new leader of sufficient local standing or notoriety would therefore have to come from outside the city. Fortunately for the Particular Baptists one was at hand, and he was Thomas Collier. [7]

'A MASTER SECTARIE'

Little is known of Collier's early life but it is fairly certain that he was born in Westbury (sub Mendip), four miles west of Wells. Although Westbury was one of the manors of the Bishop of Bath and Wells and the bishop appointed the vicar there, Purefoy Middleham, the vicar of Westbury from 1623 until 1661 was a Puritan who in 1648 became one of the Presbyterian ministers in the Wells Bruton classis. Middleham was closely connected with the Colliers who were Westbury husbandmen and churchwardens and it was almost certainly Middleham who educated Collier and influenced his radical religious views. During the civil war Collier left Westbury and became an itinerant preacher attached to the army of the Eastern Association a strongly Puritan organisation. During this time, Collier became a Baptist while still keeping a residue of Presbyterian beliefs such as predestination. He was in Yorkshire in June 1644 and was probably present to witness the parliamentary victory at Marston Moor serving with the Earl of Manchester's army. After the victory, he preached in York itself to a Baptist congregation in July 1644 and possibly took part in a baptism of converts in the River Ouse in the winter of 1644/5. His movements are then a little uncertain but it seems likely that he attached himself to the New Model Army of Fairfax and Cromwell and in June 1645 it is probable that he was at the battle of Langport with the army. He was certainly at Taunton in the early summer of that year where he helped to found a fledgling Baptist association. It is also likely that he visited Wells when the army occupied the city on July 28 1645. He then followed the army to Guernsey but was expelled by the officers for 'turbulent behaviour.' Briefly imprisoned in Portsmouth, he toured southern England and in 1646 made his way to London.

Collier was an able polemicist and in his first published work *In Certain Queries, or Points, now in Controvercy* showed that he had moved away from the views of his former vicar by attacking the Presbyterian ministers who were drafting the Directory of Worship and setting up the classis system as an alternative to episcopacy. He called upon parliament to 'dismiss that assembly of learned men [the Westminster Assembly] who are now called together for to consult about matters of religion' since he knew 'no rule in the Book of God for such an Assembly.' One of his Presbyterian enemies worried about his theology, eloquence and organising ability, called him ' a master sectarie, a man of great power among them, and hath Emissaries under him, whom he sends abroad.' From August 1647 he was chaplain to Colonel Twistleton's New Model Regiment of Horse and this enabled him to speak with 'both opportunity and freeness' at the army headquarters at Putney. In the autumn of 1647 he was present at an event of national importance – the Putney Debates and on 29 September in the old church at Putney in the presence of Cromwell, he preached a sermon entitled: *A Discovery of a New Creation* based on Isaiah 65, verse 17 'Behold I create new heavens , and a new earth.'

In this sermon Collier set out his beliefs. While he was sympathetic towards much of the Levellers' secular political programme then permeating the army such as manhood suffrage, the opening of enclosed lands, the abolition of the monarchy and the equality of men under the law, he added a spiritual dimension. He argued that the army's victory over the king and the general desire for reform came from God 'in a beam of radiance reflecting the new Jerusalem.' He saw the present time as 'the last time' when a new kingdom or new earth would be established by Jesus Christ who would come in the Spirit to renovate and renew men's minds by bringing about in them 'an internal and spiritual change.' The men who received the Spirit would then become Saints who were 'free indeed by Christ and government would be in their hands.' His idea of the 'Saints' owed much to the Presbyterian idea of the elect with which he had grown up. The characteristic of the new earth the Saints would create through the Spirit would be 'the execution of righteousness, justice and mercy without respect of persons ... to undo every yoke.' Spiritual and temporal oppression would be eradicated and the new earth would be without 'temporal oppressions in matters of conscience' such as 'tyrannical and oppressing laws, courts of justice and tithes.' The old church 'must be spiritually slain and a new one created.' Unity of purpose amongst the Saints would be brought about by the 'Spirit of light and truth.'

By 1648, Collier was back in Somerset and living in Wells. It was possibly there in the late autumn after Pride's Purge of Presbyterian members of parliament, that he drafted the Somerset petition for John Pyne already referred to. By 14 December 1648, he was back in London and speaking in the Whitehall debates opposing the civil state's right to interfere in religious matters. He later defended the execution of the king and again reiterated his basic doctrine that 'those who are saved spiritually know best what is good for the nation's temporal well-being.' By 1650 he had returned to Somerset preaching, teaching and provoking religious controversy throughout the area around Wells. His proselytising aroused the ire of religious conservatives. 'None but rogues would put down Common Prayer,' the conservative Cheddar constable fulminated. He added that he would like to see Collier hanged because he 'would not go to church.' On 6 March 1650/1 Collier was accused of blasphemy at Axbridge in a public disputation with two Presbyterians. He described the 'unchristian-like, and indeed inhuman-like reproaches and falsehoods' he had received from his opponents. He added that 'in the discourse they behaved themselves as scurrilous ... manifesting nothing but lightness, laughter and vanity, not meet to be seen in sober Christians at any time, much less in discoursing about the high things of God.' However there is no evidence of hostility by the Presbyterians in Wells to the Baptist group there. Although none of the leading men on the corporation joined it, its standing was increased by the presence of one corporation member David Barrett. Barrett joined the corporation after he gave up his post of county marshal probably in 1650 when he is mentioned as being constable of Wells. Barrett had strong links with the leading Presbyterians on the corporation and his energy, decisiveness and capacity for hard work came to play an important part in the fight against Cornelius Burges. The Baptists were also supported by Major John Jenkins and by his cornet, Samuel Bridger. [8]

Collier's highly motivated adherents needed to be guided and controlled. They were open to the influence of other developing minority sects such as the Ranters and the Quakers who were regarded with deep suspicion by both the local and national authorities. One hostile witness in Wiveliscombe in May 1652 described Collier's followers as 'furious disciples.' It was for this reason that Collier, under pressure from the Particular Baptists of London, led the movement to establish a Western Association of Particular Baptist congregations from the churches of Somerset, Wiltshire, Devon, Gloucester and Dorset which had its first meeting in Wells on 6 and 7 November 1653. The meeting solved the problem of authority by deciding the ordination procedure for Baptist ministers: 'that the imposition of hands with fasting and prayer on such as are called to office in the church or sent forth to preach the gospel to the world, is an ordinance of Christ.' A further meeting of the Baptist church was called for the Easter Monday and Tuesday of 1654. Collier's prominent position was recognised in that he was appointed by the meeting to publish its resolutions which he promptly did. These meetings almost certainly took place in the chapter house of Wells Cathedral. [9]

'THE OLD RANTERS, GARMENT AND ROBINS.'

In 1656, Thomas Collier in his published attack on the Quakers *A Looking-Glasse for the Quakers* wrote that two well known Ranters Joshua Garment and John Robins were associated with Wells [10] The Ranters who flourished between 1649 and 1654, were a small relatively uncoordinated group of men and women who believed that everyone had the Spirit within them and had no need of a risen Saviour to wash away their sins. They rejected outward forms of religion, rejected the Bible as the word of God and believed that all goods should be held in common. Consequently they were unrestrained in their behaviour. Godly men and women were scandalised by them and generally associated the Ranters with wife swapping, illicit sex, and public nudity. It did not help that alehouses were the common venue for Ranter activity. The Ranters are interesting because they provide a brief glimpse of the religious undercurrents in Wells society at this time of political and religious change.

Joshua Garment was a Wells man. The son of William Garment, he had been born in early June 1617 and baptised in St Cuthbert's church on 9 June 1617. Fortunately he left a record of his first major religious experience which occurred when he was 14 in 1631: 'as I lay waking upon my bed, the glory of the Lord shone about me, many Angels of light, in light came unto me, standing before me; the Angel that first appeared to me, spake these words unto me, *Fear not thou servant of the most high God, we are sent unto thee to protect thee from the power of the Devil*: then the Angel told me that there should be sudden and strange alterations in the world, as the taking away of Episcopacy and Kingly Monarchy; also that the things might not be spoken until I had a command from God to speak and declare the things.' Although the details about the demise of episcopacy and monarchy were probably added by Garment much later, his account is the only one we have of a religious experience by a local man during this period. On 5 October 1637, the 20 years old Garment married Dorothy Steevens possibly the daughter of a local innkeeper and was still in Wells in the early months of 1642 because he is recorded as taking the Protestation oath there. But at some time during 1642 or 1643, he enlisted in the parliamentary army and was a soldier for three years. Soon after his return to Wells at the end of the war, his wife Dorothy died and was buried in St Cuthbert's church on 21 September 1646. [11]

In 1647 Garment had his second vision in which an angel offered him bread that he ate. The angel then called him 'Josherbah' and told him 'the time draws near that the Jews, even the Hebrews must be gathered and delivered.' This emphasis on the deliverance of the Jews was a new development in Garment's thought and it is likely that by this time Garment had come under the influence of a certain John Robins who propagated such ideas. It is possible that Robins was in Wells at that time. Also it was in 1647 that Garment started to cohabit with a woman called Joan who later on became Robins's wife. Joan reported in 1651 that she had 'lived with Joshua Garment (by the Word of the Lord), as his wife three years.' By the late 1640s Garment was becoming well known amongst such former radical army chaplains as Hugh Peter and Robert Bacon suggesting that he was spending some time in London where Robins was active. Thomas Collier certainly knew of the Ranters' connection with Wells and probably witnessed their activities there. [12]

John Robins was most likely a Somerset man. He may have come from Wells because there was a Robins family in the city but his name does not appear in the church registers although Collier certainly connected him with Wells. This probably referred to the two possible visits made by Robins to Wells in 1647 and in 1650. In his younger days Robins was influenced by a Somerset minister John Traske who taught that Old Testament laws applied to Christians, that the dietary laws of the Jews should be kept and the Sabbath celebrated on Saturday. From the 1620s Traske had based himself in London but still preached occasionally in the west country. By the 1620s the Robins family was in London and in 1627 John Robins of London the father of the later Ranter, John Robins, left money to Traske in his will. Whatever John Robins's provenance, the important thing was that Robins had a tremendous effect on Garment who in 1650 had another striking vision: 'I saw the man called John Robins riding upon the wings of the wind in great glory; then the word of the Lord came unto me, saying, *this is thy Lord, Israels King, Judge and law giver...* Then the word of the Lord came unto me, saying ... This is he that shall ... divide the Seas, and lead the Hebrews to their own land ... Deliverance will be this year ... The manchild will be born this year, even he that shall come to rule with a rod of iron all nations ... The sea shall be divided, and many Jews that [are here] in England shall go thorow on dry foot towards Judea ... John Robins is the man ordained by the Creator of heaven and earth to lead the Hebrews.' By this time Joan 'Garment' had transferred her affections to Robins and by November 1650 she was pregnant with Robins's child.

Meanwhile in the summer of 1650, a couple of people from Wells were reported in late August 1650 to have had 'an immediate call from God to goe and preach the gospel in Galilee.' Robins was reported to have stated that his mission 'was to gather out of England and elsewhere, an Hundred and Forty Four Thousand men and Women, and lead them to Jerusalem to Mount Olivet, and there to make them happy: And that he would feed them with manna from heaven: And that he would divide the Red Sea, and that they should go through upon dry land.' The two people from Wells on hearing this evidently sold their property and with four likeminded people from Glastonbury believing that 'they were Jews, and that the time of their gathering together out of all Lands' especially England, was at hand, set off for London. Robins and Garment were also possibly in Wells in 1651 because it was reported in a newsletter that men claiming to be prophets were preaching in Wells and Glastonbury in 1651, one claiming that he 'and his fellow prophets 'would shortly 'walk over the River Thames' at high tide.' [13]

By 1651 the Ranters were becoming notorious and numerous sensational pamphlets were being printed in London purporting to describe in lurid detail their activities. Robins and Garment were back in London by May 1651 and on 24 May 1651 they were holding a meeting in Long-Alley, Moorfields in the early hours of the morning when they were arrested and brought before Thomas Hubbert, a Middlesex JP who committed them to the New Prison at Clerkenwell on a charge of blasphemy. With Robins and Garment was Joan Robins claiming that she had lived with the aforesaid John Robins these three quarters of a 'yeer as her flesh and bone' and said that she was now pregnant by Robins. She claimed that the child in her womb was the Lord Jesus Christ. Another Joan calling herself Joan Garment claimed that she had known Robins for a year and that he was 'her God Almighty.' Many London gentry and citizens went to the New Prison to look at and converse with these Ranters. They were fascinated by the their behaviour especially their clapping and 'hollowing and shrieking.' Joshua Garment was particularly described as 'clapping with his hands, and filliping with his fingers' (bending the last joint of a finger against the thumb and suddenly releasing it). It was in this prison on 5 June that Garment composed his testament *The Hebrews: Deliverance at hand*. which was published on 23 August 1651 by a London merchant who had formerly entertained him. How long Garment remained in prison is unclear. His case was actually raised in the House of Commons who referred it back to the Committee for Plundered Ministers. Robins was convicted of damnation and received a prison sentence. Two months after sentencing in 1652, he was released from prison after recanting his religious beliefs in a letter to Cromwell. He then stole the money which had been donated to his group, 'gave all his disciples about London the slip' and returned 'into his own Country', where it was claimed he repurchased his land and then promptly disappeared from history. Garment and his 'wife' Joan did return to Wells. In May 1654 they were living in the High Street in Wells and the St Cuthbert's parish register records the burial of their infant daughter Joan. By 1656 they had moved to Tucker Street on the south-western side of the city and two more of their children died there: a still born female child was buried on 1 June 1656 and on the 13th of the same month their son Philip was buried. Garment continued to live at Wells until at least 1660 but no more is known of him or his 'wife' after that date. [14]

THE QUAKERS

John Whiting, an eminent Quaker, who was responsible for bringing William Penn to Wells on 15 November 1695 wrote: 'In the year 1656, many people in the foresaid County of Somersett began to wayte on the Lord in silence of flesh, and denyed the worlds worship, teachers, paymt of tyths maintaining of Steeple Houses, (the which the world and their teachers call churches) ... and diverse were moved of the Lord to goe to the Steeple Houses and beare witness.' This Quaker movement which developed in Somerset from the mid 1650s in which women played a major part, was centred mainly in rural areas and small clothing towns: 62% of known adherents being agricultural labourers. Street and Shepton Mallet became the centres of Quaker activity in the Wells area. In 1668 when systematic records began, 17 meetings were held in Street, 14 in Shepton Mallet and 11 scattered between Banwell and Cheddar but none in Wells. Indeed as late as 1695 John Whiting wrote 'there is a prospect and opertunity presented that the blessed truth may be published in the City of Wells.' The reasons for the lack of success of the Quakers in Wells during this early period is no doubt due to the close eye the

Presbyterians kept on dissident sects and the open antagonism of Thomas Collier and the Baptists against the newly emerging religious group. The Quaker cause was not helped by the notoriety given it by the arrival of James Naylor and his entourage in the city in October 1656.

Naylor had served as a soldier in the New Model Army and developed a taste for preaching. In 1652 he had had a conversion experience and soon became a leading figure in the developing Quaker movement. He came to the West in the summer of 1656 but was arrested and imprisoned in Exeter gaol. Collier had published a direct attack on Naylor either before or when he came to the West and Naylor had replied in his pamphlet *Deceit brought to Daylight in answer to T. Collier what he hath declared in a Book called A Dialogue between a Minister and a Christian* so antagonism already existed between the two men which subsequent events were to intensify. Naylor was released from gaol on 20 October after one of his female followers had interceded with her employer, the wife of Major General Desborough, on his behalf and with a small band of followers journeyed to Taunton and reached Wells on 23 October en route for Bristol. His entry into Wells was sensational. The small procession was led by two of his female acolytes. Naylor, bearded and with long hair, followed riding on a horse preceded by a bare headed man. Collier who was in Wells at the time was appalled. He reported that Naylor's followers were 'singing before him sometimes *Hosanna in the Highest* and sometimes *holy, holy, holy, Lord God of Sabbath* throwing their garments under the Horses feet as they passed thorow, viz Hoods, Gloves, Hankerchiefs & refusing to receive them when offered them.' To Collier this imitation of Christ's entry into Jerusalem on Palm Sunday was sheer blasphemy. He was even more affronted that Divine Providence had chanced to 'bring him [Collier] to shame in the very place of my abode [Wells], when *at home* [author's italics]; whom he had so abused knowing in his own heart that what I had written was truth, he must come from London to discover himself in Wells. Secondly, in Wells was the seat of the old Ranters, Garment and Robins, who was proclaimed the great God, came to a shameful end: hither must this new sort of Ranters come to discover themselves. Thirdly, That what I asserted in my book ... that their principles were the same as the old Ranters, though in word they deny it, yet in act he [Naylor] must come and proclaim it.'

Naylor went on from Wells to Bristol where he made a similar triumphant entry. He met with a hostile reaction from the Presbyterian ministers there who interrogated him. He was then sent to London where he was indicted for 'horrid blasphemy' by parliament which resolved on 16 December 1656 that Naylor should be whipped through the London streets by the hangman, exposed in the pillory, have his tongue bored through with a red hot iron and have the letter B (for blasphemy) branded on his forehead. Naylor bore his hideous punishments stoically and 'embraced his executioner and behaved very handsomely and patiently.' After these draconian punishments the Quakers repudiated him and he was imprisoned in London until granted an amnesty in 1659. His health now ruined he died in 1660. Naylor's notoriety and punishment combined with the hostility of the local Presbyterians and Particular Baptists led by the polemical Collier who in 1657 published his *A Looking-Glasse for the Quakers Wherein They may behold themselves; and others also may behold their pernicious ways,* meant that it was too dangerous for Quakers to meet in Wells. The movement in Somerset would have to develop in other areas outside the city. [15]

NOTES

[1] WTH *Wells Corporation Receiver's Book 1652-1681,* folios 1-3; Matthews, A G (ed), *Calamy Revised,* Oxford 1934, pp 114 (Chetwynd) & 468-9 (Stubbes); *Wells St Cuthbert Churchwardens' Accounts* SRO D/PWStC 4/1/1.

[2] James Clutterbuck's will can be found at NA Probate 11/346; Coldham, P W, (ed), *The Bristol Registers of Servants Sent to Foreign Plantations, 1654-1686,* Baltimore, 1988, pp 25, 34, 39, 43, 75, 84, 105, 108-110, 115, 117, 125, 133, 135; Sacks, D H, *The Widening Gate: Bristol and the Atlantic Economy, 1450-1700,* London 1991, pp 282, 438; Dunn, R S, *Sugar and Slaves: The Rise of the Planter Class in the English West Indies,* North Carolina, 1972, pp 68-9, 72. WTH *Wells Corporation Receiver's Book 1652-1681,* folios 1-3: for Richard Stacie see Scrase, A J, & Hasler, J, (eds), *Wells Corporation Properties,* SRS Vol. 87, Taunton 2002, pp 23,143, 147, 172, & 207.

[3] For Ezekiel Barkham's will and early Blue School property transactions see SRO DD/WBS; Holmes, T S, *Wells & Glastonbury: A Historical and Topographical Account,* London 1903, pp 153-4; Hembry, P M, *The Bishops of Bath and Wells, 1540-1640: Social and Economic Problems,* London 1967, pp 195-6, 216, 219, 234, 244, 247; Barnes, A D, *The Church & Education in Wells Somerset from the Eve of the Reformation until 1891;* M Phil. Thesis, University of Manchester, 1990, Vol. I p 43.

[4] For John Aishe see Nott, A & Hasler, J, (eds), *Wells Convocation Acts Books 1589-1644 & 1662-65,* SRS 91, Taunton 2004, p 938; Robert Aishe's will is at

NA Prob/11/273; Colchester, L S, *Wells Cathedral School: The First Thousand Years c 909-1964*, Wells 1985 pp 30-31.

5 I am indebted to Jean Imray for information regarding the almshouse during the Interregnum.

6 Hutton, R, *The British Republic 1649-1660*, 2nd ed, London 2000, pp 43-4; Nott, A & Hasler, J, (eds), *Wells Convocation Acts Books 1589-1665: Part1: 1589-1629*, SRS 90, Taunton, 2004, pp 33-35; Humphrey Cordwent's will is at NA Prob. 11/177; Sarah Tabor's will is at NA Prob. 11/252; William Morgan's will is at NA Prob. 11/236; for a general discussion of the effect of the civil war and the years following on the position of women in society see Crawford, P, *The Challenges to Patriarchalism: How did the Revolution affect Women?* in Morrill, J, (ed) *Revolution and Restoration: England in the 1650s*, pp 112-128; for a discussion of women in the property market in early modern Wells see Scrase, A J, *Wells: The Anatomy of a Medieval and Early Modern Property Market, working Paper 30*, Faculty of the Built Environment, University of the West of England, Bristol, 1993, pp 164-179; the examples of women in Wells are taken from WTH *Wells Corporation Sessions Book 1625-50*, fos. 46v, 74v, 86, 104, 104v & 129v.

7 Coffey, J, *The Toleration Controversy during the English Revolution,*, in Durston C, & Maltby J, (eds), *Religion in Revolutionary England*, (eds), Manchester 2006, pp 45-52; Hutton R, *The British Republic 1649-1660, 2nd edition*, London, 2000, p 30.

8 DNB *Thomas Collier*, Wright, Stephen, 2004; Underdown, D, *Revel, Riot and Rebellion*, Oxford, 1985, p 232 mentions Collier as having come from Westbury sub Mendip; Woodhouse, A S P, (ed), *Puritanism and Liberty*, London 1986, pp 390-6 for Collier's sermon at Putney; Bell, M, *Freedom to form: the development of Baptist movements during the English Revolution*, in Durston, C & Maltby, J, (eds), *Religion in Revolutionary England*, Manchester, 2006, pp 181-204; Collier, T, *The heads and substance of a DISCOURSE; First private and afterwards publicke; held in Axbridge, in the County of Somerset about the 6th of March, 1650*, London 1651, BL 701.e. 24(4.) & E. 1368. (2.).

9 White, B R, (ed), *Association Records of the Particular Baptists of England, Wales and Ireland to 1660, Part 2: the West Country and Ireland*, Baptist Historical Society, pp 70 – 72; Goadby, J J, *An Early History of the Somerset Baptist Association, England*, 1871, pp 182-6.

10 Collier, Thomas, *A Looking-Glasse for the Quaker*, London 1657, BL E 896(11) p 16.

11 SRO D/P/WStC 2/1/1; Garment, Joshua, *The Hebrews Deliverance at Hand*, London Aug 23rd 1651, BL 640. (18.)

12 Garment, J, *The Hebrews Deliverance* op cit; DNB *Robins, John*, Hessayon, Ariel, 2004; see also Collier, T, *A Looking-Glasse for the Quaker* op cit, p 16.

13 DNB *Robins* op cit; *CSPD 1660-1*, Green, MAE (ed), HMSO 1860, p 7.

14 DNB. *Robins* op cit; *The Declaration of John Robins*, London 1651, BL E 629 (13); *The Ranters Creed*, London 1651, BL G 19144. (2.); *A List of some of the Grand Blasphemies, which was given in to the Committee for Religion;* London 1654, BL 816.m 20(13); SRO D/P/WStC 2/1/1.

15 Reay, B, *The Quakers and the English Revolution*, London 1985, pp 22-28;

'SOCIETY AND RELIGION: 1649-59'

Moreland, S, (ed), *Somerset Quarterly Meeting of the Society of Friends,* SRS 75, Taunton 1978, pp 2-6, 42, 242.

CHAPTER 10

RESTORATION AND REACTION: 1659-65.

The fall of the Protector Richard Cromwell and the restoration of the Rump Parliament in May 1659 were welcomed by John Pyne and his allies on the Wells Corporation. When a parliamentary ordinance of 26 July 1659 placed the county militia firmly back into Pyne's hands, he immediately appointed the mayor of Wells, William Whiting, as one of the commissioners for the militia. Pyne's dominance however was not to last for long. The army, still powerful, dismissed the Rump in October 1659 but plagued by dissension in its ranks and by hostile public opinion, was forced to reinstate it in December 1659. It was generally recognised that the Rump now consisting of just over 50 members, could not remain as the sole governing body of England. In January General George Monck invaded England with the army of Scotland. On 11 February 1659/60 he reached London and immediately declared for a 'free' parliament. To achieve this he restored the surviving MPs excluded in Pride's Purge of 1648 to enact the legislation to make this possible. This move signalled the end of Pyne's influence in the county and a new list of commissioners was drawn up which represented all shades of moderate opinion. As well as Whiting, Stephen Haskett and Thomas Meade lost their posts as commissioners for the monthly assessment to which they had been appointed only in the previous month by Pyne. On 16 March the remnant of the Long Parliament was dissolved and fresh elections were ordered for a Convention Parliament to decide the future nature of the government. A royalist restoration was now a distinct possibility.

THE ELECTIONS TO THE CONVENTION PARLIAMENT

Faced with a parliamentary election, the leading members of the Wells Corporation cast around for two suitable members. Traditionally the city recorder was usually one of the MPs but this tradition had ended in November 1640 when the candidature of the then recorder John Baber had been rejected in favour of that of the much more important Sir Ralph Hopton. Thereafter Wells had been represented by Clement Walker, Lislebone Long and the protégée of Major General Desborough, Major John Jenkins. The young recorder Thomas White, who had sat briefly in the last protectorate parliament and had lent the corporation £200, was a possible candidate in 1660 but the corporation felt that it needed somebody who was an important county figure if not a national figure to accompany White to Westminster. There was a lot at stake: the rights and property that had belonged to the former bishop, now in the hands of the corporation, were at risk in any pro-royalist settlement. John Buckland of West Harptree was the first man approached. He had topped the poll in the county election held at Wells in 1656 and could be considered in the sheriff's words as a 'pious, sober, prudent and peaceable' man. His constant support for the Protectorate however had made him unpopular and he preferred to keep a low profile and not stand for a parliamentary seat. The ruling group on the corporation then approached William Prynne. Prynne had suffered under the government of Charles I and had had his ears cut off for his anti-government writings. He had however been purged from parliament in 1648 for his Presbyterianism, opposed the execution of the king and had been an opponent of Commonwealth and Protectorate. In 1660 however he preferred to stand as MP for Bath, his political base, and was duly elected its MP. In the end the corporation chose the 29 years old Henry Bull of Shapwick, the brother-in-law of the recorder Thomas White. Bull came from an old Wells family. His grandfather William Bull (1) a wealthy linen draper, had been mayor of Wells in 1613 and his father William Bull (2), who lived at the rectorial manor of Shapwick, had been a moderate parliamentarian in 1642 and served as a county committee member in 1643. After the royalist takeover of the county in June 1643 he then became a royalist supporter during the rest of the war incurring a fine of £900 at the end of it. His son Henry had been educated at the Inner Temple and called to the bar in 1658. His family interest and the influence of Thomas White secured his election by the Wells burgesses as MP with White in the Convention Parliament which met on 25 April 1660. The parliament soon got down to business and on 1 May 1660, Charles Stuart, the son of the late king, was invited to return from exile.[1]

On 12 May 1660 King Charles II was proclaimed in Wells. The mayor Richard Casbeard and his Presbyterian colleagues on the corporation must have had mixed feelings as the trumpeters, drummers and city musicians celebrated the event. The bells of St Cuthbert's were rung and the ringers were nourished with three hogsheads of beer plus tobacco. £22 15s was spent on wine and 'other things' and the King's Arms were repaired and erected in the new town hall in the Market Place. The poor were not forgotten: money was given to the residents of the Almshouse and small change was given to the city poor at the Christopher Inn in the High Street.[2]

THE RESTORATION: THE BISHOP AND THE CATHEDRAL

The restoration of the monarchy and the inevitable return of the Anglican Church meant that the rights and lands of the bishop and the dean and chapter that had been confiscated and sold by parliament during the Interregnum would have to be returned to their previous owners. Worryingly for the Wells burgesses, the Act for Confirming Judicial Proceedings passed by the Convention Parliament at the beginning of May 1660, while it ensured that no judgements arrived at by due processes of law since May 1642 could be overturned, specifically excepted sales of land. In fact, no legislation forcing those who had bought church land during the Interregnum to return it, was ever passed but the principle of returning confiscated land to former owners was established, with the proviso that the present owners should be accommodated by being allowed to lease back their former property where practicable. The threat to the corporation's purchases was further underlined in an act of May 1661 'to preserve the person and government of the King' that stipulated that all 'pretended orders and ordinances of both or either houses of parliament … to which the royal assent was not expressly had or given ... are and so shall be taken to be null and void.' The corporation now had no legal right to the bishop's rights and lands it had bought and would have to return them. To the relief no doubt of David Barrett and other strong supporters of republican government, the Convention Parliament in August 1660 also passed an Act of General Pardon, Indemnity and Oblivion only excepting surviving regicides. The Wells radicals were safe from prosecution. [3]

The authority of the bishop over the diocese was quickly re-imposed and the dean and chapter restored. But, true to his nature, Cornelius Burges remained combative. In May 1660, he was still at the cathedral. Since the fall of Richard Cromwell in May 1659 he had been in resurgent mood. In the summer of 1659 he had dismissed Humphrey Marsh and replaced him with the elderly ex-vicar choral William Atkins but after May 1660, his ecclesiastical enemies moved in to attack him. On 29 June 1660 Charles II appointed Robert Creyghton, newly returned from exile in the Netherlands, as Dean of Wells and Bishop Piers on 18 July instituted him as dean in London. Creyghton was an inveterate enemy of Presbyterianism. While acting as chaplain to the king at The Hague he had 'preached very liberally against the Presbyterians, and the murderers of King Charles I.' Creyghton was in aggressive mood and it was not long before he moved against Burges. In October 1660 he initiated proceedings against him by granting Gyles Hunt a three-year lease of the deanery at a peppercorn rent. Burges's reaction was as expected: he denied Hunt entry to the deanery whereupon Hunt acting for Creyghton indicted Burges at the county court, won the case and evicted him from the deanery in March 1661. Burges was now a pitiful figure: bankrupt and ill, he left Wells and retired to Watford where he died of cancer in 1665. [4]

By the early autumn of 1660, the Wells Corporation, knowing that it could not retain its former purchases, drew up its final account of the bishop's rights and property that it had bought. The job was given to David Barrett who had been so instrumental in the purchase and he soon forced Samuel Bridger to pay the corporation the £100 he still owed for the Tower House.

Bishop Piers, now eighty years old, remained in London where Samuel Pepys saw him on 4 October 1660 with four other bishops in Westminster Abbey 'all in their habitts in King Henry the 7ths chapel. But Lord, at their going out, how people did most of them look upon them as strange Creatures, and few with any kind of love or Respect.'[5] Returning clergy would have much to do to regain the respect of many of the people in Wells. It had been over 15 years since the cathedral clergy had left and 20 years since the bishop had been at Wells; many of the younger men and women would have had little recollection of them. Dean Creyghton took his time, returning to Wells only for the Christmas celebrations on 20 December 1661 when the ringers at the cathedral were paid 10s to welcome him. Three pre-war residents resumed their posts: Thomas Walker as canon resident, Sebastian Smith as precentor, and William Piers, the son of the bishop, as archdeacon of Taunton. James Dugdale was appointed a canon resident and acted as communar while William Piers took on the extra job of keeper of the fabric of the cathedral in charge of repairs. The rest of the chapter appointments were soon made during the following year. Richard Busby, headmaster of Westminster School, became treasurer; Thomas Holt who had been a prebendary and had been ejected from his living of Weston Zoyland, became chancellor; Grindall Sheafe was appointed as archdeacon of Wells, and John Selleck as archdeacon of Bath. One of Thomas Holt's first acts was to order the return from St Cuthbert's of the books taken from the cathedral library during the Interregnum. The churchwardens complied on 14 May 1661 noting 'that the books remaining in the vestry were fetcht away by Mr Chancellor Holt's order as appertayninge of right to the Cathedral Church in Wells aforesaid and were deliv'd by Mr Chetwynd and the ... churchwardens.' No mention was made of the books taken by the town clerk, John Standish. It is possible that the cathedral authorities knew nothing about them and that they were never returned. Standish himself had very 'sticky fingers' and after his dismissal as town clerk in October 1662, only gave up, very grudgingly, the corporation account books and keys in his possession. The only books now remaining in the church other than the bible were 'a copy of [the sixteenth century] Bishop Jewel's book' and two copies of Foxe's Book of Martyrs! [6]

The refurbishment of the cathedral fabric began immediately on Archdeacon Piers's return. The cathedral authorities were able to pay for the repairs because of the 'faire and more than ordinary crop of profit and treasure' gained through the leases and entry fines on its newly restored property. Between 1660 and 1663 the Wells chapter received an income from property amounting to £14,000 of which

£3000 was spent on refurbishing the cathedral. The accounts for 1660-1 show that most of the money was spent on lead and tiles for the roof. The internal walls were also re-plastered; glaziers were employed to mend the windows; new Common Prayer Books were ordered for the 14 vicars and service books for the choir, The existing organ was repaired, a new little organ bought for £80 and a new large one ordered from Robert Taunton in 1662 costing over £500. This must be the one that the Dutch traveller, William Schellinks referred to on 22 July 1662 when he visited Wells: 'A very large organ was in hand to be installed in the church.' Schellinks also noted that the West Front of the cathedral 'was in a bad condition because of its great age, as well as the war, but it is all being repaired.' By the autumn of 1661, the cathedral was again functioning normally. [7]

The bishop's administration was also reconstituted. On 2 July 1660, Edmund Pierce LLD was appointed vicar general in spiritualities to hear causes relating to moral matters in the bishop's consistory court. The two Richard Hixes, father and son, were appointed to act as surveyors of the bishop's 'lordships and manors' on 21 December 1660. Arthur Mattock resumed his role as general receiver of 'all lordships, manors, lands etc of the bishop' an appointment which had been originally ratified by the dean and chapter at the last chapter meeting before it had disbanded on 28 January 1644/5. The corporation hastened to curry favour with him presenting him with a 90 lb cheese on 17 August 1661. The next three appointments were made in January 1661: Alexander Jett was re-appointed as bishop's registrar to control clergy appointments; Thomas Wesley the younger, son of the former vicar of St Cuthbert's, became keeper of the Bishop's Palace and prison; and George Walrond, son of William Walrond, was named as clerk of the bishop's courts and auditor. The appointment of Timothy Revett, son of a pre-war episcopal official, as auditor general was made on 3 October 1661 and Lord John Poulett and his son John of Hinton St George resumed their family's traditional role as chief stewards of all the bishop's hundreds and manors on 27 February 1661/2. The bishop's administration was now complete but the exact date of the bishop's return to Wells is unclear. Before he could return, the Bishop's Palace at Wells had to be repaired. According to his bailiff, Christopher Clement, Bishop Piers spent £5000 on rebuilding his palace and his house at Banwell. He pursued a conciliatory policy towards his tenants abating rents alike to those who had purchased his lands during the Interregnum and now had to lease them back from him and to those who had suffered in the royalist cause. Once the structural repairs to the palace at Wells were complete, the bishop refurbished his own quarters in sumptuous fashion. His bed, covered in purple cloth befitting his episcopal rank, was lined with 'aurora-coloured sarsnet [a fine soft silk material];' the recesses in the chamber over the parlour were also covered by purple hangings and the spaces over the great fireplaces in the chamber and parlour adorned with landscapes. These cultural delights were enhanced by music played on the bishop's virginals (a single keyboard instrument in a box) and a harpsichord. The bishop was also well equipped for travelling, having two coaches, a chariot and a horse litter in the stables. The domestic bliss of the elderly bishop was enhanced by a new wife, his first wife Anne having died in 1655. His second wife, Mary who was considered by contemporaries as being 'too young and cunning for him' finally persuaded him in the late 1660s to leave Wells and settle in Walthamstow, Essex, where he died in April 1670 aged 90 and was buried in the parish church. [8]

ST CUTHBERT'S CHURCH

Although the bishopric and the dean and chapter were restored quickly, the establishment of a new regime at the parish church took a little longer to achieve. Both Stubbes and Chetwynd remained joint ministers throughout 1660 and 1661. Stubbes was more vulnerable to attack as he had been an assistant to the commissioners appointed by parliament 'to eject ignorant and scandalous ministers.' Sometime in the summer of 1662, after the passing in May 1662 of the Act of Uniformity which deprived from their livings all ministers who refused to use the new 1662 Prayer Book and to accede to the 39 Articles of faith, Stubbes left Wells and retired to Dursley in Gloucestershire. He had certainly left by 20 November 1662 when he received a letter from a colleague comforting him on 'the loss of his employment' and promising him £5 a year paid quarterly 'whilst he was in need.' Chetwynd however accepted the new order and remained. He was still there in August 1662 when he arranged for Rev Alexander Baron to preach an annual charity sermon but probably left soon after, on the appointment of a new vicar. Thereafter he pursued his ecclesiastical career in Bristol becoming vicar of Temple Church in 1667 and preacher and lecturer at St Nicholas church in 1668. He still remembered his days in Wells however, because on his death in 1692 he left £5 to the grandchildren of Samuel Oliver his colleague at Wells 40 years before. [9]

It seems likely therefore that Thomas Westley, the previous incumbent, never returned to officiate as vicar of St Cuthbert's. He had spent the previous 14 years living in retirement at the nearby hamlet of Chilcote. At the Restoration he petitioned the king for an appointment as a residentiary canon of the cathedral. He claimed that he had been 'one of his majesties suffering and almost perishing clergy any time these 16 yeeres, having been plundered, sequestered and imprisoned to his ruyne.' His petition was successful and on 3 August 1660 he was installed as prebendary for Wiveliscombe. The government order for his appointment repeated the details of Westley's sufferings and pointed out that as Vicar of St Cuthbert's Wells he had paid £34 yearly for maintenance of the cathedral; 'parochial vicars being always resident are fittest for canons residentiary'. He did not enjoy his position for long. In late August 1661 or early September Westley, then staying at Butleigh and seriously ill, made his will. By 30 September he was dead and his successor as prebendary for Wiveliscombe appointed. This was Charles Thirlby, the newly appointed master of the Cathedral Grammar School who also became vicar of St Cuthbert's church in the following year. [10]

BAPTISTS AND QUAKERS

Just before his restoration to the throne, Charles II had issued the Declaration of Breda in April 1660 granting 'liberty to tender consciences.' This had raised the hopes of the Baptists and Quakers that they would be allowed to continue to worship in their own way unmolested. Their hopes were further raised by the Lord Chancellor's (the Earl of Clarendon) speech to parliament in May 1661 when he spoke in favour of peaceful nonconformists. This was followed by a royal proclamation forbidding the imprisonment of Quakers for refusing to take oaths. Some Quakers were released from prison but in the following months the number imprisoned for this 'offence' grew. The cause of the non-conformists had not been helped by the small rebellion in north London in January 1660/1 of men led by the cooper Thomas Venner who wished to establish the rule of the saints on earth by armed rebellion. The rebellion was put down easily but the news quickly spread to the provinces, alarming the magistrates.

In Wells the return of the cathedral chapter inevitably meant that the Baptists could no longer meet in the Chapter House. Their freedom of worship however was not seriously threatened until the late summer of 1662 when those members of the corporation who had allowed them to worship, were excluded from the corporation by the Corporation Act passed in December 1661 but not enforced until early October 1662 in Wells. The act stipulated that all municipal office holders had to take the Anglican sacrament and renounce the Presbyterian covenant. The position of nonconformists was further weakened by the passing of the Quaker Act of 1662 and the Conventicle Act of 1664. The latter Act provided for a series of escalating fines for any who attended nonconformist meetings – £5 (or three months' imprisonment) for the first offence, £10 (or six months' imprisonment for the second) and £100 (or transportation) for the third. These acts meant that the Baptist congregation in Wells was forced to meet in small groups in private houses. However there is no evidence that Baptists were persecuted in Wells at this time and Thomas Collier continued to preach locally to committed groups. In 1669 he was reported as teaching in Axbridge and no doubt was active in Wells. The Western Association he had founded continued and Collier was still writing pamphlets until his death in 1691. Just before his death he raged against the selfishness and materialism of the age as he saw it. He was a disappointed man: 'the glorious kingdom of the saints' had not come to pass as he had hoped; there had been no 'new heavens' or 'new earth!' His angry words echo down the years and have a curious modern resonance: 'self it is that rules, in city and country, self profit and advantage it is, that manageth all callings ... self honour, self pride and self will it is that is the cause of most of the wars and blood in the world.'

At the Restoration it was the Anglican vision of religion that won the day. In many respects it was initially a narrow intolerant Episcopalian church that was re-established. Anglicans gained a monopoly on office holding, worship and education. However not all Anglicans were against nonconformists: some were sympathetic to their plight and wished for the relaxation of the re-introduced

Elizabethan penal laws punishing non-attendance at church. It is likely that the new pro-royalist administration in Wells, appointed in October 1662, continued the lenient policy towards non-attendance at the parish church that had been traditionally practised by the pre-war corporation. [11]

MAKING ADJUSTMENTS

The Convention Parliament dissolved in December 1660 and the new parliament, which came to be known as the Cavalier Parliament, met for the first time on 8 May 1661. The Wells Corporation determined to choose two new MPs who, because of their social position, would be able to advance the city's interests more effectively than White or Bull could have done. The more prestigious but the less effective of the two new MPs was the 21 year old Lord Richard Butler, fifth son of the 1st Duke of Ormonde recently created Lord Lieutenant of Somerset and the choice of Butler was made purely as a compliment to his father. Butler turned out to be of little use to the city and became a well-known libertine. A contemporary described him as 'singularly adroit in all kinds of exercises notably tennis and the guitar, his amorous and alcoholic proclivities made him a symbol of the baseness and looseness of the court.' The second choice was the more important one, that of the 33 year old Sir Maurice Berkeley eldest son of Sir Charles Berkeley of Bruton. Berkeley had been too young to fight in the civil war and during the Interregnum had held local office under the Protectorate becoming a commissioner for the monthly assessment in 1657 and 1660-1. His subsequent career made him an extremely desirable person to represent Wells in parliament. As well as being appointed as a JP for Somerset in March 1660 and a captain of the militia horse in the county from April 1660, he became a judicial commissioner in the western circuit in July 1660 and commissioner for sewers in December 1660. Berkeley was also well known in London. He had on 17 April 1660 been given a pass beyond the seas to carry to the court of the exiled Charles Stuart in the Netherlands the news that General George Monck, the most powerful man in England, had declared for a restoration of the monarchy. On the king's return he had been rewarded with a baronetcy and a post in the Duke of Gloucester's household; the Duke being the younger brother of the king. The position however was only a short-lived one as the Duke died before the year was out. In June 1660 he was also made a gentleman of the Privy Chamber with access to the king. Berkeley was certainly a man to cultivate. At the end of the first parliamentary session in September 1661, Sir Maurice came to Wells where he was entertained by the corporation – Mr Cox being paid 13s for 'wine for Sir Maurice Berkeley by Mr Mayor's order.' [12]

The summer of 1661 must have been an anxious one for the Wells Corporation because it was almost certainly at this time that it had to return to the restored bishop all his rights and property it had bought from 1647 onwards. The quarter sessions of January 1660/1 had been held in the 'the new hall' but this was to be the last time. John Stafford was paid 4s.8d for replacing roof tiles 'against the justices came.' During 1661 the corporation was assiduous in propitiating its former opponents. The coronation of the king in early May 1661 was celebrated in great style in the city. Civic pomp was on show: the civic swords were 'dressed' and the two sergeants who carried them were given new gowns to head the civic procession; a hogshead of beer was given to the poor and wine to the two captains of the militia. A large bonfire made up of a hundred faggots was lit and the corporation members regaled themselves by consuming two gallons of French wine. The general celebratory mood was extended to Ascension Day on 23 May which the corporation members celebrated with 'wine, beare, bread, tobacco and pipes.' [13]

On 31 July 1661 the corporation received the news that it feared: a copy of the royal proclamation 'for clayme to ye lands in England.' The rights and lands belonging to the bishop now had to be returned to him and this was done quietly and without fuss. The immediate reaction by the corporation to this setback was to launch a charm campaign in the autumn of 1661 in an attempt to ingratiate itself with the restored authorities. Sir Maurice Berkeley was entertained as we have seen, wine and six sugar loaves were presented to the assize judges and Captain Coward's soldiers were entertained with a hogshead of beer. Last minute repairs were made to the roof of the 'new hall' before it was handed back to Archdeacon Piers as a canonical house. [14]

The Wells Corporation was not however disheartened by the setback of losing its gains in the past fourteen years and soon formulated a new plan to enhance the city's market facilities and provide a new home for corporation meetings, the assizes and the quarter sessions. Claiming to act 'with the consent and approbation of the Bishop,' it decided to build a new dual market and town hall in the Market Place immediately in front of Archdeacon Piers's house. The agreement of the bishop was necessary because the Market Place was 'part of the waste of ye manor of Wells belonging to the Bishop.' Because of the unfortunate loss of the corporation acts' books from 1644-62, no evidence has survived concerning any negotiations that may have taken place between the corporation and the bishop's officials about the constuction of new facilities to house what was again the bishop's market, although the presentation of the large cheese to Arthur Mattock, the bishop's receiver general, may have had something to do with assisting the negotiations. Evidence does survive of the conditions laid down for maintenance by the bishop: the corporation was allowed to use the two upper storey rooms above the main market hall on condition that it kept the building 'tiled and whited.' [15]

Archdeacon Piers was not happy about the new project because he had repaired the canonical house and 'converted it again into an habitable house.' The work had been expensive and the cathedral chapter had contributed £700 to the cost probably in the form of a loan. After about two years, when the building of the new market house was moving towards completion, Piers moved to the Tower House home of the absentee precentor Sebastian Smith because, as the records of the dean and chapter state, 'there is a great market house built before the dore of this canonical house which hath drawn the market from other partes to the dores of this house, to the greate annoyance of the said house.' The corporation as it was constituted in the spring and summer of 1662 was not however to be left to finish the construction it had started. A new threat to the membership of the corporation had emerged with the passing by the Cavalier Parliament of the Corporation Act in December 1661. Corporations were now to be purged of those men who had vigorously supported the Commonwealth and Protectorate. During the summer of 1662, the members of the Wells Corporation waited no doubt nervously for the arrival of the commissioners who were to enforce the act.[16]

AN ACT FOR THE 'WELL GOVERNING AND REGULATING OF CORPORATIONS'.

The commissioners chosen by the king were all royalists and strong supporters of episcopacy. They reached Wells in early October 1662 and met at the Crown Inn where they were supplied with wine, bread and beer paid for by the corporation they were to purge. Their immediate targets were the ten surviving men who had been most dominant in the Wells Corporation during the Interregnum. The local royalist gentry resented the fact that while they had been excluded from county government during the Interregnum, these men who had supported the republic were still in power in Wells. The local gentry were also keen to gain personal influence in Wells as it contained two parliamentary seats. All corporation members were required by the Act to sign a declaration against the Presbyterian Solemn League and Covenant and to take an oath against the principle of resistance to the king but the commissioners had power to displace even those who signed and swore the oath and they often did. Three of the men who had been firm supporters of the republic were already dead: Robert Morgan in 1653, Thomas Salmon in 1658 and William Whiting in 1660. Stephen Haskett, Thomas Meade, David Barrett in particular had no hope of surviving the purge: their long record of opposing the royalist government during the civil war and their involvement in county government during the Interregnum made their expulsion from the corporation inevitable. It is highly likely that they refused to sign or swear.

Also purged were men who had served as the corporation's general receivers and had been involved in the corporation's purchases of episcopal land during the Interregnum: William Andrews, William Atwell, Samuel Reade and Thomas Nixon. Joseph Gallington a staunch Presbyterian who had served as mayor in 1654-5 and Robert Hole who had occupied the canonical house in the Market Place and had leased The Rib canonical house in the Liberty were also casualties. The last man to be excluded was the elderly James Hurman. He had become a burgess only in 1658 and had joined the corporation some time after that. The only evidence suggestive of a misdemeanour is a note at the first meeting of the reformed corporation on 16 October 1662 about 'a paper in question ... of Mr James Hurman who was sent for but was out of town.' Two other corporation officials had to go. On 15 October the Corporation Act commissioners meeting in Wells informed the Privy Council in London 'we have displaced Thomas White esq. from being Recorder of the city of Wells and in his room and stead have placed John Lord

Poulett, Baron of Hinton St George, Recorder of ye city which election and charge we said commissioners do ratify and allow by these presents.' The choice of Baron Poulett to be the new recorder of Wells was somewhat ironic considering he was the son of the man who had stirred up such feelings of animosity in Wells in 1642 by his tirade against those he considered his social inferiors. The town clerk since 1653, John Standish was also forced to resign for his part in the property deals. [17]

The ten new men were led by four of minor gentry status reflecting the pre-war establishment: George Walrond, the new mayor, the son of William Walrond, William Coward brother of the royalist militia officer Thomas Coward, John Piers the younger son of the bishop and Tristram Towse the younger, son-in-law of the bishop's registrar, Alexander Jett. The other six men brought on to the corporation were local men, merchants and artisans who had played no part in the administration of the city during the Interregnum: William Fricker, Edmund Lovell, Thomas Davidge, John Cordwent, Thomas Heath and Edward Watts. The ten excluded men never served on the corporation again but a gesture was made by Walrond, Cordwent, Coward and William Baron to Joseph Gallington and James Hurman. Because they had lost the prestigious church seats they enjoyed when they were corporation members, they were promised new seats as soon as 'such seats may fall' and in the meantime they were allowed to sit 'where they may get a place.' The same privilege was not extended to the other excluded members! [18]

Following Thomas White's dismissal, the reformed corporation met on the day following in some confusion as witnessed by the crossings through and deletions on the written record of the meeting. The ex-town clerk John Standish still had several books of accounts and arrears of rent, plus the key to the desk in the exchequer in his possession and these were sent for. Standish only released them grudgingly over the next few weeks. A sign of the ascendancy of the small group of gentlemen on the corporation was the order that was passed 'that the gentlemen newly elected have the seniority as masters.' The main policy decision to emerge from the first meeting was the decision to press on with building of the town hall which as William Schellinks had noted on 22 July 1662 was already under construction. [19]

THE CONSTRUCTION OF THE NEW MARKET/TOWN HALL

The new hall to be built in Wells was not a building to be compared with such fine, surviving market/town halls in other small Somerset towns such as Somerton, Martock or Milborne Port. It was however the best structure the impoverished city corporation could afford after the financial catastrophe of having to return to the bishop the purchases it had made during the Interregnum.

The new hall which was a dual purpose building providing shelter for market traders and a meeting place for the corporation, was not to be built in stone but was to be a predominantly wooden structure. It was rectangular in shape and was some 120 feet in length and about 25 feet wide with the roof supported on 10 pairs of stone pillars. The space between each pillar was capped by a small gable (see the plan by William Simes of 1735). However a drawing of the plan of the market house dated 1767 shows that by then some pillars had been extended possibly with boarding to give more shelter. It was to be an open structure with a staircase on the north side in the middle of the building leading to the two chambers for the use of the corporation. The eastern end of the new building was later to be walled in to provide accommodation for the justices at the quarter sessions in Wells. The arrangement was never very satisfactory because the quarter sessions were traditionally held in January and the justices over the years complained vigorously of the cold and the draughts. The floor was paved with slabs into which the pillar bases and freestone pillars, made probably with oolitic limestone from Doulting, east of Shepton Mallet, were inserted. Richard Cole was paid £1 10s. 'for the remainder of the car[ry]ing of the freestones' and William Barnard was paid 5s. 6d for 'footing up the pillars,' The pillars were joined longitudinally at the top by timbers which formed the base for the long shed-like roof supported on rafters spanning the gaps between the pillars and fastened to the pillars by 'irons.' 256 feet of rafters were purchased for £4 17s 6d with just over 4000 lasts to construct the roof and the upper chambers. The roof was in the form of a tiled gabled canopy over the open space beneath topped with 'creases' or ridge tiles. In all likelihood the floor of the two upstairs rooms was built on lateral beams secured to three of the outside pairs of pillars and supported by three pillars in the centre of the building.

Four windows in the side gables provided the light and ventilation for these rooms which were accessed by a staircase on the north side.

The building work was carried out by local craftsmen but with the advice of two carpenters from Sherborne and financed by the members of the seven trade companies in the city, 'divers gentlemen' and the inhabitants generally. Money was slow to come in. On 13 May 1663 the corporation reported that the work on the hall had stopped. The 'impediment' was lack of money to pay the contractors and workmen. Richard Hole and Edmund Meadows were 'desired to go in the town to the inhabitants to collect what moneys they [could] get towards the building of the hall.' By 5 June 1663 the funding crisis had deepened and the corporation ordered that a conference be held with the trade companies 'for carrying on the work of the hall.' The conference achieved little because on 14 September the corporation ordered the masters of the trade companies to bring in the money they were holding on pain of being fined. Things did not improve. On 3 November 1663, in desperation, the corporation ordered that the goods and chattels of those refusing to pay should be sold and the proceeds used to finance the hall. Even this draconian measure was not effective and the new hall still remained uncompleted. The corporation then returned to a policy of gentle persuasion and by June 1665 the fitting out of the hall was nearly complete. The catalyst was the need to provide a 'hall fit for the assizes' due to be held in August. The plan for reserving a part of the new hall for the assizes and quarter sessions had been made in the previous May and consisted of 'the erecting and making fit a bench, table, board, bar and other materials for the reception of the judges at the hithermost end of the new hall.' (the east end) Seats were also to be provided for the magistrates' wives at the quarter sessions.

Bishop Piers, in giving his agreement for the construction, had followed the same conciliatory course as he had with the granting of leases knowing that an enhancement of the market facilities was in his own best interests. However the relationship between the bishop and the corporation soon became strained over the terms of the agreement. In 1670 Bishop Creyghton demanded that the corporation should pay an entry fine for the new building but the corporation decided that 'no fine shall be paid to ye bishop for ye town hall but persons to wait on his lordship to know what acknowledgement he pleases to demand.' The bishop then demanded rent for the new building but the corporation refused to pay it alleging that the bishop's bailiff was 'neglecting his service'. By 1675 another problem was emerging: 'whereas the mayor, masters and burgesses [of Wells] 'about fourteen years since at ye great charges and expense ... have erected and built a common hall in the town of Wells ... [because of] some default in building of ye hall, ye same is in danger of becoming ruinous.' The corporation consequently changed its strategy and decided, with the consent of Bishop Mews, to take over sole control of the building by endeavouring 'to get an act of parlt for settling ye town hall on ye corporation.' Unfortunately for the corporation nothing came of this and the ownership of the market/town hall and control of the market was not to be resolved until 1779 when, due to the ruinous structure of the seventeenth century building, the corporation bought the canonical house in the Market Place from the bishop, demolished it, and on obtaining an Act of Parliament, built the present town hall on the site. [20]

EXITS AND ENTRANCES

The domination of the city's government by the imported gentry did not last for long. Lord John Poulett soon delegated his powers as recorder to William Coward the younger son of William Coward, mayor 1663-4. On Poulett's death in September 1665, Coward became the most dominant man in the city. He was immediately appointed as recorder, an office he kept until his death in 1705 and also served as MP for the city in seven parliaments between 1679 and 1702. He was an acquisitive, ambitious man of conservative views who brooked little opposition. In 1684 he moved to what is now 17 the Liberty, leasing it from the dean and chapter. However in 1689 he refused to pay what he considered an exorbitant fine for renewal of his lease and 'gutted the house and carried the materials to repair his house in Chamberlain St.' [21]

The other gentleman who did not remain on the corporation for long was John Piers the son of the bishop and brother of Archdeacon Piers. John resigned from the corporation on 4 February 1664/5 because he found difficulty in attending convocation meetings as his home was at Denton in Oxfordshire. George Walrond continued in office and lived in the Liberty until his death in 1680 and Tristram

Towse (the younger) mayor in 1664-5, remained on the corporation until his death in 1674. The rest of the corporation was made up of merchants, tradesmen and artisans as before. [22]

Of the excluded members Stephen Haskett may have left the city while David Barrett continued to live unmolested in the house opposite Jacob's Well at the junction of High St and Wet Lane until possibly 1686. An Elizabeth Barrett (his wife or daughter) was still there in 1703. Thomas Meade, the 'arch incendiary' died in 1668 and was buried on 23 December in St Cuthbert's Church. Wily old Richard Casbeard finally succumbed to death in January 1662/3 but his son John took some time to be reconciled to the new regime. [23]

John Casbeard had business and property interests in Bristol as well as Wells and other places. However he seems to have been rather intemperate in his criticism of the new royalist government. In July 1663, six of his enemies in Bristol alleged that Casbeard had said that ' he expected to see [General] Monck's quarters hang where others are now [a reference to the exhibition of the exhumed body parts of Oliver Cromwell and other regicides hanging from the towers of London Bridge].' Casbeard was also alleged to have called the new king 'an arrant tyrant but for the good men in Parliament and a bastard and said he would venture his blood before kingly authority should rule.' Casbeard was arrested and sent to the Gatehouse Prison in Westminster but was released without trial and on his return to Bristol arrested his chief accuser, an Irishman called Fawns Urrey for a debt of £10,000 and kept him in Newgate Gaol in Bristol for nineteen and a half weeks. Undeterred, Urrey tried to incriminate Casbeard a second time alleging that Casbeard had spoken of 'adventuring all he had on the good old cause and joining the well affected in Ireland.' He was again unsuccessful, and financially ruined by Casbeard, returned to Ireland and out of the historical records. Casbeard continued to thrive and became a pillar of the south Bristol community. On the death of his wife Mary in 1676, he and his son Theophilus granted to the churchwardens and overseers of the poor in the parish of St Mary Redcliff an annuity of 40s per annum 'issuing out of pasture ground called Ridings in Bishford, Bedminster to be given to between 4 and 10 families in the parish.' [24]

Casbeard remained a thorn in the flesh of his enemies in the Wells clerical establishment. He had inherited from his father Richard an area of land next to the Christopher Inn in the High Street (now the entrance to Guardhouse Lane.) This piece of undeveloped land had been the main point of access to the pool behind the High Street (La Poole) useful for watering the horses and cattle driven into the city on market days. Casbeard took out a new lease of the ground in 1679 and if Nathaniel Chyle writing in 1680 is to be believed, he closed off the land and built on it cutting off part of the access to La Poole. Access to La Poole however was still available through Mill Street but this would have meant animals passing the front doors of people's houses which in itself could have been very unpopular. Chyle made the most of the situation by alleging that horses and cattle could now only be watered in the palace moat to the 'greate Nusance and affront to the Bishopp and his Authority as can be possible. Nay this Indulgence encourages all the neighbourhood about the Palace to carry and wheel all the dirt, and filth of theire Houses, through the palace gate making their common Dunghill within the Palace Walls under the Bishop's nose.' Whether Chyles's allegations were right or wrong, one fact is clear: John Casbeard, twenty years after the restoration of the king, was still able to infuriate the ecclesiastical authorities. If Chyle were right, then the citizens of Wells still harboured a thoroughly disrespectful attitude to the restored clerical hierarchy.[25]

EPILOGUE

The civil war and its aftermath had been a chastening experience for the people of Wells, an experience they would not wish to repeat. No men from Wells were involved in the Monmouth rebellion of 1685. When on 1 July 1685 the Duke of Monmouth, in rebellion against James II, arrived in Wells with his army and lodged in the archdeacon's house on Cathedral Green, a Wells resident reported: 'my uncle knew a man who came with a dish of strawberries. "Where be going with they?" says he. "To give un to King Monmouth," says he. "Now, you just take my advice," says he. "Car'un along back, or eat them yourself" And so he did and so he escaped hanging.' [26]

    The corporation had always been made up of a broad coalition of views and interests and although it had become more radical in the 1650s it had still contained some men of moderate views. The lack of vituperation by the winners after the Restoration only meant that although the hardliners were permanently excluded from participation in the government of the city, most still remained as residents. There had also been no abrupt change of policy; the market/town hall project being continued by the new administration.

The prosperity of the city remained the main aim of the city government and its citizens and when Celia Fiennes visited Wells in 1698 she noted that 'the assizes was in the town which filled it like a fair, and little stands for selling things was in all the streets; there I saw the Town hall – the streetes are well pitched – and a large market place and shambles ...' Everything in fact was as it should be in a small prosperous town. Despite the penal legislation against the nonconformist sects in the early 1660s, as soon as the political climate became a little more benign, the Presbyterians made a quiet comeback in 1674 acquiring two tenements in Southover which were registered as a Presbyterian church two years later. Finally in 1695 the Quaker William Penn was able to preach to a crowd of 2000 people from the upper storey of the Crown Inn. When the mayor, Matthew Baron, arrested him he found to his chagrin that Penn held a licence to preach from Bishop Kidder himself. As the eighteenth century dawned, Wells moved into a more genteel existence despite the occasional trade or election riot and the conflicts of the mid seventeenth century became a distant memory to its citizens. [27]

NOTES

[1] Henning, B D, (ed), *The History of Parliament: The House of Commons 1660-1690*, London 1983, Vol. I pp 379,381, 746-7, Vol.3 p 706; Underdown, D, *Somerset in the Civil War and Interregnum*, Newton Abbot, 1973, pp 34,39,69,124,182,192.

[2] WTH *Wells Corporation Receiver's Book 1652-1681*, fos. 28 & 29.

[3] Holmes, G, *The Making Of A Great Power: Late Stuart and Early Georgian Britain 1660-1722*, London 1993, pp 27-28.

[4] Underdown, D, *A Case Concerning Bishops' Lands: Cornelius Burges and the Corporation of Wells*, EHR 1963, p 46; *Wells Cathedral; A History*, Colchester, L.S. (ed.), p 160; DNB. *Creighton, Robert*, Macauley, J.S., 2004.

[5] Latham R., & Matthews, W., (eds), *The Diary of Samuel Pepys Vol. 1 1660*, Berkeley and Los Angeles, 1970, p 259.

[6] *Calendar of the Manuscripts of the Dean and Chapter of Wells Vol. II*, H.M.S.O., London 1914, pp 430-432; *Wells St Cuthbert, Churchwardens' Accounts 1649-65*, SRO D/P WStC. 4/1/1.

[7] *Calendar of the Manuscripts of the Dean and Chapter*, op cit, p 432; Colchester, L S, (ed), *Wells Cathedral: A History*, op cit, pp 160-162; William Schellinks's description is quoted in Rodwell, W, *Wells Cathedral Excavations and Structural*

Studies 1978-93, English Heritage, 2001, Archaeological Report 21, pp 6-7.

[8] *Calendar of the Manuscripts of the Dean and Chapter*, op cit, pp 430-433, DNB *William Piers*, Dorman, M, 2004; Hembry, P, *The Bishops of Bath and Wells 1540-1640: Social and Economic Problems*, London, 1967, pp 250-253; Dunning, R, *The Bishop's Palace*, in Colchester, L S, (ed) *Wells Cathedral: A History*, op cit, pp 240-241.

[9] Matthews, A G, (ed), *Calamy Revised*, Oxford 1934, pp 114 (Chetwynd) & 468-9 (Stubbes); WTH *Wells Corporation Receiver's Book* fos 40 & 41.

[10] Thomas Westley's will can be found in NA Prob 11/309; Everett Green, M A E, (ed), *CSPD 1660-1661*, HMSO London, 1860, no 126 p 250; Serel, T, *Historical Notes on the Church of St Cuthbert in Wells*, Wells 1875, p 118.

[11] DNB *Thomas Collier*, Wright, Stephen, 2004.

[12] Henning, B D, (ed), *The History of Parliament: The House of Commons 1660-1690*, Vol. 1 pp 632-3 & 755-6; WTH *Wells Corporation Receiver's Book*, fo. 33v.

[13] WTH *Wells Corporation Receiver's Book* fos. 29v. & 33.

[14] WTH *Wells Corporation Receiver's Book* fo. 33v.

[15] WTH *Untitled Memorandum Book*, Vol P, p 77, c 1675 Draft of an Act of Parliament for 'ye setting and re-establishing of ye hall.'

[16] *Calendar of the Manuscripts of the Dean and Chapter of Wells Vol.II*, op cit, p 431; Bailey, D S, *The Canonical Houses of Wells*, Gloucester, 1982, pp 161-2; the conditions attached to the use of the new town hall are mentioned in Baines, A, *The Monmouth Rebellion in Wells*, Wells, nd., p 8; the evidence suggesting the George Inn as a possible venue for the quarter sessions comes from WTH *Wells Corporation Receiver's Book fo.39* 'Pd for the use of the hall at the sessions by ye order of Mr May;' the May family being the bailiffs of the Ayleworth estate of which the George Inn was a part. Another payment in 1663/4 was made to William Ford 'for the use of his chambers at the sessions,' fo. 41v. William Ford cannot be traced but A J Scrase has suggested that he might be linked to the Star Inn for which records have not survived. Both inns were in prime positions in the High Street and thus would have been suitable venues.

[17] For a discussion of the Corporation Act of 1661 see Hutton, R, *The Restoration*, Oxford 1985, pp 158-161; biographical details of the men purged see Nott A, & Hasler, J, (eds), *Wells Convocation Acts Books 1589-1665, Part 2 1629-44; 1662-65*, SRS 91, Taunton 2004, p 938 passim; WTH *Wells Corporation Receiver's Book* fo. 39.

[18] The 14 corporation members who were not purged were: Humphrey Cordwent, William Baron, Hodges Cook, Robert Frier, Hugh Merefield, Henry Baron, Joseph Plummer, Henry Webster, John Middleham, John Davidge, Richard Casbeard, William Smith, Robert Hill and Robert Thomas.

[19] Nott A & Hasler, J, (eds), *Wells Convocation Acts Books 1589-1665, Part 2 1629-44; 1662-5*, op cit, pp 882-886; *Wells St Cuthbert Churchwardens' Accounts*, SRO D/P/WStC 4/1/1. For Schellinks see note 7 in this chapter.

[20] Nott A & Hasler, J, (eds), *Wells Corporation Acts Books Part 2 1629-44; 1662-5*, op cit, pp 882-922 passim. There is some difference of opinion about the date of the building of the town hall. A J Scrase suggests in *Wells: A Small City*, Stroud,

2006 p 70, that a new market house may have been built by Bishop Knight in 1542-3 and that this was the market house that was repaired and extended in 1662-5. I initially agreed with him in my introduction to SRS 90 p. 28 but now think that the available evidence shows that Bishop Knight built only the High Cross and that the market house/town hall was a new construction undertaken by the Wells Corporation in 1661-5; the 1767 plan of the market hall can be found at SRS DD/WM/1/C *Case involving the Market House also used for an assize and sessions hall in Wells with ink drawing of the Market Place 1767*; see also WTH *Untitled Memorandum Book E*, pp 202,203, 260 & WTH *Untitled Memorandum Book P*, p 77 which show almost certainly that market hall/town hall was built soon after the Restoration.

[21] Nott A, & Hasler, J, (eds), *Wells Corporation Acts Books Part 2 1629-44; 1662-5,*op cit, pp 960-1 & 1001.

[22] Nott, A & Hasler, J, (eds) *Wells Corporation Acts Books part 2 1629-44; 1662-5,* op cit, pp 1000, 1015 & 1017.

[23] Nott, A & Hasler, J, (eds) *Wells Corporation Acts Books part 2 1629-44; 1662-5,* op cit, p 945; Bailey, D S, *Wells Manor of Canon Grange,* Gloucester, 1985, pp 136-7.

[24] Everett Green, M A E, (ed), *C.S.P.D. 1663-4,* London 1862 pp 220-1; BRO *P St MR/Ch/19/ff.*

[25] Reynolds, H E, (ed), *Wells Cathedral; Its Foundation, Constitutional History and Statutes,* Wells, 1881, p. cxlv

[26] Baines, A, *The Monmouth Rebellion in Wells,* op cit, pp. 1-2.

[27] Celia Fiennes's comments can be found in Rodwell, W, *Wells Cathedral: Excavations and Structural Studies, 1978-93,* English Heritage 2001, p 7; Scrase, T, *Wells: A Small City,* Stroud 2006, pp 101 & 105.

APPENDIX : MAYORS OF WELLS

The mayor of Wells was appointed on 30 September each year and was in office for one calendar year.

1640-41:	Thomas Jones
1641-42:	Robert Morgan
1642-43:	Robert Rowley
1643-44:	William West
1644-45:	Richard Casbeard
1645-46:	Henry Foster
1646-47:	Robert Morgan
1647-48;	Thomas Salmon
1648-49:	Bartholomew Cox
1649-50:	William Smith
1650-51:	William Whiting
1651-52:	(unknown)
1652-53:	William Baron
1653-54:	Thomas Mead
1654-55:	Joseph Gallington
1655-56;	Stephen Haskett
1656-57:	Thomas Salmon
1657-58:	William Smith
1658-59:	William Whiting
1659-60:	Richard Casbeard
1660-61:	William Baron
1661-62:	Humphrey Cordwent
1662-63:	George Walrond
1663-64:	William Coward (died 24the August 1664)
1664-65:	Tristram Towse

PRIMARY MANUSCRIPT SOURCES

NA: Probates 11 for cited PCC wills.

SRO: Sir Edward Rodney's Account of his family: DD/TB Box 20/1;
Wells Diocesan letters 1640-1759: DD/OC/1878 Box 2;
Wells St Cuthbert, Churchwardens' Accounts 1649-54, D/P/WStC 4/1/1;
Wells St Cuthbert Parish Register 1609-1665, D/P/WStC 2/1/1;

WTH: Wells Corporation Sessions Book 1625-50;
Wells Corporation Receiver's Book 1652-81;

WCL: Untitled Memorandum Books, E & P

PRINTED PRIMARY SOURCES

BL:

A Coppie of a Letter, Read in the House of Commons: Sent from Master Sampford 26 August 1642, BL E 114 (18);

A List of the Grand Blasphemies which was given in to the Committee for Religion, London 1654, BL 816 m 20 (13);

A Memento for Yeomen, Merchants, Citizens And all the Commons in England, August 22nd 1642, BL E 113(13);

A Perfect Relation of All the passages and proceedings of the Marquesse Hartford, the Lord Paulet and the rest of the Cavelleers that were with them in Wels, London, 12 August 1642, pp 3-8, BL E 111. (5.);

A Second Letter Sent from John Ashe Esquire ... , London, August 16 1642, pp 3-16, BL E 112 (13);

A True and Exact Relation of all the Proceedings of Marquesse Hartford, Lord Pawlet, Lord Seymor, Lord Coventry, Sir Ralph Hopton, and other His Maiesties Commissioners in the publishing of the Commission of Array in his Maiesties County of Somerset, London 19th August 1642, (no BL reference or pagination);

A True and Sad Relation Of divers passages in Somersetshire, between the Country and the Cavaleers concerning the Militia and the Commission of Array, August 5 1642, p 5, BL E 109 (34.);

A case concerning the Buying of Bishops Lands with the Lawfulness thereof and the Difference between the Contractors for sale of those lands and the Corporation of Wells, Burges, Cornelius, London, 1659, BL 108. g 33;

Certain and true News from Somerset-shire with the besieging of Sir Ralph Hopton's House ..., London, October 15, 1642, BL E. 122 (18);

Collier, T, *The heads and substance of a DISCOURSE; First private and afterwards publicke; held in Axbridge in the County of Somerset about the 6th of March 1650*, BL 701.e.24(4);

Collier, T, *A Looking-Glasse for the Quaker*, London, 1657, BL E 896 (11);

Exceeding Joyfull Newes from the Earl of Bedford ..., London August 23 1642, [no pagination] BL E 113 (17).

Garment, J, *The Hebrews Deliverance at Hand*, London, 1651, BL 640 (18);

Joyful Newes from Wells in Somerset-Shire, London 12 August 1642 (no BL reference);

Rodney, Sir Edward- Manuscript writings – BL Add 34239;

The Declaration of John Robins: the False Prophet otherwise the Shakers' God London 1651, BL E 629 (13);

The Lord Marquesse of Hertford, His Letter, Sent to the Queen in Holland. Also a letter from the Committee in Sommersetshire, to the Houses of Parliament, London, August 8 1642, BL E109. (24),

The Ranters Creed, London, 1651, BL G 19144 (2);

PARLIAMENTARY RECORDS

Journal of the House of Commons, History of Parliament Trust, 1802.
Journal of the House of Lords, History of Parliament Trust, 1802.

BIBLIOGRAPHY

Adamson, J, *The Noble Revolt*, London, 2007.
Bailey, D S, (ed), *Wells Cathedral Chapter Act Book 1666-83*, London, 1973.
Bailey, D S, *The Canonical Houses of Wells*, Gloucester, 1982.
Bailey, D S, *Wells Manor of Canon Grange*, Gloucester, 1985.
Baines, A, *The Monmouth Rebellion in Wells*, Wells, no date.
Barnes, A D, *The Church and Education in Wells, Somerset from the Eve of the Reformation until 1891*, M Phil Thesis, University of Manchester, 1990.
Barnes, T G (ed), *Somerset Assize Orders 1629-40*, SRS 65, Taunton, 1959.
Barnes, T G, *Somerset 1635-1640: A County's Government during the Personal Rule*, London, 1961.
Bates Harbin, E H, (ed), *Quarter Sessions Records for the County of Somerset Vol 3, Commonwealth 1646-60*, SRS Vol 28, Taunton, 1912.
Bell, M, *Freedom to Form: The Development of Baptist Movements during the English Revolution* in Durston, C & Maltby, J, (eds), *Religion in Revolutionary England*, Manchester, 2006.
Bettey, J, (ed), *Calendar of the Correspondence of the Smyth Family of Ashton Court 1542-1642*, BRS Vol XXXV, Bristol, 1982.
Bruce, J, (ed), *Calendar of State Papers Domestic, 1625-1626*, London, 1858.
Bruce, J, (ed), *Calendar of State Papers Domestic, Charles I 1635*, London, 1872.
Calamy, E, *Account of the Ministers, Lecturers, Masters and Fellows of Colleges and Schoolmasters who were Ejected or Silenced aftyer the Restoration in 1660*, 2nd ed, London, 1713.
Calendar of Manuscripts of the Dean and Chapter of Wells Vol II, HMSO, 1914.
Chadwyck Healey, C E, (ed), *Bellum Civile, Hopton's Narrative of the Campaign in the West (1642-44)*, SRS, Vol 18, Taunton, 1902.
Clarendon, Edward Earl of, Macray, W D, (ed), *The History of the Rebellionand Civil Wars in England*, Oxford, 1888, 6 volumes.
Clark, P, *The Ramoth-Gilead of the Good: Urban Change and Political Radicalism at Gloucester 1540-1640*, in Barry, J, (ed), *The Tudor and Stuart Town: A Reader in English Urban History 1530-1688*, London, 1990.
Cockburn, J S, (ed), *Somerset Assize Orders 1640-59*, SRS Vol 71, Taunton, 1971.
Cockburn, J S, (ed) *Western Circuit Assize orders 1629-1648*, Camden 4th Series, London, 1976.
Colchester, L S, *Wells Cathedral School: The First Thousand Years c 909-1964*, Wells, (no date.)

Colchester, L S, (ed), *Wells Cathedral: A History*, Wells 1982.
Coldham, P W, (ed), *The Bristol Registers of Servants Sent to Foreighn Plantations, 1654-1686*, Baltimore 1988.
Coffey, J, *The Toleration Controversy during the English Revolution, in* Durston, C & Maltby, J, (eds), *Religion in Revolutionary England*, Manchester, 2006.
Crawford, P, *The Challenges to Patriarchalism: How did the Revolution affect Women?* in Morrill, J, (ed), *Revolution and Restoration: England in the 1650s*, London, 1992.
Cressey, D, *England On Edge: Crisis and Revolution*, Oxford, 2006.
Dunn, R S, *Sugar and Slaves: The Rise of the Planter Class in the English West Indies*, North Carolina, 1972.
Dunning, R, *The Bishop's Palace* in Colchester, L S, (ed), *Wells Cathedral: A History*, Wells 1982.
Dunning, R, *Somerset Families*, Tiverton, 2002.
Edgar, F T R, *Sir Ralph Hopton*, Oxford, 1968.
Everett Green, M A, (ed) *Calendar of State Papers Domestic 1660-61*, HMSO, London, 1860.
Everett Green, M A, (ed), *Calendar of State Papers Domestic, 1663-4*, London, 1862.
Everett Green, M A (ed), *Calendar of State Papers Domestic 1650*, HMSO, London, 1873.
Everett Green, M A, (ed), *Calendar of State Papers Domestic 1651*, HMSO, London, 1877.
Everett Green, M A, (ed), *Calendar of State Papers Domestic 1652-3*, HMSO, London, 1880.
Everett Green, M A, (ed), *Calendar of State Papers Domestic Interregnum 1657-58*, HMSO, London, 1884.
Everett Green, M A, (ed), *Calendar of the Committee for the Advance of Money Part 1, 1642-5*, HMSO, London, 1888.
Everett Green, M A, (ed), *Calendar of the Proceedings of the Committee for Compounding, Vol II 1643-46*, HMSO, London, 1890.
Firth, C H, & Rait, R S, (eds), *Acts and Ordinances of the Interregnum 1642-60*, London, 1911.
Firth, C H, & Davies, G, *A Regimental History of Cromwell's Army Vol* , Oxford, 1940.
Fletcher, A, *The Outbreak Of the English Civil War*, London, 1981.
Foster, J, (ed), *Alumni Oxonienses: The Members of the University of Oxford 1500-1714*, Oxford, 1891/2.
Fox, A, *Oral and Literate Culture in England 1500-1800*, Oxford, 2001.
Gardiner, S R, (ed), *The Constitutional Documents of the Puritan Revolution 1625-1660*, 3rd ed, Oxford, 1906.
Goadby, J J, *An Early History of the Somerset Baptist Association, England. 1871.*
Green, E, *The King's March through Somerset*, SANHS 24, Part 2, 1878.
Gristwood, S, *Arbella: England's Lost Queen*, London, 2003.
Hasler, J & Luker, B, *The Parish of Wookey: A New History*, Stroud, 1997.

BIBLIOGRAPHY

Hayden, R, (ed), *The Records of a Church of Christ in Bristol 1640-87*, BRS Vol 27, Bristol 1974.

Hembry, P, *The Bishops of Bath and Wells, 1540-1640,: Social and Economic Problems*, London, 1967.

Henning, B D, (ed), *The History of Parliament: The House of Commons 1660-90*, London, 1983.

Hill, R, *The Christopher Inn*, History Round Wells, Issue 5, 2002.

Holmes, G, *The Making of a Great Power: Late Stuart and Early Georgian Britain 1660-1722*, London, 1993.

Holmes, T S, *Wells and Glastonbury: A Historical and Topograpghical Account*, London, 1903.

Howard, A J & Stoate, T J, (eds), *Somerset Protestation Returns and Subsidy Rolls*, Almondsbury, 1974.

Hutton, R, *The Restoration*, Oxford, 1985.

Hutton, R, *The British Republic 1649-1660*, 2nd ed, London, 2000.

Hutton, R, *The Royalist War Effort 1642-1646*, 2nd ed, London, 2003.

Jeffs, R, (ed), *Mercurius Aulicus: The English Revolution III Newsbooks Vol 1*, London, 1971.

Lake, P, *The Laudian Style: Order, Uniformity and the Pursuit of the Beauty of Holiness in the 1630s*, in Fincham, K, (ed), *The Early Stuart Church 1603-1642*, Stamford, California, 1993.

Latham, R & Matthews, W, (eds), *The Diary of Samuel Pepys Vol 1*, Berkeley and Los Angeles, 1970.

Lynch, J, *For King and Parliament: Bristol and the Civil War*. Stroud, 1999.

Manning, B, *The English People and the English Revolution*, London, 1976.

Manning, B, *1649, The Crisis of the English Revolution*, London 1992.

Matthews, A G, (ed), *A Revision of John Walker's Sufferings of the Clergy during the Grand Rebellion 1642-60*, Oxford, 1948.

Moreland, S, (ed), *Somerset Quarterly Meeting of the Society of Friends*, SRS 75, Taunton, 1978.

Morrill, J, *The Church in England 1642-9* in Morrill, J, (ed), *Reactions to the English Civil War 1642-9*, London, 1982.

Morrill, J, (ed), *Revolution and Restoration*, London, 1992.

Morrill, J, *The Religious Context of the English Civil War* in Cust, R, & Hughes, A, (eds), *The English Civil War*, London, 1997.

Nott, T, *Poxe, Puncke and Puritane*, History Round Wells, Issue 4, Wells, 2001.

Nott, A & Hasler, J, (eds), *Wells Convocation Acts Books 1589-1665, parts 1 & 2 1589-1629 & 1629-44; 1662-5*, SRS Vols 90 & 91, Taunton, 2004.

Reynolds, H E, (ed), *Wells Cathedral: Its Foundation, Constitutional History and Statutes*, Wells, 1881.

Reay, B, *The Quakers and the English Revolution*, London, 1985.

Robinson, A, (ed), *Laudian Documents* in Palmer, T F, (ed), *Collectanea II*, SRS 43, Taunton, 1928.

Rodwell, W, *Wells Cathedral Excavations and Structural Studies 1978-93*, English Heritage, 2001, Archaeological Report 21.

Royle, T, *Civil War: The Wars of the Three Kingdoms 1638-1660*, London, 2004.

Russell, C, *Parliaments and English Politics 1621-1629*, Oxford, 1979.

Sacks, D H, *The Widening Gate: Bristol and the Atlantic Economy 1450-1700*, London, 1991.

Scrase, A J, *The Anatomy of a Medieval and Early Modern Property Market*, Working Paper 30, Faculty of the Built Environment, University of the West of England, 1993.

Scrase, A J, & Dunning, R, *The Bishop's Palace, Wells*, Somerset and Dorset Notes & Queries Vol xxxv, Part 354, September 2001.

Scrase, A J, & Hasler, J, (eds), *Wells Corporation Properties*, SRS 87, Taunton, 2002.

Scrase, A J, *The Inhabitants of Wells 1600-49*, History Round Wells, Issue 7, 2003.

Scrase, A J, *Wells: A Small City*, Stroud, 2006.

Serel, T, *Historical Notes on the Church of St Cuthberts in Wells*, Wells, 1875.

Shaw, W A, *A History of the English Church during the Civil Wars and under the Commonwealth 1640-1660*, Vol 2, London. 1900.

Slack, P, *Poverty and Politics in Salisbury 1597-1666* in Clark, P, and Slack, P, (eds), *Crisis and Order in English Towns 1500-1700*, London 1972.

Slack, P, *The Impact of the Plague in Tudor and Stuart England*, Oxford, 1985.

Slack, P, *Poverty and Policy in Tudor and Stuart England*, London, 1988.

Steig, M, *Laud's Laboratory: the Diocese of Bath and Wells in the Early Seventeenth Century*, London and Toronto, 1982.

Stokes, J, (ed), *Records of Early English Drama: Somerset*, 2 Volumes, Toronto, 1996.

Stokes, J, *The Wells Cordwainers' Show: New Evidence concerning Child Entertainments in Somerset*, Comparative Drama 27, 2, 1993.

Stoyle, M, *From Deliverance to Destruction*, Exeter, 1996.

Symonds, H, *A Bypath of the Civil War*, SANHS 65, 1919.

Thornbury, W, *Old and New London*, London, 1878.

Tinniswood, A, *The Verneys*, London, 2007.

Trevelyan, W C, & Trevelyan C E, *Trevelyan Papers*, Camden Series 105, London 1872.

Underdown, D, *Royalist Conspiracy in the Civil War and Interregnum*, Newhaven, 1960.

Underdown, D, *A Case Concerning the Bishops' Lands: Cornelius Burges and the Corporation of Wells*, New Series 78, English Historical Review, 1963.

Underdown, D, *Pride's Purge: Politics in the Puritan Revolution*, London, 1972

Underdown, D, *Somerset in the Civil War and Interregnum*, Newton Abbot, 1973.

Underdown, D, *Riot, Revel and Rebellion: Popular Politics and Culture in England 1603-1660*, Oxford, 1985.

Underdown, D, *Fire From Heaven*, London, 1992.

Vernon, E, *A Ministry of the Gospel: the Presbyterians during the English Revolution* in Durstan, C, & Maltby J, (eds), *Religion in Revolutionary England*, Manchester, 2006.

Walker, J, (abridged by Whittaker, R), *The Sufferings of the Clergy during the Great Rebellion*, London 1863.

White, B R, (ed), *Association Records of the Particular Baptists of England, Wales and Ireland to 1660, Part 2: the West Country and Ireland,* Baptist Historical Society.

White, P, *The Via Media in the Early Stuart Church* in Fincham, K, (ed), *The Early Stuart Church 1603-1642,* Stamford, California, 1993.

Williams, M, *The Draining of the Somerset Levels,* Cambridge, 1970.

Woodhouse, A S P, (ed), *Puritanism and Liberty,* London, 1986.

Woolrych, A, *Britain in Revolution 1625-1660,* Oxford, 2002.

Wroughton, J, *The Civil War in Bath and North Somerset,* Bath, 1973.

Wroughton, J, *An Unhappy Civil War: The Experience of Ordinary People in Gloucestershire, Somerset and Wiltshire 1642-46,* Bath, 1999.

Young, P, (ed), *Military memoirs: The Civil War: The Vindication of Richard Atkyns,* London, 1967.

INDEX

Notes
1. As **Wells** is the subject of the entire book, it is omitted as an entry in this index.
2. **Bold** page numbers indicate **chapter** extents.
3. *Italicised* plate numbers indicate *illustrations*
4. Sub-entries are arranged alphabetically, except where chronological order is more logical (e.g. Raleigh's funeral is after his murder)

Act for 'Well Governing and Regulating of Corporation' 214–16
'Act for Yearly Holding of Parliaments' (1640) 54
Adams, John (of Dulcote) 145
Adamson, J. 65
adultery, punishment for 179
aftermath of war (1645-49) **127–58**
    Bishop's rights and lands purchased 149–53
    cathedral and church affairs 139–43, 148–9
    Dean Raleigh, 'villanous' murder of 146–8, 157
    economic crisis 129–31
    national, county and city politics 132–5
    parliamentary bye-election 137–9
    Presbyterian MPs purged and imprisoned by army 154–5
    Royalists punished 135–7
    'sickness' (bubonic plague or typhus) 124, 127–9
    social problems 143–7
    end of decade 153–5
'aged and impotent and like to perish' 185–6
agriculture 129–30, 163
Aishe, John (died 1657) 184, 199
Aishe, Mary (later Evans) 184
Aishe, (Ashe) Robert (son of John, schoolmaster) 95, 184, 199–200
alcohol *see* drinks and drunkenness; inns
Alderley, Arthur 157, 158

alehouses *see* inns
ales (celebrations) *see* church ales
Alford, Elizabeth 145, 187
Allen, Richard and brother: witness crucifix destruction 58
Allen, Robert 155
almshouses 13, 14, 62, 143, 147
    Almshouse Hall 170
    Beggar Street 140
    Bubwith 13, 62, 170
    for elderly 185–6
    and Standish 143
American colonies and emigration to 72, 179, 181–2
Amor, John (carpenter/'mungrel-Joyner') 171
Andrews, William 175, 215
Anglicans 189, 211
Ann, Queen (consort of James I) 6
apprentices 51, 131
archbishops 108, 149
    of Canterbury *see* Laud
Archdeacons
    of Bath 12, 57
    see also Wood, Dr Gerard
    of Taunton *see under* Taunton
    of Wells 57
arms and armoury 76, 92–3
army
    Army Council 154
    billeting 43–6, 108, 153–4
    control of 132
    coup of 1648 189
    desertion, vandalism and murder by 45–6
    levy to support 131
    pay 93–4
        dean and chapter lands sold 153
        subsidies to raise money for 61–2
artisans 12–13
Ash Lane 7
Ash and Well Inn 169, 187
Ashburnham, John 115
Ashe, John (clothier from Freshford) 72, 73, 77, 80, 84, 85, 88

Assembly of Divines (Westminster) 109, 141, 191
Atkins, William 157, 206
Atkyns, Captain (*later* Major) Richard *Plate VII*, 100, 101, 102
Attwood, Henry 34
Atwell, Richard 61, 186
Atwell, William 22, 134, 175, 215
August of 1642 ('combustion at Wells') 66, **66–85**
  Monday August 1st 74–6
  Tuesday August 2nd 76
  Wednesday August 3rd 76
  Thursday August 4th 77–9
  Friday August 5th 79–82
  Saturday August 6th 82–4
Axbridge 17, 39, 192, 228
  Particular Baptists in 190, 211

Baber, George 130
Baber, John (MP) 10, 16, 21, 106, 204
  and Bartholomew Cox 50, 113
  and gunpowder purchase 112, 113
  national government and local affairs (1625-40) 43–4
  'service of the country' (1639-42) 49, 53, 59, 61
  and Wykes 50, 113
  death (1644) 113
Back Lane 7
Back Liberty 6, 7
Bacon, Robert 195
Bailey, D. S. 27, 104, 124, 125, 176, 177, 223
baileywicks purchased 168
bailiff 19
  of bishop 26
  fines 150
  wages of 151
Baines, A. 223, 2224
Baker, Edward 102
bakers 13
Bampfield, George 173
Bankes, Sir John 68
Banwell 96, 109, 147, 166–7, 208
Baptists 34, 133, 165, 189
  and Chapter House 172, 211
  General 190
  meetings in homes 211
  Particular 118, 123, 160, 190, 193, 211
  preacher *see* Collier
  and Presbyterians in dispute 191, 192–3
  and Quakers 198, 210–12
Barbados, indentured servants sent to 181, 182, 183
Barebone's Parliament (1653) 162
Barkeley, Sir Charles (of Bruton) see Berkeley

Barkham, Ezekiel 143, 170, 199
  secretary of *see* Bellamy, William
  will provides for charity school 183
Barkham, Margaret (widow of Ezekiel): founds school 183
barley shortage 130–1
Barlow, Henry 137
Barnard, William 217
Barnes, A.D. 199
Barnes, T.G. 46, 47, 84, 85
Barnstaple 90
Baron, Reverend Alexander 209–10
Baron, Henry (draper) 131, 134, 175, 223
  signature *Plate IX*, 165
Baron, Matthew (mayor) 222
Baron, Thomas: will (1634) 32
Baron, William (Mayor of Wells) 88, 134, 223
  and 1639/40 election 49
  in 1652-53 and 1660-1 225
  in Group of Eight 159
  as justice (1641) 61
  signature *Plate IX*
  death 21
Barons of the Exchequer 112, 149
Barrett, David (Puritan shoemaker and constable) 124, 133, 175, 193, 206
  and Baptists 172
  and canonical house restoration 170
  disenfranchised 105–6
  and Doctor Godwin's house 171
  elected as burgess (1640) 51, 53
  guilty of 'villainous' murder of Dean Raleigh (1646) 147–8
  takes Walrond to Ilchester 136
  visits London with Standish 168
  Western Association members arrested 160
  death (possibly 1674) 215, 220
Barrett, Elizabeth 220
Barrington Court 72
Barry, J. 27
bastardy case: woman treated more harshly than man 61
Batcombe parish 58, 135, 144, 155
Bates Harbin, E.H. 156, 176
Bath 3, 4, 6, 80, 119
  Abbey 141
  Archdeacons of, *see also* Wood, Dr Gerard
  besieged 121
  king visits (July 1644) 114
  Prynne as MP for 154
  Road 7
Bath and Wells, See of 15, 51
  Bishops *see* Godwin, Thomas; Laud, William; Piers, William

236

INDEX

Batt, Marie 122–3
battles, significant
  Dunbar 161
  Landsdown 103
  Langport 120, 191
  Lostwithiel 116
  map of 66
  Marston Moor 114, 191
  Naseby 120, 164
  Newburn 52
  Preston 164
Bayley, Philip 94
Beaminster (Dorset) 112
Beauchamp, Lord 160, 161
Beaumont, John and Anthony 27, 64
Beaumont, Thomas 157
Beaumont, William (d. 1633) 27
Beckington church and altar disagreement (1638) 37–8
Bedford, Earl of 53, 67, 88–9, 228
beer-brewing 131
Beggar Street 7
  Almshouse 140
Bekynton, Bishop 9, 33
Bekynton conduit *Plate XVII*
Bell, M. 200
Bellamy, William 26, 55–6, 58–9
Bendle, Matthew 182
benefices, bill against plurality of 56
'benevolences' ('voluntary' loans/ship money) 38–43, 54, 61, 106, 131
  abolished (1641) 43
Benford, Augustine 157
bequests, charitable 13
Berkeley, Sir Edward 89, 90
Berkeley, Sir Maurice 212–13
Berkeley of Bruton, Sir Charles 70, 115, 160, 212
Berkeley of Yarlington, Sir Henry 70
Berrow 118
Beryl 66, 81
Bettey, J.H. 784
Beverley (Yorkshire) 2
Bicknall, John 157
billeting militia 43–6, 108, 153–4
Binegar Fair 150
bishops
  abolition discussed 18, 139
    petition to keep (1641) 57
    by Parliament (1646) 108
    Piers impeached 54–9
    and Presbyterians 132
    retained 132
  and land
    purchase 151, 152–3
    rights purchased 168
    sale of 150, 151, 168–9
  restored (1659-65) 205–9, 211
  Wars against Scots and (1638 and 1640) 43, 44–6, 52
  woodlands, warden of 26
  see also archbishops; Godwin, Thomas; Guildhall; Laud, William; Piers, William
Bishop's Eye (Palace Gate) *Plate* XVII
Bishop's Lydyard 52
Bishop's Palace 1, 9, 10, 83
  in 1665 Plate XVII
  and Burges 166, 167
  keeper of 26
  looted 84, 96
  prison in 168
Bishop's Park 1
blacksmiths 115
Blagdon 35
Blake, Robert 119
blasphemy, Naylor indicted for 199
Blinman, John 173
Blue School founded in 1654 183
Bodmin 138
Boroughbridge 78
Bourne, Dr Gilbert (vicar general of Bath and Wells) 16
Bourne, Jane *see* Wykes, Jane
Bourne, Richard 18, 50
Bourne, Roger 18, 173
  sister *see* Wykes, Jane
Bower, Adrian (father of Edmund no.2) 17, 18, 43
  will of 27, 32
Bower, Edmund (no.1, son of Walter) 17, 27, 91
Bower, Edmund (no.2, son of Adrian) 17, 18
Bower, Walter (canon) 17
Bowerman, Andrew 17, 18, 110
  will of 27, 123, 126
Bowerman, Elizabeth 13
Bradford, John: will 32
Bratton, Ellinor 120
Breda, Declaration of (1660) 210
Brick, Walter 14, 18, 21, 57, 134
Brick almshouse 185
Bridger, Cornet Samuel 169, 171, 172, 193, 206
  marries Robert Morgan's daughter 164, 170
Bridges, Sir Thomas: of Keynsham 106, 137
Bridgwater 98, 110, 138
  arms caches 87
  besieged and captured (1643 and 1645) 97, 121, 146, 147
  quarter sessions meeting (1646) 133
  Stawell's meeting 115
Bridport 114

237

Brinte, Thomas: murders Thomas Foster 113, 124
Bristol 4, 6
  and aftermath of war (1645-49) 129, 136, 137
  and 'combustion at Wells' (1642) 76, 80
  Naylor in 199
  Newgate Gaol 220
  plague in 127
  Puritans worship in 34
  and Royalist Wells 105, 118, 124
  St Philip's Church 180
  society and religion (1649-59) 179, 180, 181, 182
  stormed (1643 and 1645) 105, 121
Bristol Road 7
Broadmead (Bristol) 34
Browne, Edward 61
Brown's Gate 171
'broyles and sharp contentions' (1649-59) **159–77**
  bishops' rights and property, disputes over 166–72
  Burges damages bishop's palace 166–7
  cathedral, dissension in 172–5
  corporation, changes in 159–60
  'every railing Shimei' 166–7
  national and local government 161–6
  royalist plotting (1649-50) 160–1
  'vexatious, frivolous and contentious jar' 167–72
Bruce, J. 47, 65
Bruton 45, 70, 115, 142, 212
bubonic plague *see* plague
Bubwith Almshouse 13, 62, 170, 185, 186
Buckingham, Duke of 43, 72
Buckland, John 204
Buckley, Daniel 31, 64
Bull, George 18, 41, 143
Bull, Henry 204
Bull, Lawrence 75
Bull, Thomas 101
Bull, William (linen draper, mayor 1613, died 1622) 13, 204
Bull, William (of Shapwick) 18, 204-5
Burges, Dr Cornelius 24, 56, 177, 206
  on Aishe 184
  on Amor 171
  arrival in 1649 149
  and bishop's lands purchase 151, 152–3
  and Bridger 171
  disagreements and conflict with others 157, 179, 193
  asserts rights to cathedral 174–5
  chancery suit against corporation (1649-63) 153
  damages palace to refurbish deanery 166–7
  and Dr Walker's house 169, 170
  labelled as 'vexatious, frivolous and contentious jar' 167–72
  and social ostracism 167
  and Marsh 148
  and Mead 171
  as pluralist (more than one living) 173
  son John 159
  and The Rib *Plate XIV*
  and Walrond group 172
  on wives of burgesses ('proud wifelings') 186, 187
burgesses 51, 53, 60
  capital 19, 22
  wives *see* 'wifelings, proud'
Burial Farm, (Beryl) lane to 7
burling chamber 14
Burnham 118
Burrington church 35
Busby, Richard 207
Bush, Edward 146
Bushell, William 44
butchers 13
Butler, Humfrie 155
Butler, Lord Richard 212
by-elections 137–9

Caernarvon, Earl of 99, 100
Calamy, E. 156
Calvinism 32
Camely, Samuel Oliver as Vicar of 141
Camery (Cathedral land) 37, 112
campaigns of 1644 and 1649 113–18, 164
Canonical Houses (The Rib/The Deanery) 166, 168–9, 170, 171, 215, 219
  illustrated *Plates XII, XIII, XIV* and *XVII*
Canterbury
  Archbishop of *see* Laud
  Prerogative Court wills still extant 30
Capell, Lord 119
capital burgesses 19, 22
Cardiff 89
card-playing in alehouses 145
carrier service disrupted 122
Casbeard, John 18, 134, 141, 175
  criticises new royalist government 220–1
  father *see* Casbeard, Richard
  and purchase of former bishop's rights and property 149–51, 152, 168
  arrested 153
Casbeard, Mary (wife of John) 220
Casbeard, Richard 13, 22, 107, 115, 175
  as justice 141
  as Mayor of Wells (1645-46 and 1659-60) 31, 141, 205, 225

INDEX

not purged 223
as shoemaker 117–18, 122
son *see* Casbeard, John
will 32
death (1662/3) 220
Casbeard, Theophilus (son of John and Mary) 220
Castle Cary 120
catechising 142
Cathedral (Wells) 187
  in 1735 *Plate XV*
  and aftermath of war 139–43, 148–9
  Camery (land) 37, 112
  Chapter House 172, 193, 211
  clergy 18–19
  Cloister *Plate XVII*
  Company 84
  dissension in 172–5
  establishment, threat to 108–12
  fashionable area to live near 15
  Green 15, 16, 147, 171
  Lady Chapel *Plate XVII* 112
  parliamentary soldiers damage (1643) *Plate* VI, 96
  Puritans and 34
  restored (1659-65) 205–9
  see also Liberty
Cathedral School
  Grammar *see* 'Free Grammar School'
  Lechlade's House (College Road) *Plate XII*, 16
Catholicism
  Protestation against 62
  Rebellion, Irish 2, 136
  recusants (1642) 25–6, 64
  tolerated 144
cattle market 10
Cavalier Parliament and local MPs 212–14
Chadwyck Healey, C.E. 6, 85
Chain Gate *Plate XVII*
Chamberlain Street 7, 15, 17, 50, 76, 123, 219
Chancery, Court of 169
chandlers 12, 22
Chapter House (Cathedral) 172, 193, 211
chapters abolished by Parliament 108, 149
  land sold 153
Chard (Somerset) 109, 112, 114, 117
Charity School *see* Blue School
Charles I, King (1600-49, r. 1625-49) 1–2, 11, 35, 49, 61, 161, 206
  and army 43, 45
  arrives in Bath 114
  and 'combustion at Wells' 67, 68
  nephew of *see* Maurice, Prince
  Royal Arms in St Cuthbert's Church *Plate XVII*

and Royalist Wells 116, 117, 119
and Scottish Presbyterians *see* Wars *under* bishops
and ship money 40, 131
and 'Short' parliament 51
surrender to Scots (1646) 132
trial 155
death of 110, 155
see also Royalist Wells
Charles II, King (1630-85, r. 1660-85)
  and Declaration of Breda (1660) 210
  as Prince of Wales 110, 119, 155, 160–1, 205, 206
Charterhouse on Mendip 138–9
Cheddar 109, 190, 192
  Road 7
Chedzoy (near Bridgwater) 110, 147
Chetwynd, Edward and John 180, 207, 209–10
Chew Magna 180
Chew Stoke 35
Chewton (Mendip) 6, 76, 77, 99, 100, 106
Chief Justice of Common Pleas (Bankes) 68
Chilcote 139
Child Okeford (Dorset) 111
children, working 14
Chrighton, Doctor *see* Creighton
Christ Church College *see under* Oxford
Christmas: observance banned 109
Christopher Inn 13, 22, 172
church 179–81
  and aftermath of war (1645-49) 139–43, 148–9
  ales (celebrations) and controversy (1607) 11, 20, 22
  penalty for non-attendance 189, 211
  see also Cathedral; Catholicism; clergy; religion
Church of England 62, 111
churchwardens 64, 113, 134, 227
Chute, Robert 19
Chyle, Nathaniel: *History of Wells* (1680) 96, 166, 176, 221
Ciniox, Ralph 22, 118, 134
Cirencester 94
city politics and aftermath of war (1645-49) 133–5
Civil War, English (1642-9) 23, 31, 60, **66–126**, 132, 190
  sequence of events *see* August of 1642
  see also aftermath of war (1645-49); 'combustion at Wells'
Clarendon, Edward Earl of 4, 6, 9
  and 'combustion at Wells' (1642) 68, 72–3, 84
  as Lord Chancellor 210
Clark, P. 27

239

classis system of presbyteries and parishes 141–2, 191
Clement, Christopher 208
clergy 11, 15, 18–19, 172
Close Hall (Vicars. Hall) *Plate XVII* 153
clothiers/drapers/mercers 13, 14, 22, 23, 92
  decline 12
  trade 24–5
  and wartime demand 122
  see also Baron, Henry
Clubman movement (1645) 80, 120
Clutterbuck, Benedick 116
Clutterbuck, James 159, 181, 199
cobblers *see* shoemakers
Cockburn, J.S. 6, 157, 176
Coffey, J. 200
Coke, Sir John 35–6
Colchester, L.S. 125, 176, 222
Coldham, P.W. 199
Cole, Richard 217
College Lane/Road 1, 6, 7, 15, 167
  Lechlade's House *Plate XII* 16
Colles, John 13
Collier, Thomas 195
  Discourse ....in Axbridge 228
  Looking-Glass for Quakers (1642) 193, 198, 199, 200, 228
  as 'Master Sectarie' 190–3
  petition on army 154
  preaches in York 191
  on Presbyterianism, frivolity of 191, 192–3
  death (1691) 211
colonies, usefulness of 181–2, 188
'combustion at Wells' (1642) **66–85**, 123
  map of battles fought 66
  Parliamentarians as protagonists 71–4
  Royalists as protagonists 67–71
  see also August of 1642; Civil War
Commission of Array 2, 3, 73, 76, 83
Committees
  for Advance of Money 135
  of Compounding 26, 136
  for Removal of Obstructions 168
  for Sequestrations 149
  Somerset County 23, 91, 139
common land enclosed 5
Common Pleas, Chief Justice of (Bankes) 68
Common Prayer, Book of: abolished and illegal 108–9, 143, 147
communion table, unornamented 35–6
Compounding, Committee for 26, 128, 136, 137
Compter/Counter (London prison) 90–1
Compton Bishop 16
Compton Dando 71, 77, 110
Compton Dundon 78

Coniers, Ralph (Corporation) 18
Contractors for Sale of Bishops' Lands 168
Conventicle Act (1664) 211
Convention Parliament elections 204–5
Convocation Acts Books (1589-1644 and 1662-65) v
Cook, Hodges 223
Cooke, Josiah (churchwarden) 64, 134
Cordwainers 11
Cordwent, Frances (widow of Humphrey, later marries Mayor Robert Morgan) 22, 188
Cordwent, Humphrey (died 1638) 188, 200
Cordwent, Humphrey (Mayor of Wells, 1661-62 – stepson of Robert Morgan, innkeeper and draper) 169, 170, 175, 223
Cordwent, John 216
Cork, Lord of 58
Cornwall 89, 115–16, 124
Corporation v 12, 167, 173
  'Act for Well Governing and Regulating of' (1661) 211, 214–16
  changes in 159–60
  finances 13–14
  in 'Pleasant City' 19–25
  Receiver 134, 170
  recorder *see* Dodington, Christopher
  records 227
  signatures of leading parliamentarians in *Plate XII*
Cothelstone 52, 76
Cottington, Francis, elder and younger (recusants) 64
Cottington, Dr James (d. 1605) 26
Coulin, Richard 119
Councell, Elizabeth 183
Council of State 172
county politics and aftermath of war (1645-49) 133
Courts
  of Chancery 169
  High Commission suppressed 56
  Prerogative, extant wills of 30
Couth, John 31, 73, 74
Coventry, John 70, 77
Coventry, Thomas, Lord Keeper 70, 227
Coward, Mary (later wife of William Piers, son of the bishop) 111
Coward, Thomas (Mayor of Wells, 1611-1612 and 1619-1620, died 1621) 17
Coward, Thomas (militia captain, 1640s) 17, 45, 76, 93, 115–16, 137, 173, 183, 213
Coward, William (brother of Thomas of militia, mayor of Wells 1663-4) 17, 18, 27, 216, 219

INDEX

Cox, Bartholomew (Town Clerk and Mayor of Wells, 1648-49) 18, 19, 20-1, 88, 146, 225
  and alehouses 145, 213
  and Baber 50, 113
  and bishops's rights purchase 151
  retirement 159
  will 32
Cox, John (burgess, nephew of Bartholomew) 22, 134
Coxley 83
Crane, Alice 176
Crawford, Anne (Wells Cathedral archivist) 104
Crawford, P. (on patriarchalism) 200
Creed, George 145
Creese, Robert (burgess) 22
Creighton (Creyghton/Crightone), Dr Robert (Dean) 16, 18
  and new market/town hall 218
  and restoration and reaction (1659-65) 206, 207
  and parliamentary Wells 95, 101
  and Royalist Wells 109, 110, 120
Creighton, Frances (wife of Robert) 110
Cressey, D. 65
Crewkerne 113
Creyghton/Crighton *see* Creighton
crime
  juvenile 146
  see also murder
Croker, William (d. 1624) 24
Cromwell, Oliver 119, 161, 163, 189, 197
  appointed Lord Protector (1653) 162
    see also Protectorate
  and Major Generals 164, 165
  petition from Wells 173
  death (1658) 165
  exhumed remains 220
Cromwell, Richard 165-6, 203, 206
Croscombe 24
Crosse, Bailiff William 19
Crown Inn (Market Place, Wells) *Plate X* 113, 118, 172, 215
Cuddesdon (Oxfordshire) 111
Culme, Robert 182
Culpepper, Lord 119
Curle, Bishop of Bath & Wells (1629-32) 34, 36
Curll, Edward 135, 144, 157
Curry Mallett 72, 133
Curse, Robert 176
Cuthbert, Saint *see* St Cuthbert

Daniell, Christopher 119
dates, old and new styles of v
David, King 177

Davidge, John 175, 223
Davidge, Thomas 216
Davis, Daniel 157, 158
Davis, Joan (first death from 'the sickness') 124
Davis, Richard 124
Davis, William (archdeacon of Bath) 112
De Vita Christi (Ludolphus) *Plate VI* 97
Deane, Richard 31
Deanery, The *see* Canonical Houses
deans
  abolished by Parliament 108
  Dean's Lodging 16, 44
  of Gloucester 35
  of Winchester 110
  see also Creighton; Raleigh, Dean Walter
death penalty for adultery 179
Declaration of Breda (1660) 210
'Defence of King, Parliament and Kingdom' (1642-3) 92-5
Denton (Oxfordshire) and Piers family 219
  William Piers retires to 9, 58-9
depreciation in value of wages 13
Dericke, William: alehouse 155
Desborough, Colonel/Major General 161, 163, 164-5, 172, 204
  wife of 198
Devon 89, 193
Dewbery, James and Mary 157
Digby, Sir John 70, 75, 76, 78
Dinham, Jasper 92
Directory of Public Worship 109, 143, 191
Ditcheat 111
Doctor Godwin's house 171
Dodington, Christopher (Corporation recorder) 109, 133, 138, 168
Dodington, Sir Francis (brother of Christopher) 70, 76, 133
Dorman, M. 223
Dorset 106, 111, 112, 193
Doulting limestone 217
Dove, Colonel John 168, 169
Downe, John 146
drapers *see* clothiers/drapers/mercers
drinks and drunkenness 145, 187
  see also inns and alehouses
Duck, Dr Arthur (bishop's vicar general) 19, 51, 58
Duffett, Richard 61
Dugdale, Dr James 90, 207
Dulcote 124, 145
Dulverton: vicar appointed (1642/3) 95
Dunbar, battle of (1650) 161
Dunn, R.S. 199
Dunning, R. 176, 177, 223
Dunster Castle: captured (1643) 97
Dursley (Gloucestershire) 209

241

Durston, C. 200

East Brent 118, 139
East Curry 140
East Liberty 6, 7, 15
'East Ruin' 171
Easter: observance banned 109
Eastern Association 164, 190
economy and crises 11–14, 129–31
Edgar, T.F.R. 65
Edmunds, John 148
education 183–5
   Blue School 183
   of women 187
   see also Cathedral School; 'Free Grammar School'
elderly, almshouses for 185–6
elections 49, 53, 165
   by-elections 137–9
   Convention Parliament 204–5
   and Piers 50–1
Ellesmere, Lord Chancellor 4–5
emigration to America 179, 181–2
employment 11–14
enclosure of common land 5
episcopacy *see* bishops
Episcopalian church 211
Erbury, William (preacher) 34–5
Essex, Earl of 4, 67, 113–14, 115, 116
Estibrooke, John 101
Eure, Lieutenant: murdered 46
Evangelicalism 30, 31
Evans family 18, 27
Evans, Mary (née Aishe) 184
Evans, William (recusant) 64
Evans, William (schoolmaster) 26
Evelyn, John (diarist) 110
Evercreech 42
Everett Green, M.A.E. 104, 125, 156, 157, 176, 223, 224
Exchequer, Barons of 112, 149
excise rates 131
Exeter 11, 114, 116
   captured (1643) 97
   gaol, Naylor in 198
   market 130
Exeter College (Oxford) 141
Exmoor 89

Fairfax, Sir Thomas: New Model Army 120–1, 137, 138, 191
fairs *see* markets and fairs
Farleigh Castle 80
farming 129–30, 163
Farnborough 99
Fatt, Thomas: will 32

feudalism 2
Fiennes, Celia 222, 224
finances of corporation 13–14
Fincham, K. 46, 47
Firth, C.H. 125
fish shambles 10, 169–70
Fletcher, A. 65
Flower de Luce Inn 155, 166
Ford, William 223
Forestallers 131
Foster, Henry (Mayor of Wells, 1645-46) 20, 22, 134, 225
   and Royalist Wells 107, 113
   son *see* Foster, Thomas
Foster, Joan 46, 156
Foster, Sir Robert 3, 124
Foster, Thomas (constable/tanner) 22, 107
   father *see* Foster, Henry
   murdered by Brinte 113, 124
Fowey 117
France 54
   Creighton's escape to 110
   War with (1626-27) 43, 44
'Free Grammar School', Cathedral *Plate XVII* 15, 26, 112, 183–5, 210
   masters *see* Ashe, Robert; Thirlby
freedom bonus 182
freedom of worship (1650) 190
Fricker, William 216
Frier, Robert 223
Frome 7
   plague in 127
   riot in 131
Front Library 6, 7
Fryer, Richard 24, 90, 175

Gaik, John 155
Gallington, Joseph (Mayor of Wells, 1654-55) 24, 175, 225
   and aftermath of war (1645-49) 134, 142, 145
   in group of eight 159
   and restoration and reaction (1659-65) 215, 216
   signature of *Plate IX* 165
gaol *see* prison
Gardiner, S.R. 65
Garment, Dorothy (née Stephens/Steevens, wife of Joshua) 194
Garment, Joan (and John Robins) 196
Garment, Joan ('wife' of Joshua) 195, 197
Garment, Joshua (Ranter) 124, 193–7, 198
   Hebrews Deliverance written by 196, 200, 228
Garment, Philip 197
Garment, William 194
Gatehouse Prison (Westminster) 220

INDEX

Gates, Lieutenant 43
'Genevan tyranny', Presbyterianism as 110
gentry
  in 1642 14–18
  in Liberty 11, 15, 172
George Inn 22, 223
Glastonbury 78, 83, 112, 119
  couples from, married in Wells 123
  houses pillaged 102
  and parliamentary Wells 89–90, 95, 97, 98, 101
  'prophets' preaching in 196
  Road 7
Gloucester
  Cathedral organ 112
  dean of (Warburton) 35
  Duke of (died 1660) 212–13
  economic depression (1620s-30s) 11–12
  fair cancelled (1625) 92
  Particular Baptists in 193
  prison 34, 94
Gloucestershire 4, 80, 209
Goadby, J.J. 200
Godney Moor enclosure 5
Godwin, James (d. 1616) 13, 26
Godwin, James (1642) 25–6
Godwin, Joseph 25–6
Godwin, Dr Paul (canon and son of Bishop Thomas Godwin) 38 16, 18, 112, 171
Godwin, Robert 25, 26
Godwin, Thomas (Bishop of Bath and Wells 1584-90) 18, 38, 41
Godwin family recusants 64
Goldsmith's Hall 138
Gorges, Sir Ferdinando 70, 74, 76, 89
Goring, Lord George 118, 119, 120, 146
Gorren, Gray Holliner: murdered 124
Gorway, Widow 130
Grammar School *see* 'Free Grammar School'
Grand Remonstrance (1641) 63
green wax profits (from fines) 150
Grenville, Sir Richard 119
Grey, Earl Henry 93
Gristwood, S. 65
grocers 13, 24
Grope Lane 7
Guardhouse Lane 22
Guernsey 191
Guildhall 62, 151, 152, 168, 171

haberdashers 13
  Haberdashers Hall 138
Haines, Ralph 34
Hampden, John 54
Hampshire 106, 110, 116
Hance, John: murder of 124
Hardwich, Thomas and Joseph 182

Hare and Hounds Inn 22
Harperly, Thomas 176
Harris, William 101, 124
Hartford, Marquesse see Seymour Edward
Hartlepool, defence of 165
harvests, poor (1646) 129–30
Haskett, Stephen (Mayor of Wells, 1655-56) 23–4, 57, 60, 142, 175, 220, 225
  chooses Jenkins to represent Wells 165
  in group of eight 159
  move to Bristol 124
  and parliamentary Wells 89, 90, 102–3
  signature of *Plate IX* 215
  as tax commissioner 163
Hasler, Joan v, 230, 231, 232
havock' (soldiers raid cathedral) 95–7
Hawley, Sir Francis 70, 78, 79
Hayden, R 46
Hayward, Lieutenant 90
Healey, Chadwyck 104
Heath, Thomas 216
Hellyer, Richard 94–5
Hembry, P. 65, 84, 199, 223
Henning, B.D. 222, 223
Henrietta Maria, Queen 2, 110
Henstridge 111
Herbert, Lord Philip 5
Hertford Earl of, Lord Lieutenant (1601, grandfather of Marquis) 4–5
  Marquis of *see* Seymour, William
Hiett, William (constable) 22, 64, 118
Higgins (cook): on hypocrisy of Puritans 144, 157
High Commission Court suppressed 56
High Cross *Plate XVII*, *Plate XI*, 38
High Littleton 99
High Street 22, 220
  Christopher Inn 13, 22, 172
  Garment living in 197
  George Inn (now Nat West) 22, 223
  Hare and Hounds Inn (now no. 33) 22
  long term occupation of rented houses 123
  number 6: 19
  number 8: 19
  number 28: 169
  number 78: 17
  tenements 10, 16
Hill, John (burgess) 22, 134
Hill, Joseph 24
Hill, Robert (constable) 22, 27, 64, 175, 223
  signature of *Plate IX*
Hinton St George, Baron of see Poulett
Hixe, Richard (father and son) 208
Hole, Dorothy (*later* Mercer) 176
Hole, John 11, 12, 20, 24, 25, 134, 169, 184
  will 32

243

Hole, Richard 218
Hole, Robert 134, 135, 171, 175
  purged 215
  signature of *Plate IX*
  and The Rib *Plate XIII*
Hollis, Denzill 4
Holmes, G. 222
Holmes, T.S. 199
Holt, Thomas 207
Holy Communion: access controlled 142
holy days: observance banned by parliament 109
Hopton, Sir Ralph *Plate II* 4, 23, 204, 227
  appoints Nurton as postmaster 107–8
  besieged 104, 228
  and 'combustion at Wells' 68, 70, 73-7 *passim*, 80-3 *passim*
  house at Witham 115
  impeached by parliament 137
  and impressment of soldiers 106
  and Long Parliament 53
  as MP for Wells 59, 62, 63–4
  and parliamentary Wells (1642-43) 90, 93, 94, 97-101 *passim*
  recommendations by 133
  and Royalist Wells 108, 117
  and William Morgan 106
  wounded and flees 138
Hopton, Robert 53
Horler, John 186
Horner family 133
Horner, Sir John 72, 73, 79, 82, 138
  home of 77, 114
Horse Pool 177
horse-requisitioning 107
house of correction in prison loft 14
House, Elizabeth and Hester: sent to Barbados 182
House, Mary: sent to Virginia 182
Houses of Parliament *see under* Parliament
Howard, A.J. 65
Howard, Captain 96
Hubbert, Thomas (JP) 196
hucksters 131, 187
Hundred of Wells Forum 42, 112–13, 116, 150, 168
Hungerford family 133
  Sir Edward 80
Hunt, Gyles 200
Hurman, James 175, 215, 216
  signature of *Plate IX*
Hutchins, Henry 34
Hutton, R. 125, 200, 223

Ilchester 49, 53
  gaol 88, 111, 146–7
  King visits 115

Strode as MP for 154
illegitimate births 119–20
Ilminster, vicar of 111
impeachment
  of Piers 18, 54–9
  of Strafford 54, 59–60
impressment of soldiers 106
Imray, Jean 157, 200
indentured servants sent abroad 14, 179, 181-3
Independents 132, 133
  religious 162, 189
inflation 13
Ingrossers 131
inns and alehouses 13, 42, 223
  Ash and Well 169, 187
  card-playing in 145
  Christopher 13, 22, '72
  Crown *Plate X* 113, 118, 172
  Flower de Luce 155, 166
  George 22, 223
  Hare and Hounds 22
  on High Street 13, 22, 172, 223
  illegal sales 122
  innkeeper *see* Cordwent
  proliferation and crusades against 144
  regulation of 131
  Star 223
  Swan 13, 42
  work for women in 187
  see also drinks and drunkenness
Instrument of Government 163, 165
"intelligencers" 52, 130
Interregnum 110, 124, 212, 215
investment in Propositions scheme 93, 103
Ireland 111
  army in 114
  campaign against (1649) 164
  Catholic Rebellion 2, 136
  Lord Lieutenant of 54
  Stubbes exiled to 180
  Walrond from 136
Isle Brewers (near Taunton) 16

Jacob's Well 220
James I, King of England 6, 35, 39, 54
James II, King of England 221
Jeffs, R. 104
Jenkins, Major John 125, 163, 164–5, 176, 193, 204
  cornet of *see* Bridger
Jetson, Bernard 101
Jett, Alexander 18, 19, 51, 58, 173, 175
  Bellamy's letter to 55–6
  as bishop's registrar 208, 216
  as clerk to county committee 106
  fined for working with royalists 137

INDEX

letter to Sandford 57
  as Sarah Tabor's executor 188
  as West's executor 159
Jett, Margaret (daughter of Alexander) 173
Jews 194, 195
Johnson, Gabriel 92
Jones, Henry (glazier/unlicensed alehouse) 122, 187
Jones, Henry (hammerman) 64
Jones, Katherine (wife of Henry the glazier) 186, 187
Jones, Thomas (justice) 64
Jones, Thomas (Mayor of Wells, 1640-41) 21, 33, 52, 225
juvenile crime 146

Keene, Francis (son-in-law of Sarah Tabor) 96, 97, 188
Keene, Walter 188
Kellow, Elizabeth, Margaret and Ann (daughters of Henry) 129
Kellow, Ellinor (wife of Henry) 129
Kellow, Captain Henry 101
  loss of remaining seven family members to plague 129
Kellow, James and John 129
Kellow, William 101
Keynes, Alexander 160
Keynsham 137
Kidder, Bishop 222
King, Edmund 145
'King, Parliament and Kingdom, Defence of' (1642-3) 92–5
King's Moor 115
Kingsbury Episcopi 111
Kingweston (near Glastonbury) 112
Kinsale (Ireland) 111
Kirkby, Patrick: photographs by *Plates V, XIII, XIV*
Kirton, Edward 54, 70, 77, 133
Knapfee 140
Knight, Bishop 9, 36, 224

Lady Chapel of Cathedral *Plate XVII* 112
Lake, Bishop Arthur 30, 60, 183
Lake, P. 46
Lamport (Langport) 106
Lancaster, Elizabeth: and 'base' child 119–20
land
  Bishops' *see under* bishops
  purchased by church, Bishop's rights and 168
  sold to finance army 153
Landsdown, battle of 103
Lane, John (mariner) 182
Lane, Robert 21, 22, 25, 134

visit to London (1641) 59–60
Langport, battle of (1645) 120, 191
Latham, R. 222
Laud, William, Archbishop of Canterbury 19, 51
  as bishop of Bath and Wells (1626-28) 34, 37, 183
  high church policies 18, 29
  Laudian altar removed 142
  Laudianism and Puritanism 35
  protégés of 35
  and Warburton 36, 58
  executed 110
law
  lawyers 15
    see also Morgan, William
  property, women and 188
  recorder (legal officer) 19
Lawpool 7
Lay, Mary 179
Lay Subsidy returns (1641) 15
lead mining 151, 152
lead-stripping by thieves 148
leases, property 188
Lechlade's House *Plate XI* 16
Lee, Katherine 61
Levellers 164, 191
Lewce, William 12, 22, 34
'liable to bear office' 59–60
liberty of subject 3
Liberty, The (area near cathedral) 9, 18, 59–60, 64, 117
  in 1735 *Plate XV*
  Back 6, 7
  Dean's Lodging 16, 44
  Duck's house in 51
  East 15
  gentry and clergy in 11, 15, 172
  houses sold 168
  Lechlade's House *Plate XII* 16
  North *see* College Lane
  number 17 219
  payment 42
  Robert Chute in 19
  Robert Toope of 26
  William Laud in 19
  see also Canonical House
libraries 6, 7, 173, 180, 207
Lightfoot, Robert 122
limestone 217
Little Entry 7
Litton 42
Llewellyn, Henry 14
Llewellyn almshouse 185
loans *see* 'benevolences'
local affairs *see* national government and local affairs

Loggins, John 134
London 109, 168
  carrier service disrupted 92, 122
  Collier in 191
  Committee for Advance of Money 135
  Committee for Removal of Obstructions 168
  Naylor in 199
  prison 18, 54–9, 90–1
  Putney Debates (1647) 191
  see also Parliament
Long, Lislebone (died 1659) 204
  and aftermath of war 133, 138, 139, 150, 154
  'broyles and sharpe contentions' 162, 165, 166
Long, Sir Robert 101
Long, William 75
Long Ashton 89
Long Parliament/the Rump (164-53) 38, 52–4, 161–2, 166
Lords, House of 57–8
Lostwithiel and battle of 115, 116
Lovell, Edmund 216
Lovell, Richard (cutler) 34
Low Ham 76
Luker, Brian, v, 230
Ludolphus de Saxonia: *De Vita Christi*/'Vita Jesu Christi' *Plate VI* 97
Lund, John 27
Lund, Maurice (Morris) recusant, 26, 27 64
Lunsford, Colonel Henry 1, 70–1, 78–9, 81, 83
Lunsford, Sir Thomas 70–1
Lydford Fair 77
Lyme Regis 92, 108, 114
  siege of 113
Lympsham 118
Lynch, J. 155

Macauley, John S. 124
Maintenance of Ministers, Trustees for 149, 173
Major Generals, rule of 161, 163, 164–5
Malett, Thomas 60
Maltby, J. 200
Maltsters 131
Manning, B. 156
maps 7, 66
Mark (place) 118
Market Hall *see* New Market/Town Hall
Market House *see* Town Hall
Market Place 188
  in 1665 *Plate XVII*
  in 1735 *Plate XV*
  Crown Inn *Plate X* 113, 118, 172
  New Works 9, 15, 188

Number *25* 16
Numbers *16, 19, 21* and *24* 19
punishments in 179
see also Canonical Houses; Guildhall; New Market; Town Hall
markets and fairs 12, 56, 150, 163
  cancelled 92, 128
  cattle 10
  cross, Bishop Knight's Late Gothic 9
  illegal activities 122
  profits from 167
  and sale of bishop's land 151
  six annual 13
Marks, Richard 145
Marlborough 2–3, 4, 9
Marley, Captain John 119
Marquis, the *see* Hopton, Sir Ralph
Marsh, Humphrey (sexton) 112, 148, 157, 172–3, 174, 175
  dismissed 206
  son-in-law *see* Edmunds, John
Marshals Elm 78, 79, 81
Marston Moor, battle of (1644) 114, 191
Martock 217
'Master Sectarie', Thomas Collier as 190–3
Matthews, A.G. 46, 125, 156, 157, 199, 223
Matthews, W. 222
Mattock, Arthur 19, 109, 214
  bribed with 90lb cheese 208
Maurice, Prince of Rhine (1621-52) *Plate VIII*, 97, 98–9, 100, 102, 106, 108, 113–14
  Prince Maurice's Regiment of Horse *Plate VII*
May family (bailiffs) 223
May (month): customs/maypoles 11, 34
Mayne, John (musician) 34, 41, 42
mayors 19
  listed (1640-65) 225
Mead, Hugh (pewterer, died 1639) 14, 24, 25, 32
Mead, Thomas (Mayor of Wells, 1653-54, son of Hugh) 24, 64, 159, 163, 165, 169, 171, 175, 203, 215, 220, 225,
  signature of *Plate IX*
Meadows, Edmund 218
Mells Court 77, 114, 115
Mendip Hills 4, 5, 6, 77, 80, 82, 98, 99, 138–9
  lead from 151, 152
Mercer, David 176
Mercer, Dorothy (*née* Hole) 176
mercers *see* clothiers/drapers/mercers
Merefield, Hugh (chandler) 134, 175, 223
Meres, John 130
Mews, Bishop 219
Middle Row 10

INDEX

Middleham, James 175, 184
Middleham, John 223
Middleham, Purefoy (vicar of Westbury, 1623-61) 190
Middleham, Thomas 41
Middleton, John, Lieutenant General, 116–17
Milborne Port 116, 217
Militia
  billeting 43–6, 108, 153–4
  Ordinance 2, 83, 87
Mill Lane 7
Millard, Florence (widow of William) 187
Millard, Hugh and Alice 129
millers 22
Milton (hamlet) 6
Milward, George 75, 93
Minehead 71, 89, 138
Moderate Intelligencer, The 130
Mogge, Richard 135
monarchy restored *see* Restoration
Monck, General George 203, 212, 220
Monmouth, Duke of (1685) 221
Montacute 49, 72
moral reformation of society 179
moral turpitude 60–1
Moreland, S. 201
Morgan, Ann (prostitute) 61, 145–6, 186, 187
Morgan, Frances (wife of Robert, widow of Humphrey Cordwent) 22, 188
Morgan, John 137
Morgan, Robert (Mayor of Wells, 1641-42 and 1646-47) 106, 115, 225
  and aftermath of war (1645-49) 133, 134, 138, 141, 144, 151, 152, 153
  bishop's rights purchase 149, 150
  brother *see* Morgan, William (lawyer)
  and 'broyles and sharp contentions' (1649-59) 159
  'combustion at Wells' (1642) 76, 83
  daughter marries Samuel Bridger 164, 170
  father William 22
  freed from captivity 114, 143–4
  increased number of petty sessions 144
  marries Frances Cordwent (widow of Humphrey Cordwent, died 1638) 22, 188
  parliamentary Wells 87, 88, 89, 90, 93, 102, 122
  'Pleasant city' (1642) 13, 17, 22–3
  rents house 169
  'service of the country' (1639-42) 57, 60, 64, 163
  stepson *see* Cordwent, Humphrey (Mayor)
  death (1653) 153, 168, 175, 215

Morgan, William (father of Robert) 22
Morgan, William (lawyer) 17, 22, 93, 103, 106, 116, 119, 124, 137, 188
Morrill, J. 46, 125, 157, 200
Moss, John 157, 158
Mowrie, Anthony 157
Mowrie, Mary 157
Mundays Meadow 153
murder
  of Dean Raleigh 146–8, 157
  of Gray Gorren 124
  of John Hance 124
  of Lieutenant Eure 46
  murderers caught 113, 124, 147–8
  of Thomas Foster 113, 124
  threats of 112–13
Museum, Wells 171
music in church 37, 112, 143

Naseby, battle of (1645) 120, 164
national government
  and aftermath of war 132
  and local affairs (1625-40) **29–47**
    Bishop Piers 32–5
    'in a mist of ceremonies' 35–8
    militia and billeting 43–6, 108
    religion 29–30
    St Cuthbert's Church 30–2
    ship money 38–43
  and local affairs (1649-59) 161–6
Navy, Treasurer of 42
Naylor, James 198–9
Nedge, near Chewton (Mendip) 100
Netherlands 110, 160
Nettlebury (Dorset) 112
New Market/Town Hall/Market Hall *Plate XI*, *Plate XVII* 213–14, 217–19
New Model Army 120–1, 129, 136, 137, 138, 164, 191, 198
New Street 6, 7, 15, 123
New Works 9, 15, 188
Newark 132
Newburn, battle of (1640) 52
Newgate Gaol (Bristol) 220
Newport (Isle of Wight) 154
news culture 51–2
Newton Percy 185
Niblett, John 53, 160
Niblett, Nicholas 188
Nixon, Thomas 175, 215
  signature of *Plate IX*
non-attendance at church 212
  penalised 189, 211
Non-conformists
  laws against 211
  punishments (fines, prison and transportation) 211

247

see also Baptists; Congregational; Methodists; Puritanism; Quakers
North Curry 110, 140
North Liberty *see* College Lane
North Petherton 116
Nott, A. 27, 223, 224
Nurton, Joseph (postmaster) 107–8, 124
Nurton, Ursula (wife of Joseph, and later of Samuel Robinson) 107–8, 176, 186

Obstructions, Committee for Removal of 168
Okehampton 117
Oker, John (organist) 112, 157, 184
Old Bristol Road 6
old people, almshouses for 185–6
Oliver, Samuel (Pastor of St Cuthbert's) 140, 141, 142, 180, 210
Ordinance, Militia 2, 83
organs (musical) 37, 112
Ormonde, 1st Duke of (Lord Lieutenant of Somerset) 212
ornaments in cathedral 37
Osmond, Joseph 78, 79
Ottington (Devon) 101
Ouse River, converts baptised in 191
outworkers in cloth trade 12
Oxford 112
   Christ Church Cathedral 31
   Christ Church College, Westley and Piers at 30–1
   Exeter College 141
Oxfordshire 111
   see also Denton
Ozwell, Thomizen and Henry ('base child') 120

Palace Gate (*now Bishop's Eye*) *Plate* XVII
Palm Sunday entry of Christ imitated by Naylor 198
Palmer, Humphrey (grocer d. 1641) 24
Palmer, T.F. 46
pamphlet of 1642 ('Combustion at Wells') *Plate IV*
Parliament 20, 76, 92
   archbishops, bishops, deans and chapters abolished 108, 149
   and Baber 44
   death penalty for adultery 179
   House of Commons 4, 63, 91
   House of Lords 57, 91, 149
      Piers' impeachment by 55
   Presbyterians purged from 189
   records 228
   representatives in 212–13
   'short' (1640) 51, 55

signatures of leading parliamentarians *Plate IX*
subsidies (taxes) 38–9
see also bye-elections; Houses of Parliament
Parliamentary Association of Western Counties 114
Parliamentary Pamphlet *Plate IV*
Parliamentary Wells (August 1642-June 1643) **87–104**, 131
   Sir Edward Rodney imprisoned 90–2, 105, 161
   'For Defence of King, Parliament and Kingdom' 92–5
   'havock' (soldiers raid church) 95–7
   Royalist victory of June 1643 97–103
   plague 127–9
Parret river 78
Parsons, John 130
Particular Baptists 118, 123, 160, 190, 193, 211
Pawlet, Lord (see Poulett) 227
Pearce, James 144, 157
Pearse, Thomas 182
Pen Hill 6
Penn, William 197, 222
Penniless Porch *Plate XVII*
Penruddock, John 164
Pepys, Samuel: on Piers 206
Percy, Lord 115
Perkins, John (of Ottington) 101
Perry, Marie 186
Perry, William 134
Peter, Hugh 195
Petition of Right (1628) 3
Petty Sessions records 143
pewterers 12, 24
Phelips, Edward: of Montacute 49
Phelips, Sir Thomas 72
Phelps, Elizabeth 61
Phelps, Sir Robert 43–4
Phillips, Richard: refuses burgess role 60
Phippen, Robert (died 1656) 134
Pierce, Edmund 208
Piers, Anne (first wife of Bishop William) 209
Piers, John 219
Piers, Mary (second wife of Bishop William) 111, 209
Piers, William (Archdeacon of Taunton and son of Bishop William) 95, 111, 207, 213–14, 219
Piers, William, Bishop of Bath and Wells (from 1632) 206
   'beauty of holiness' policy 29
   and bishops 56–7
   disgruntled 33

INDEX

and elections 50–1
impeached and imprisoned in Tower of London for corruption of religion (1640) 18, 54–9
as lord of manor of Wells 56
and market and fairs 56–7
and national government and local affairs 32–5
and New Market/Town Hall 218
and parliament 49
portrayed *Plate V*
restores palace and Banwell house 166–7, 208–9
sons *see* Piers, John; Piers, William (Archdeacon)
and The Rib *Plate XIII*
and Vicar General's visit 58
and Warburton/Wood animosity 37–8
and Westley 30–1, 139–40
retirement to Denton 9, 58
remarries, moves to Walthamstowe and dies (1670) 111, 209
pig market 10
Pile, Sir Francis 103
Pilton 87, 138
Pilton Park 50
plague
  in 1625 92, 127
  deaths (1645-6) 129
  post-war 124, 127–9
  wandering victims punished 128
plan of Wells (1735) *Plate XI*, *Plate XV*, 10, 217
Player, Timothy 130
'pleasant city' **9–27**
  Catholic recusants 25–6
  clergy and ecclesiastical office holders 18–19
  economy 11–14
  gentry 14–18
  social and political scene 10–11
'Pleasant City' concept 19–25
Plummer, Joseph (mercer) 64, 134, 175, 223
  signature of *Plate IX*
Plundered Ministers, Committee for 197
plurality of benefices, bill against 56
Plymouth 93
politics 132–5
  see also elections
poll tax 62
poor rate 13
Pope, Henry 157
Popery 62
Popham family 133
Popham, Alexander 2, 6, 164
  and 'combustion at Wells' 70, 71–2, 77, 80

parliamentary Wells 87, 88, 95, 96, 97, 98
Popham, Sir Francis 71, 72, 73
Popham, Sir John 71, 75, 79
Popham, Sir Thomas 72
population increase 11
Portsmouth 191
Portway 7
Portway Avenue 50
postmaster *see* Nurton
Poulett, Baron John the elder (of Hinton St George) 208
  as Chief Steward of Bishop's Hundreds 143
  and 'combustion at Wells' 68–70, 76, 77, 81, 85
  delegates powers 150, 219
  and parliamentary Wells 88, 89
  as Recorder of Wells 148, 215–16
  'service of the country' (1639-42) 50, 51, 58, 63, 64
  death (1665) 219
Poulett, Baron John the younger 76, 208
poverty 13–14
Powell, Samuel 16–17, 44
Powell, Dr William 17
Prayer Book 58, 141
  of 1662 209
preaching 143
  'in the quire' 36
  payment for 31
precentor of Bath 57
predestination doctrine 32
Prerogative Court of Canterbury: wills extant 30
Presbyterianism 141, 175
  and Baptists in dispute 191, 192–3
  and card-playing 145
  classis system of presbyteries 141–2, 191
  Commissioners from Scotland 109
  Creighton attacks 110
  and episcopacy 132
  frivolity of, Collier attacks 191, 192–3
  Jenkins and 165
  MPs purged and imprisoned by army 154
  Naylor and 199
  power of elders 180
  Pride's Purge of MPs (1648) 192
  renunciation required for municipal office holders 211
  and St Cuthbert's Church 189, 190
  'Saints' idea 192
  Solemn League 215
  takeover of parish church 143
  and Walker 139
Preston, Captain 78, 79
Preston (Lancashire), battle of 164
Prickman, John 173

249

Priddy 150, 152
Pride's Purge of Presbyterian MPs (1648) 192
Priest Row 7, 14, 169, 185
  vestry house converted into library 180
primary sources 227–8
  Regiment of Horse 1643 *Plate VII*
Prince, Nicholas 120
Prince of Wales 67, 118, 120, 138
  Charles II as 110, 119, 155, 160–1, 205, 206
Prior's Hill 66, 80
prison
  in Bishop's Palace 168
  Cirencester 94
  Exeter, Naylor in 198
  Gloucester 34, 94
  house of correction in loft 14
  Ilchester 88, 111, 146–7
  London 18, 54–9, 90–1
  MPs in 154–5
    Sir Edward Rodney 90–2, 105, 161
  for non-conformists 211
  Piers in 18, 54–9
  in Westminster 220
Privy Council 67
  and clothing trade 12
  and militia levy 45
  and plague control 127–8
  and ship money 42
  'voluntary' loan requested by (and not paid) 39
property law 188
Propositions scheme investments 93, 103
prostitution 145–6, 187
Protectorate 162
  fall of (1659) 172
  Protector's Council 173, 174
Protestation of 1641/Protestantism 19, 62–5, 124, 194
'proud wifelings'
Prowse, William 16
Prynne, William 133, 154, 204
punishments 38, 128, 135–7, 146, 157, 179
  for non-conformists 211
  see also prison
Puritanism 14, 71–2, 140, 143, 180, 190
  in Batcombe 58
  and Bishop Piers 37–8, 140
  and Corporation 22, 23, 24, 25
  county gentry and 55
  criticism of church establishment 33–4
  Eastern Association and army of 164, 190
  hypocrisy of 144
  and Laudianism 35
  and local customs 11
  radical/extreme 32, 34
  and St Cuthbert's Church 34, 37

  and Sunday sports 34
Putney Debates (1647) 191
Pym family 90, 133
Pyne, Hugh 72
Pyne, John (of Curry Mallett) 54, 160, 192, 203
  career and end of 162, 163
  and 'combustion at Wells' (1642) 67–8, 72, 78–9, 81, 83
  aftermath of 1645-49) 133, 135, 138, 139, 154 **SORT UNDA WORD**

Quakers 193, 197, 199
  Act of 1662 211
  and Baptists 198, 210–12
  Collier on *Plate IV* 193, 198, 199
  imprisonment forbidden 210
  see also Naylor
Quantock 78
quarantine 128
quarter sessions 15
Queen Camel 115
Queen Street 7
'Quire' of Wells Cathedral 36

Rait, R.S. 125
Raleigh, Dean Walter 18
  eldest son 147–8
  and parliamentary Wells 95, 101
  and Royalist Wells 109, 110
  'villainous' murder of 146–7, 157
  funeral 148–9
Ranters 124, 189
  Creed 200, 228
  John Robins 193–7, 198, 200
  Joshua Garment 124, 193–7, 198, 200
'rayling Shimei' 166–7
Read, Edward 119
Reade, Samuel 175, 215
  signature of *Plate IX*
Reay, B. 201
Receiver, Corporation 134, 170
recorder (legal officer) 19
recusants 25–6, 64
Redland Court 182
religion *see* Catholicism; church; clergy; society and religion
rents, increased 13, 123
'respectable' poor 14
Restoration and reaction (1659-65) **203–24**
  Act for 'Well Governing and Regulating of Corporation' 214–16
  adjustments, making 212–14
  Baptists and Quakers 210–12
  Bishop and Cathedral restored 205–9
  Cavalier Parliament and local MPs 212–14
  Convention Parliament elections 204–5

250

INDEX

exits and entrances 219–21
New Market/Town Hall 217–19
St Cuthbert's Church 31, 209–10
epilogue 221–2
retail trade 12–13, 24–5
Revett, Dr Timothy (1634, Archdeacon) 30
Revett, Timothy (1661, son of Archdeacon) 208
Reynolds, H.E. 156, 158, 176, 224
Rib, The *see* Canonical Houses
roads 5–6
Robins, John (Ranter) 193–7, 198, 200
'declaration of' *Plate XIII* 228
Robinson, Dean Armitage 46
Robinson, Samuel 176
Robinson, Ursula (*earlier* Nurton, wife of Samuel) 107–8, 176, 186
Rodney, Sir Edward (MP) *Plate III* 5, 49, 51, 138, 176
  account of family 227
  on army 44
  captured 90–2
  and combustion of 1642 68, 75, 76, 77, 79, 81, 82
  and Dodington 133
  impeached by parliament 137
  as MP for Wells 50, 53, 54, 59, 62
  and parliamentary Wells 87–8, 91
  prison and release from 90–2, 105, 161
  questioned about taxation 39–40
  refusal to serve in Second Bishops' War 45
  and Royalist Wells 106, 115
  theological works by 32
  and Western Association 160
  writings 32, 228
Rodney Stoke manor 50
Rodwell, W. 222, 224
Rogation, observance banned by parliamentary ordinance 109
Rolle family 16
  Henry 60
Rowley, Robert (Mayor of Wells, 1642-43, died 1651) 18, 21, 225
  and Parliamentary Wells 89, 93, 102, 122
Royal Arms of Charles I *Plate XVII*
Royal Charter
  of 1589 19
  new, not recommended 60
royal prerogative 40
Royalist Wells (1642 and before) 9, 15, 20, 21, 23–4, 26, 67–71
Royalist Wells (1643-1645) 5, **105–26**, 220
  1643 victory 97–103
  1644 campaign 113–18
  Cathedral establishment, threat to 108–12
  demands, threats and murder 112–13
  paying for war 106

postmaster problems 107–8
Royalist Association created (1644) 114
end of war 118–21
effects of war 121–4
see also Charles I
Royalist Wells (after 1645) 14, 135–7, 153–4, 160–1
'Royalty of the Town' 150
Royle, T. 104
Rump, the *see* Long Parliament
Rupert, Prince 94, 97, 111, 114, 120–1
Russell, C. 47
Ruthin, Colonel William 93

Sabbath, Jewish 195
Sacah, James 101
Sacks, D.H. 199
saddlers 22
Sadler, William 145
Sadler Street 6, 7
  Swan Inn in 13, 42
St Andrew's Cathedral, Wells *Plate XVII*
St Andrew's Church (see Wells Cathedral) 175
St Andrew's Fair 92, 128
St Andrew's Street 15, 171
St Calixtus Fair 12, 92, 128
St Cuthbert's Church *Plate XVIII*, v, 15, 164, 169, 187, 220
  almshouses near 185
  ammunition and gunpowder in 16, 76, 79, 112
  cathedral, use of 174
  churchwarden (Josiah Cooke) 64, 134
  churchwarden (Thomas Brinte) 113, 124
  communion service changes 142–3
  curates *see* Buckley, Daniel; Standish
  and gentry 15
  King's Arms taken down 155
  locked 174
  manuscript sources 227
  military burials at 101
  and morality 179, 180
  and national government 30–2
  parish 42, 64, 174
    clerk disagreement 33
    petition from parishioners 174
    poor rate 13
  pastor (Oliver) 140, 141, 142, 180, 210
  pastor (William Thomas) 140, 141, 142, 156, 180
  Piers and 139
  on plan of 1665 *Plate XVII*
  Presbyterians and 189, 190
  Puritans and 34, 37
  Restoration and reaction (1659-65) 31, 209–10

251

Royal Arms of Charles I in *Plate XVII*
special pews in 187
taken over 143
traditional parochial structure maintained 142
vestry house 173, 226
vicars of 210
St Cuthbert's Street 7, 123
St John Street 7
St John's Hospital 26
St Kitts, indentured servants sent to 14
St Margaret's Church (Westminster) 91
St Nicholas Church (Bristol) 210
St Paul's Cathedral (London) 149
St Peter and Paul' Church (Shepton Mallet) 31
St Thomas Street 64, 169
saints' days observance banned 109
'Saints' idea of Presbyterians 192
Salisbury 11, 163–4
Salmon, Dorothy 176
Salmon, Thomas (Mayor of Wells, 1647-48 and 1656-57) 88, 107, 225
and aftermath of war (1645-49) 134, 146, 150
and alehouses 144
and 'broyles and sharp contentions' (1649-59) 165, 175
Burges writes to 168
as church elder 142
in group of eight 159
and 'Pleasant City' 15, 24, 25
rights 152
death (1658) 215
Sampford, Master 227
Sampson (teacher, 1657) 184–5
Sandford, James (Bishop Bekynton's secretary/servant) 33, 57
Sandford, Peter (tailor) 155
Sands, Captain 78, 79
Saunders, William: disenfranchised 105–6
Schellinks, William 208, 216, 222
schools *see* education
Scot, Thomas 160
Scotland
army of 61–2, 132
Bishops' Wars against (1638-1640) 43, 44–6, 52, 54
invasion of England (1640) 53
lieutenant from *see* Middleton, John
Presbyterian Commissioners from 109
surrender to (1646) 132
Scrase, A.J. 27, 65, 125, 157, 177, 199, 200, 223–4
Second Bishops' War 45–6
selfishness condemned by Collier 211
Selleck, John 207

Sequestrations, Committee for 149
Serel, T. 156, 157, 223
sermons, payment for 6
servants 33, 57
indentured 14, 179, 181–3
'service of country' (1639-1642) **49–65**
Earl of Strafford impeached 54, 59–60
Lane's visit to London 59–60
Long Parliament 38, 52–4
moral turpitude 60–1
Piers as 'impious and turbulent Pilate' 54–9
Protestation of 1641 62–5
subsidies to raise money for armies 61–2
Seymour, Sir Francis 2–3, 54
Seymour, William, Marquis/Earl of Hertford and Lord Lieutenant
of Somerset *Plate*, 1-6 *passim* 135, 160, 227
and 'combustion at Wells' (1642) 67–84 *passim*
letter to Queen in Holland 228
and parliamentary Wells 87, 88, 91, 94, 97, 98, 99, 102
and 'Pleasant City' 9, 10, 20, 23
'service of the country' (1639-42) 53, 57
son *see* Beauchamp, Lord
Shaftesbury 121
shambles, fish 10, 169–70
Shapwick 13
Shaw, W.A. 156
Sheafe, Grindall 207
Sheares, Francis 130
Sheldon, Major Thomas 102
Shepton Mallet 93
church 31
and 'combustion at Wells' (1642) 71, 73, 75–6, 81
House of Correction 173, 179
and Quakers 197
Road 7
Sherborne 75, 83, 94, 106
carpenters from 218
Castle 88, 121
siege of (1642) 89
fair cancelled (1625) 92
Sherbourne Lane 7
'Shimei, rayling' 166–7, 177
ship money *see* 'benevolences'
Shipham farm 188
shoemakers and cobblers 12, 13, 22, 34
king's demand for 500 pairs of shoes 117–18
see also Barrett, David; Casbeard, Richard
shops *see* retailers
'Short' Parliament (1640) 51, 55
'sickness, the *see* plague

INDEX

silver bowl gift, Bishop Piers demands explanation for absence of 33
Silver Street 7
Simes, William: plan of Wells (1735) *Plates XVII, XVIII* and *XI*, 10, 217
Skinners Close 146
Slack, P. 27, 155
Small, Mistress 31
Smith, Captain (died 1650?) 164
Smith, Edward (grocer, died 1623) 25
Smith, Sebastian (precentor of Wells Cathedral) 18, 95, 207, 214
Smith, (Smyth) William 18, 175
  and Bower brothers (1640s) 18
  as city receiver 94
  in group of eight (1649) 159
  and Jenkins 125, 165
  as Mayor of Wells (1649-50 and 1657-58) 225
  as mercer 24–5
  not purged 223
  visits Glastonbury (1642) 90
  death (1663) 25
smiths 10, 12
Smyth, Thomas 69, 70, 74, 76, 80
Smythe, Florence and Thomas 89
social problems and aftermath of war 143–7
social relations, amicable 10–11
society and religion (1649-59) 29–30, 62, **179–201**
  education 183–5
    Blue School founded (1654) 183
    see also 'Free Grammar School'
  elderly, provision for 185–6
  indentured servants 179, 181–3
  'Master Sectarie', Thomas Collier as 190–3
  Piers impeached for corruption of 18, 54–9
  toleration of other churches 189–90
  women: status of 'proud wifelings' 186–9
  see also church; Quakers; Ranters
Solemn League, Presbyterian 215
Somerset, Captain 145–6
Somerset (county) 2, 4, 23–4, 46, 52
  Chard 109, 112, 114, 117
  County Committee 23, 91, 139
  Kingsbury Episcopi 111
  Lord Lieutenant of *see* Ormonde, 1st Duke; Seymour, William
  militia 71–2, 80
  Petition (1641) 57
  posse comitatus 116
  and Royalist Wells 109, 110, 111, 112, 114, 117
Somerton 87, 98, 99, 217
sources listed 227–8

South Brent 118
South Petherton 78
Southover (street) 7, 10, 83, 94, 123
  animal pound 167
Sports, Book of (1633) 34, 55
Stacie, Richard 182, 199
Stafford, John (tiler) 213
Stamford, Earl of *see* Grey, Earl
Standish, Francis (curate) v, 31, 119
  and aftermath of war (1645-49) 140, 142, 147, 156, 157, 158
  and almshouses 143, 185, 186
  church services by 148–9
  as teacher 183
Standish, John (Town Clerk) 17, 159, 169, 216
  petition organised by 173
  signature of *Plate IX*
  takes books from cathedral library 173, 207
  visits London with Barrett 168
Star Chamber 5, 20, 21, 24, 25, 50
Star Inn 223
Stawell, (Stowell) John (son of Sir John) 78, 79, 99
Stawell, (Stowell) Sir John 52, 53, 70, 76, 77–8, 79, 87, 88, 115
Steig, M. 46, 156
Stephens/Steevens, Dorothy *see* Garment, Dorothy
Still, John (Bishop of Bath and Wells, 1593-1608) 14, 17, 185
  grandsons *see* Morgan, Robert; Morgan, William
Still almshouse 185, 186
Stoate, T.L. 65
Stoberry Park 66, 81
stocking production 12
stocks as punishment 146, 179
Stokes, J. 6, 26, 27, 46
Stone, Edward 92
Stone, William and Peternell 129
Stoyle 27
Strafford, Earl of (Thomas Wentworth) 62
  impeachment, trial and execution (1641) 54, 59–60
Stratton-on-the-Fosse 139
Street 78, 197
Strode, Thomas 75, 81, 83
Strode, William 154
  and 'combustion at Wells' (1642) 72, 73, 74–5
  and parliamentary Wells 87, 88, 92, 93, 97
Stuart, Arbella 53
Stuart, Charles 212
Stubbes, Pastor Henry 180–1, 209

253

subsidies 15
  parliamentary 38-9
  to raise money for armies 61-2
Sunday observance, strict 24, 34, 141
Swan Inn (Sadler Street) 13, 42
Symes, John 94
Symonds, H. 124
Symonds, Martin (died 1658) 157

Tabor, Jane 188
Tabor, Mark 19, 38, 96, 97
Tabor, Sarah (widow of Mark) 187-8, 200
  son-in-law *see* Keene, Francis
Tailor, John 182
tailors 12
Tanner, Samuel 101
tanners 10, 12, 22
Tarleton, John (vicar of Ilminster) 111
Taunton, Anthony: disenfranchised 105-6
Taunton, Robert 208
Taunton 6, 16, 42, 78, 93, 106, 138
  Archdeacons of
    Dr Gerard Wood 171
    Dr Samuel Ward 171, *Plate XIII*
    William Piers 95, 111
  attacked/besieged 117-19, 121
  Baptists in 191
  captured 97, 98, 99, 118
  Castle 92, 102, 114, 160
  Isle Brewers near 16
  Naylor and followers visit 198
  plague in 127
Taverner, William (burgess) 22, 134
taxation 54
  high rate of 131
  horse-taking as 107
  increased 153, 163
  on land 15
  non-parliamentary (to provide ships) *see* 'benevolences'
  parliamentary and parliamentary subsidies 38-9, 93, 94
  poll 62
  to relieve sick 128
  and war 121
Taylor, John 148
Temple Church (Bristol) 210
tenements, High Street 10, 16
Tetbury 130
textile industry *see* cloth
The Hague 110
Thirlby, Charles 185, 210
39 Articles of Faith 209
Thomas, Grace 187
Thomas, Richard (of Corporation) 18
Thomas, Robert (constable) 107-8, 223

Thomas, Pastor William 140, 141, 142, 156, 180
Thornbury, W. 104
Thwaites, Susan 182
Tinsbury 99
Tiverton 117
tolerance, religious 144, 189-90
Tom, John 101
Toope, Robert (of Liberty) 26
Tor Hill 66, 83, 146
Tor Lane 7
Tor Street 64
Torrington 138
Tower House (precentor's house) 169, 214
Tower of London, bishops in (1641-2) 58
Town Hall 169
  construction of 216, 217-19
  see also New Market
Towse, Tristram, the younger (Mayor of Wells, 1664-65, died 1674) 19, 137, 225
  and restoration and reaction (1659-65) 216, 219-20
  and Royalist Wells (1643-45) 109, 123
transportation as punishment 211
Traske, John 195
travellers helped 181
Trevelyan, Sir C.E. and Sir W.C. 104
Truro 138
Trustees for Sale of Bishops' Lands 150
Trym, David 16
Trym, Valentine 16, 106, 136-7, 159, 173, 175
Tucker Street 7, 123, 197
Twist, Farmer 88
Twistleton, Colonel 191
typhus *see* 'sickness'

Ubley 3, 141
Underdown, D. 6, 27, 65, 103, 200, 222
  and aftermath (1645-49) 155, 156, 157, 158
  and 'broyles and sharp contentions' (1649-59) 176, 177
  and Royalist Wells 124, 125
Uniformity, Act of (1662) 209
unmarried women 188-9
Urrey, Fawns 220
Utrecht, Dr Robert Creighton in 110

Venner, Thomas 211
Verney, Edmund 110
Verney, Sir Ralph 110
Vernon, E.A. 157
vestry houses converted into library 180
Vicar General 16, 19, 51, 58
Vicars Choral 13, 112, 148-9

INDEX

Vicars Close 149, 169
  vicars' Hall (Close Hall) *Plate XVII* 153
victuallers *see* innkeeping
vintners 22
Virginia (America) 179, 181, 182
'voluntary' loans *see* 'benevolences'
voting, women barred from 186

wages, decline in value of 13
Walcombe 6
Wales 94
  see also Prince of Wales
Walker, Clement 88, 92, 138–9, 150, 154, 155, 160, 162, 169, 170, 204
Walker, John 111, 124
Walker, Rev. J. 157
Walker, Thomas 95, 112, 207
Walkley, Anthony 157
Wallbanck, Edward and Joane 101–2
Waller, Sir William 97–8, 99–100, 103, 106, 119
Wallop (Hampshire) 110
Walot, Stephen 182
Walrond, George (son of William, Mayor of Wells, 1662-63) 16, 18, 136, 137, 208, 219, 225
Walrond, Humphrey 16, 173
Walrond, William (JP) 16, 25–6, 79, 106, 208, 216
  daughter (Frances Creighton) 110
  fined 136
  gunpowder purchase 112
  leader of group of ex-royalists 172–3, 175
  Lechlade's House of *Plate XI*
  will of 27
Walthamstow (Essex) 30, 209
war *see* aftermath of war; Civil War; Royalist Wells
Warburton, George (Dean of Wells) 35–8, 58
Ward, Dr Samuel (Archdeacon of Taunton) 171
  house *Plate XIII*
Warminster 119
Warwick, Earl of 53
water supply to city cut off by Bishop Piers 33
Watts, Cornelius: and wife 143
Watts, Edward 216
Watts, William 111
weapons, search for 87
Webb, Sir John 128–9, 134
Webster, Henry 223
Wedmore, Particular Baptists in 190
Weiting, Mary and Thomas 182
Weldon, Colonel Ralph 119
'Well Governing and Regulating of Corporation', Act for 214–16
Wellington (Somerset) 46
Wells *see* preliminary note to index *and also* aftermath of war; 'broyles'; 'combustion'; Corporation; national government; parliament; 'pleasant city'; Restoration; royalist Wells; 'service of country'; society and religion
Wells Forum, Hundred of 42, 112–13, 116, 150
Wentworth, Thomas *see* Strafford, Earl of
Wesley, Thomas 208
West Indies 179, 182
West Pennard 111
'West Ruin' 171
West, William (Mayor of Wells, 1643-44) 22, 137, 225
  death (1652) and will 159, 175
  as inn-keeper 155
  and Royalist Wells 108, 115, 116, 123, 124
Westbury 50, 138
  wildfowl stolen from pool 167
  vicar of (Middleham, Purefoy) 190
Western Association of Particular Baptists 118, 123, 160, 190, 193, 211
Westley, Sarah (Francis Keene's daughter) 97
Westley, Thomas (vicar of St Cuthbert's) 32, 64, 156
  expelled 23
  wrongly described as an 'old malignant' 157
  and Piers 30–1, 139–40
  wife buried in Walthamstow (1659) 30
  as Wiveliscombe prebendary 210
  death and will (1661) 210, 223
Westminster
  Abbey 149
  Assembly of Divines 109, 141, 191
  Gatehouse Prison 220
  St Margaret's Church 91
  see also Parliament
Weston Zoyland 207
Wet Lane 220
Weymouth 114
whipping as punishment 179
Whit Sunday, observance banned by parliamentary ordinance 109
White, B.R. 200
White, Mr 74
White, P. 46
White, Thomas (recorder and MP, 1656-62) 1166, 168, 173, 184, 204, 205
  'displaced' (dismissed) 215, 216
Whiting, Elizabeth 61, 186

255

Whiting, John (of Axbridge) 17
Whiting, John (Quaker, 1695) 197
Whiting, William (Mayor of Wells, 1650-51 and 1658-59) 159, 170, 175, 203, 225
　death (1660) 215
Whittaker, Rev. R. 157
widows 187
'wifelings, proud', status of 186–9
Wight, Isle of 154
Williams, M. 6
Williams, William (alias Morgan) 22
Wiltshire 80, 119
　Particular Baptists in 193
Wincanton 73
Winchester
　bishop and see of 36
　Dean of (Young) 110
Windsor 2
Witham 115
Wiveliscombe 193, 210
Wokey, John 41–2
women
　as alcoholics 187
　barred from voting 186
　in cloth trade 12
　education of 187
　and property law 188
　prostitution 145–6, 187
　status of 186–9
　work for 187
Wood, Dr Gerard (Archdeacon of Bath, died 1645) 18, 32, 36–7, 38, 95, 109, 111, 171
Wood, Dr Roger 109, 112
wooden horse punishment 157

Woodhouse, A.S.P. 200
Woodhouse (near Longleat) 70
woodlands, warden of bishop's 26
Wookey 42
　manor house 16
　rectory 25
Wool (Dorset) 130
Woolman, Richard 9
Woolrych, A. 65, 125
workhouse 14
Worminster 137
worsted cloth production 12
Wright, Stephen 200
Wroth, Sir Thomas 185
Wroughton, J. 6, 85, 104
Wykes, Edward 17–18, 26, 106, 117
　and Baber 50, 113
　death and will of 27, 133
　as recorder 113, 114, 173
　widow see Wykes, Jane
Wykes, Jane (sister of Roger Bourne, widow of Edward) 16, 173
Wykes, Nicholas 16
Wyndham, Colonel Edmund 70, 78

Yarlington 70
Yeamans, Robert 182
Yorkshire 2, 190
　Marston Moor, battle of (1644) 114, 191
　troops from 68
York 2, 69
　Collier preaches in 191
Young, John (chancellor and chaplain) 110
Young, P. 104